Business Glossary
English-French/French-English

General Editor
PH Collin

French Editor
Françoise Collin

PETER COLLIN PUBLISHING

First Published in Great Britain 1995

published by
Peter Collin Publishing Ltd
1 Cambridge Road, Teddington, Middlesex, TW11 8DT

Business Glossary Text
© Copyright P.H. Collin 1995

British Library Cataloguing in Publications Data

A Catalogue record for this book is available from the British Library

ISBN 0-948549-52-1

Text computer typeset by PCP
Printed and bound in Finland by WSOY

Cover illustration by Gary Weston

Preface

This glossary is for any business person or traveller who needs to deal with a foreign business language. It contains over 5,000 essential business terms with clear and accurate translations.

How to use this glossary

This glossary is aranged in two main sections. The first lists English terms with a French translation, the second half lists French terms with equivalent English translation.

Throughout the Business Glossary we have used a number of abbreviations:

adj	adjectif	adjective
adv	adverbe	adverb
f	féminin	feminine
fpl	féminin pluriel	feminine plural
m	masculin	masculine
mf	masculin ou féminin	masculine or feminine
mpl	masculin pluriel	masculine plural
n	nom	noun
v	verbe	verb

Preface

Ce glossaire vous offre 5 000 mots et expressions indispensables lors de vos voyages d'affaires à l'étranger. Le format étudié, la liste de mots choisis avec soin et les traductions au point en font un outil tout à fait convivial.

Comment utiliser ce glossaire

La première section contient la liste des mots anglais avec leurs traductions ou équivalents français, alors que dans la deuxième section figurent la liste des expressions françaises suivies des traductions ou équivalents en anglais.

Les abréviations ont été réduites au minimum, en voici la liste:

adj	adjectif	adjective
adv	adverbe	adverb
f	féminin	feminine
fpl	féminin pluriel	feminine plural
m	masculin	masculine
mf	masculin ou féminin	masculine or feminine
mpl	masculin pluriel	masculine plural
n	nom	noun
v	verbe	verb

English-French
Anglais-Français

Aa

A1 *[condition]* excellent(e) *ou* parfait(e)

abandon (v) abandonner *ou* renoncer à

abandon an action *[legal]* renoncer aux poursuites *ou* à un procès

abatement (n) réduction (f)

abroad à l'étranger

absence absence (f)

absence: in the absence of en l'absence de

absent (adj) absent(e)

absolute monopoly monopole (m) absolu

accelerated depreciation amortissement (m) accéléré

accept (v) *[agree]* accepter

accept (v) *[take something]* accepter

accept a bill accepter une traite

accept delivery of a shipment réceptionner des marchandises *ou* prendre livraison d'un envoi

accept liability for something accepter la responsabilité de quelque chose

acceptable (adj) acceptable

acceptance (n) acceptation (f)

acceptance of an offer acceptation (f) d'une offre

acceptance sampling test (m) sur échantillon

accommodation address adresse (f) postale *ou* boîte (f) à lettre

accommodation bill billet (m) de complaisance *ou* effet (m) de complaisance

according to selon *ou* suivant *ou* conformément (à)

account (n) compte (m)

account: on account en acompte

account executive responsable (mf) de clientèle *ou* responsable de la gestion du budget d'un client

account for (v) rendre compte de *ou* justifier

account in credit compte (m) créditeur

account on stop compte (m) bloqué

accountant (n) comptable (mf)

accounting (n) comptabilité (f)

accounting procedures méthodes (fpl) comptables

accounts department service (m) de la comptabilité

accounts payable comptes (mpl) fournisseurs *ou* dettes (fpl)

accounts receivable comptes (mpl) clients (mpl) *ou* créances (fpl)

accrual (n) accumulation (f) *ou* capitalisation (f)

accrual of interest capitalisation (f) des intérêts

accruals (n) compte (m) de régularisation

accrue (v) courir *ou* s'accumuler

accrued interest intérêt (m) couru

accumulate (v) accumuler *ou* s'accumuler

accurate (adj) exact(e) *ou* précis(e) *ou* correct(e)

acknowledge (v) receipt of a letter accuser réception d'une lettre

acknowledgement (n) accusé (m) de réception

acquire (v) a company faire l'acquisition d'une société *ou* acheter une société

acquisition acquisition (f)

across-the-board (adj) général(e) *ou* généralisé(e)

act (n) loi (f)

act (v) agir

act of God catastrophe (f) naturelle

acting (adj) intérimaire

acting manager directeur (-trice) intérimaire

action *[thing done]* action (f)

action *[lawsuit]* procès (m) *ou* poursuite (f) *ou* action (f)

action for damages poursuite (f) en dommages-intérêts

actual (adj) réel (-elle) *ou* véritable

actuals (n) chiffres (mpl) réels

actuarial tables tables (fpl) de mortalité

actuary (n) actuaire (mf)

ad *or* **advert (n)** annonce (n) (publicitaire)

add (v) ajouter *ou* augmenter

add on (v) **10% for service** ajouter 10% pour le service

add up (v) **a column of figures** additionner une colonne de chiffres

addition (f) *[calculation]* addition (f) *ou* somme (f)

addition *[thing added]* addition (f)

additional (adj) supplémentaire

additional charges frais (mpl) supplémentaires *ou* supplément (m)

additional premium prime (f) additionnelle

address (n) adresse (f)

address (v) adresser

address a letter *or* **a parcel** adresser une lettre *ou* un colis

address a meeting prendre la parole à une réunion

address label étiquette (f) (avec *ou* pour) adresse

address list répertoire (m) *ou* fichier (m) d'adresses

addressee (n) destinataire (mf)

adequate (adj) adéquat(e) *ou* suffisant(e)

adjourn (v) ajourner *ou* remettre

adjourn a meeting lever la séance; ajourner une réunion

adjudicate (v) **in a dispute** se prononcer sur un litige *ou* sur un conflit

adjudication (n) jugement (m) *ou* décision (f) *ou* arrêt (m)

adjudication tribunal conseil (m) d'arbitrage

adjudicator (n) arbitre (m) *ou* juge (m)

adjust (v) ajuster *ou* modifier

adjustment (n) ajustement (m) *ou* modification (f)

admin (n) *[informal: administration]* (d') administration; administratif (-ive)

admin costs frais (mpl) adminsitratifs *ou* de gestion

administration (n) administration (f) *ou* gestion (f)

administrative (adj) administratif (-ive)

administrative expenses frais administratifs *ou* frais de gestion

admission (n) admission (f) *ou* entrée (f)

admission charge entrée (f)

admit (v) *[confess]* avouer *ou* reconnaître

admit (v) *[let in]* admettre (quelqu'un) *ou* laisser entrer (quelqu'un)

ad valorem ad valorem *ou* proportionnel(-elle) (à la valeur)

ad valorem tax taxe proportionnelle

advance (adj) anticipé(e)

advance (n) *[increase]* hausse (f) *ou* augmentation (f)

advance (n) *[loan]* avance (f)

advance (v) *[increase]* augmenter

advance (v) *[lend]* avancer (de l'argent) *ou* prêter (de l'argent)

advance booking réservation (f) à l'avance

advance on account avance (f) *ou* acompte (m) *ou* provision (f)

advance payment paiement anticipé

advertise (v) mettre *ou* insérer une annonce; faire de la publicité

advertise a new product faire de la publicité pour un produit nouveau

advertise a vacancy annoncer un poste (dans un journal)

advertisement (n) annonce (f); publicité (f)

advertiser (n) annonceur (m)

advertising (n) publicité (f) *ou* réclame (f)

advertising agency agence (f) de publicité

advertising budget budget (m) de publicité

advertising campaign campagne (f) publicitaire *ou* campagne de publicité

advertising manager responsable (mf) de la publicité

advertising rates tarifs (mpl) publicitaires

advertising space espace (m) publicitaire

advice note avis (m) d'expédition

advise (v) *[tell what happened]* informer *ou* aviser (de)

advise (v) *[what should be done]* conseiller

adviser *or* **advisor** (n) conseiller (-ère)

affidavit (n) déclaration (f) sous serment

affiliated (adj) affilié(e)

affirmative (adj) affirmatif (-ive)

afford (v) pouvoir se payer *ou* s'acheter *ou* s'offrir quelque chose

after-sales service service (m) après-vente (SAV)

after-tax profit bénéfice (m) après impôts

agency (n) agence (f)

agenda (n) ordre du jour (m)

agent (n) *[representative]* représentant(e)

agent (n) *[working in an agency]* agent (m)

AGM (annual general meeting) assemblée (f) générale annuelle

agree (v) *[accept]* accepter *ou* convenir de

agree (v) *[approve]* accepter *ou* approuver

agree (v) *[be same as]* concorder (avec)

agree to do something accepter de faire quelque chose

agree with *[be same as]* concorder (avec) *ou* correspondre (à)

agree with *[of same opinion]* être d'accord avec quelqu'un

agreed (adj) accepté(e) *ou* convenu(e)

agreed price prix convenu

agreement (n) contrat (m) *ou* accord (m) *ou* convention (f)

agricultural (adj) agricole

aim (n) objectif (m) *ou* but (m)

aim (v) viser (à) *ou* avoir pour but (de)

air (n) air (m)

air freight transport (m) par avion *ou* fret (m) aérien

air freight charges *or* **rates** tarifs (mpl) de transport par avion

air letter aérogramme (m)

air terminal aérogare (f)

airfreight (v) expédier par avion

airline (n) compagnie (f) (de navigation) aérienne

airmail (n) poste (f) aérienne

airmail (v) envoyer par avion

airmail sticker étiquette (f) 'par avion'

airport (n) aéroport (m)

airport bus autobus (m) de l'aéroport

airport tax taxe (f) d'aéroport

airport terminal terminal (m) (d'aéroport)

airtight packaging emballage (m) hermétique

all expenses paid tous frais payés

all-in tout compris; toutes taxes comprises (TTC)

all-in price prix (m) net *ou* tarif (m) tout compris

all-out strike grève (f) totale *ou* générale

all-risks policy assurance (f) tous risques

allocate (v) affecter *ou* attribuer *ou* distribuer

allow *[permit]* permettre

allow a discount accorder *ou* consentir une remise

allow 10% for carriage ajouter 10% pour le transport

allowance (n) allocation (f) *ou* indemnité (f)

allowance (n) **for depreciation** provisions (fpl) pour dépréciation

alphabetical order ordre (m) alphabétique

alter (v) changer *ou* modifier

alteration (n) changement (m) *ou* modification (f)

alternative (adj) autre *ou* de remplacement

alternative (n) alternative (f); solution (f)

amend (v) rectifier *ou* modifier *ou* corriger

amendment amendement (m) *ou* modification (f) *ou* correction (f)

American (adj) américain (-aine)

American (n) Américain (-aine)

American dollar dollar (m) (américain)

amortization (n) amortissement (m)

amortize (v) amortir *ou* rembourser (un prêt *ou* une dette)

amount *[of money]* montant (m) *ou* somme (f)

amount owing somme (f) due

amount paid montant (m) versé *ou* versement (m)

amount to (v) s'élever à *ou* se monter à

analyse *or* **analyze** (v) analyser

analyse the market potential étudier le potentiel du marché

analysis (n) analyse (f)

announce (v) annoncer

announcement (n) déclaration (f) *ou* annonce (f)

annual (adj) annuel (-elle)

annual accounts comptes (mpl) annuels *ou* comptes de l'exercice

annual general meeting (AGM) assemblée (f) générale annuelle

annual report rapport (m) annuel

annual return rendement (m) annuel

annualize (v) annualiser

annualized percentage rate (APR) taux (m) effectif global (TEG)

annually (adv) annuellement *ou* chaque année

annuity (n) rente (f)

annul (v) *[contract]* annuler *ou* résilier (un contrat)

answer (n) réponse (f)

answer (v) répondre

answer a letter répondre à une lettre

answer the telephone répondre au téléphone *ou* prendre un appel

answering machine *or* **answerphone (n)** répondeur (m) téléphonique

answering service permanence (f) téléphonique

antedate (v) antidater

anti-inflationary measures mesures (fpl) anti-inflationnistes

apologize (v) s'excuser

apology (n) excuse (f)

appeal (n) *[against a decision]* appel (m) (d'un jugement)

appeal (n) *[attraction]* attrait (m)

appeal (v) *[against a decision]* faire appel (d'un jugement)

appeal to (v) *[attract]* attirer *ou* séduire

appear (v) *[seem]* paraître *ou* sembler

appendix (n) annexe (f)

applicant for a job candidat(e) à un emploi

application (n) demande (f)

application for a job candidature (f) à un poste *ou* demande (f) d'emploi

application form formulaire (m) de candidature *ou* de demande (d'emploi)

apply for (v) *[ask for]* demander *ou* solliciter

apply for a job solliciter un emploi *ou* poser sa candidature à un poste

apply in writing faire une demande par écrit

apply to (v) *[affect]* concerner

appoint (v) nommer

appointee (n) personne nommée à un poste; candidat(e) retenu(e)

appointment (n) *[job]* poste (m) *ou* emploi (m)

appointment *[meeting]* rendez-vous (m)

appointment *[to a job]* nomination (f)

appointments book carnet (m) de rendez-vous

appointments vacant offres (f) d'emploi

appreciate (v) *[how good something is]* apprécier

appreciate *[increase in value]* augmenter en valeur *ou* s'apprécier

appreciation (n) *[how good something is]* appréciation (f)

appreciation *[in value]* augmentation (f) en valeur *ou* appréciation (f)

appropriate (v) *[funds]* affecter *ou* destiner *[une somme à un projet]*

approval (n) approbation (f)

approval: on approval *or* **on appro** à l'essai *ou* à condition

approve (v) the terms of a contract approuver les termes d'un contrat

approximate (adj) approximatif (-ive)

approximately (adv) environ *ou* approximativement

APR (annualized percentage rate) TEG (taux effectif global)

arbitrate (v) in a dispute arbitrer un conflit

arbitration (n) arbitrage (m) *ou* médiation (f)

arbitration board *or* **arbitration tribunal** comité (m) de conciliation

arbitrator (n) arbitre (mf)

area (n) *[of town]* secteur (m) *ou* quartier (m)

area *[region]* région (f) *ou* zone (f)

area *[subject]* secteur (m) *ou* domaine (m)

area *[surface]* surface (f)

area code *[telephone]* indicatif (m) de zone

area manager directeur (-trice) régional(e)

argument (n) discussion (f) *ou* dispute (f)

arrange (v) *[meeting]* arranger *ou* organiser

arrange *[set out]* arranger *ou* disposer

arrangement (n) *[compromise]* accord (m) *ou* compromis (m)

arrangement *[system]* organisation (f)

arrears (n) arriéré (m)

arrival (n) arrivée (f)

arrivals *[at airport, etc.]* arrivées (fpl)

arrive (v) arriver

article (n) *[clause]* article (m) *ou* clause (f)

article *[item]* article (m)

articles of association statuts (mpl) d'une société

articulated lorry *or* **articulated vehicle** semi-remorque (m *ou* f); poids lourd (m)

as per advice suivant avis

as per invoice selon facture

as per sample selon échantillon *ou* conformément à l'échantillon

asap (as soon as possible) aussitôt que possible *ou* dès que possible

ask (v) demander

ask someone to do something demander à quelqu'un de faire quelque chose

ask for (v) *[ask a price]* demander (un prix)

ask for *[something]* demander *ou* réclamer quelque chose

ask for a refund demander un remboursement

ask for further details *or* **particulars** demander des renseignements supplémentaires

assembly (n) *[meeting]* assemblée (f)

assembly *[putting together]* assemblage (m) *ou* montage (m)

assembly line chaîne (f) de montage

assess (v) évaluer *ou* estimer

assess damages évaluer les dommages

assessment (n) of damages évaluation (f) des dommages

asset (n) actif (m)

asset stripping dépeçage (m) d'une entreprise (après son rachat)

asset value valeur (f) de l'actif

assets and liabilities l'actif et le passif *ou* doit (m) et avoir (m)

assign a right to someone attribuer un droit à quelqu'un

assignee (n) cessionnaire (mf)

assignment (n) *[cession]* cession (f) *ou* transfert (m)

assignment *[work]* tâche (f)

assignor (n) cédant(e)

assist (v) aider

assistance (n) aide (f) *ou* assistance (f)

assistant (n) assistant(e)

assistant manager directeur (-trice) adjoint(e)

associate (adj) associé(e)

associate (n) associé(e); collègue (mf)

associate company société (f) affiliée *ou* filiale (f)

association (n) association (f)

assurance (n) assurance (f)

assurance company compagnie (f) d'assurance-vie

assurance policy police (f) d'assurance-vie

assure (v) someone's life assurer quelqu'un sur la vie

attach (v) attacher *ou* joindre

attack (v) attaquer

attend (v) *[meeting]* assister à *[une réunion]*

attend to (v) s'occuper de (quelque chose)

attention (n) attention (f)

attorney (n) fondé (m) de pouvoir

attract (v) attirer

attractive salary salaire attrayant *ou* intéressant

auction (n) enchère (f) *ou* vente (f) aux enchères

auction (v) vendre aux enchères

auction rooms salle (f) des ventes *ou* hôtel (m) des ventes *[enchères]*

audit (n) audit (m)

audit (v) vérifier *ou* réviser

audit (v) the accounts vérifier les comptes

auditing (n) vérification (f) *ou* révision (f) comptable

auditor (n) audit (m) *ou* auditeur (m); commissaire (m) aux comptes

authenticate (v) authentifier *ou* homologuer

authority (n) autorité (f)

authorization (n) autorisation (f)

authorize (v) *[give permission]* autoriser

authorize payment autoriser le paiement

authorized (adj) autorisé(e)

availability (n) disponibilité (f)

available (adj) disponible

available capital capital disponible

average (adj) moyen (-enne)

average (n) moyenne (f)

average: on average en moyenne

average (n) *[insurance]* avaries (f)

average (v) établir une moyenne; atteindre une moyenne

average price prix moyen

avoid (v) éviter

await (v) instructions attendre les instructions

award (n) *[decision]* décision (f) *ou* sentence (f)

award (v) attribuer

award a contract to someone donner *ou* adjuger un contrat à quelqu'un

Bb

back (n) dos (m)

back orders commandes (f) en attente

back pay rappel (m) *ou* arriéré (m) (de salaire)

back up (v) *[computer file]* sauvegarder

back up (v) *[financially]* appuyer *ou* étayer

backdate antidater

backer (n) sponsor (m); bailleur (m) de fonds

backhander (n) pot-de-vin (m)

backing (n) *[financial]* appui (m) (financier)

backlog (n) travail (m) en retard *ou* en attente

back office (n) back office (m)

backup (adj) *[computer]* de sauvegarde

backup copy disquette (f) de sauvergarde

backwardation déport (m)

bad buy mauvais achat (m)

bad debt créance (f) douteuse

bag sac (m)

bail (v) someone out cautionner quelqu'un

balance (n) solde (m) *[d'un compte]*

balance (v) équilibrer *ou* solder *ou* arrêter *[compte]*

balance (v) (a budget) équilibrer (un budget)

balance brought down *or* **brought forward** solde (m) à nouveau; ancien solde; solde reporté

balance carried down *or* **carrried forward** solde (m) à ce jour; solde à reporter

balance due to us solde (m) à recevoir

balance of payments balance (f) des paiements

balance of trade balance (f) commerciale

balance sheet bilan (m)

ban (n) interdiction (f); embargo (m)

ban (v) interdire

bank (n) banque (f)

bank (v) *[cheque]* mettre *ou* déposer à la banque

bank with (v) avoir un compte en banque (à *ou* au)

bank account compte (m) bancaire

bank balance *[bank account]* solde (m) *ou* position (f) (d'un compte)

bank base rate taux (m) de base bancaire

bank bill *[GB]* effet (m) bancaire *ou* traite (f) bancaire

bank bill *[US]* billet (m) de banque

bank book livret (m) *ou* carnet (m) de banque

bank borrowings emprunts (m) bancaires

bank charges frais (mpl) bancaires *ou* agios (mpl)

bank credit crédit (m) bancaire

bank deposits dépôts (mpl) bancaires

bank draft traite (f) bancaire

bank holiday jour (m) férié

bank loan prêt (m) bancaire

bank manager directeur (-trice) d'agence

bank mandate mandat (m) de paiement

bank statement relevé (m) de compte (bancaire)

bank reserves réserves (fpl) bancaires

bank transfer virement (m) bancaire

bankable paper effet (m) escomptable *ou* bancable

banker banquier (m)

banker's draft traite (f) bancaire

banker's order ordre (m) de virement bancaire

banking (n) banque (f) *[activité bancaire]*

banking hours heures (fpl) d'ouverture des banques

banknote billet (m) de banque

bankrupt (adj) failli(e) (adj)

bankrupt (n) failli(e) (n)

bankrupt (v) causer *ou* entraîner une faillite

bankruptcy (n) faillite (f)

bar chart diagramme (m) en bâtons; histogramme (m)

bar code code (m) (à) barres

bargain (n) *[cheaper than usual]* affaire (f) *ou* occasion (f)

bargain (n) *[deal]* marché (m) *ou* affaire (f)

bargain (n) *[Stock Exchange]* vente (f) d'un lot d'actions

bargain (v) discuter *ou* marchander

bargain offer offre (f) exceptionnelle

bargain price prix (m) sacrifié *ou* prix exceptionnel

bargaining (n) marchandage (m) *ou* négociation (f)

bargaining position prise (f) de position dans les négociations

bargaining power position (f) de force dans les négociations

barrier barrière (f) *ou* obstacle (m)

barter (n) troc (m)

barter (v) troquer

bartering échange (m) *ou* troc (m)

base (n) *[initial position]* base (f)

base (n) *[place]* siège (m)

base (v) *[in a place]* avoir son siège

base (v) *[start to calculate from]* (se) baser sur *ou* calculer à partir de

base year année (f) de référence

basic (adj) *[most important]* de base *ou* essentiel (-elle)

basic (adj) *[simple]* de base

basic discount remise (f) de base *ou* remise habituelle

basic tax taux (m) d'impôt moyen

basis base (f)

batch (n) *[of orders]* paquet (m) *ou* liasse (f)

batch (n) *[of products]* lot (m)

batch (v) grouper

batch number numéro (m) de lot

batch processing traitement (m) par lots

bear (n) *[Stock Exchange]* baissier (m) *ou* spéculateur (m) à la baisse

bear (v) *[carry]* porter

bear (v) *[interest]* porter intérêt

bear (v) *[pay for]* supporter *[frais]*

bear market marché (m) à la baisse *ou* marché baissier

bearer (n) porteur (m)

bearer bond titre (m) *ou* obligation (f) au porteur

begin (v) commencer

beginning début (m)

behalf: on behalf of au nom de

belong to (v) appartenir à

below-the-line expenditure dépense (f) exceptionnelle (hors bilan)

benchmark (n) (point de) référence (f) *ou* repère (m)

beneficiary (n) bénéficiaire (mf) *ou* ayant droit (m)

benefit (n) allocation (f) *ou* prestation (f) *ou* indemnité (f)

benefit from (v) profiter de *ou* bénéficier de

berth (n) poste (m) d'amarrage

berth (v) accoster *ou* mouiller *ou* arriver à quai

best (adj) le meilleur, la meilleure

best (n) le mieux

best-selling car voiture la plus en demande

bid (n) *[at an auction]* offre (f) *ou* enchère (f)

bid (n) *[offer to buy]* offre (f) *ou* mise (f)

bid (n) *[offer to do work]* devis (m)

bid (n) *[tender]* soumission (f)

bid (v) faire une soumission *ou* une offre

bidder (n) *[at an auction]* enchérisseur (m)

bidder *[for tender]* soumissionnaire (m)

bidding (n) *[at an auction]* enchère (f)

bilateral (adj) bilatéral(e)

bill (v) facturer *ou* présenter la facture

bill (n) *[US]* billet (m) de banque

bill (n) *[in a restaurant]* addition (f)

bill (n) *[in Parliament]* projet (m) de loi

bill (n) *[list of charges]* facture (f) *ou* note (f)

bill (n) *[written promise to pay]* traite (f)

bill of exchange lettre (f) de change

bill of lading connaissement (m)

bill of sale contrat (m) de vente *ou* acte (m) de vente

billing (n) facturation (f)

billion milliard (m)

bills for collection effets (mpl) à recevoir

bills payable effets (mpl) à payer

bills receivable effets (mpl) à recevoir

binding (adj) qui lie *[par contrat]*

black economy économie (f) parallèle; travail (m) au noir

black list (n) liste (f) noire

black market marché (m) noir

blacklist (v) mettre sur la liste noire

blame (n) reproche (m); responsabilité (f)

blame (v) reprocher

blank (adj) blanc (blanche)

blank (n) *[empty square]* blanc (m)

blank cheque chèque (m) en blanc

blister pack blister (m)

block (n) *[building]* bloc (m) d'immeubles

block (n) of shares paquet (m) *ou* bloc (m) d'actions

block (v) bloquer

block booking réservation (f) en bloc

blocked currency devises (fpl) non convertibles

blue chip titre (m) de premier ordre *ou* valeur (f) sûre

blue-chip investments placements (mpl) de père de famille

board (n) *[group of people]* conseil (m) *ou* comité (m)

board (v) monter à bord de

board meeting *[of directors]* réunion (f) du conseil d'administration

board of directors conseil (m) d'administration; directoire (m)

board: on board à bord

boarding card *or* **boarding pass** carte (f) d'embarquement *ou* d'accès à bord

boardroom (n) salle (f) de réunion (du conseil d'administration)

bona fide de bonne foi

bond *[borrowing by government]* bon (m) (du Trésor) *ou* obligation (f)

bonded warehouse entrepôt (m) de la douane

bonus (n) bonus (n) *ou* prime (f)

bonus issue émission (f) d'actions gratuites

book (n) livre (m)

book (v) réserver

book sales ventes (fpl) enregistrées

book value valeur (f) comptable

booking (n) réservation (f)

booking clerk préposé(e) à la vente des billets

booking office bureau (m) de location *ou* des réservations

bookkeeper employé(e) (n) aux écritures

bookkeeping comptabilité (f) *ou* tenue (f) de livres

boom (n) période (f) d'expansion *ou* boom (m)

boom (v) devenir prospère

boom industry industrie (f) en pleine croissance *ou* en pleine expansion

booming (adj) prospère (adj) *ou* florissant(e) (adj)

boost (n) poussée (f)

boost (v) pousser *ou* relancer *ou* réactiver

border (n) frontière (f)

borrow (v) emprunter

borrower (n) emprunteur (-euse)

borrowing (n) emprunt (m)

borrowing power capacité (f) d'emprunt

boss (n) *[informal]* patron (-onne)

bottleneck (n) goulot (m) *ou* goulet (m) d'étranglement

bottom (n) fond (m)

bottom line résultat (m) net *ou* bénéfice (m) net

bought ledger grand livre (m) des achats

bought ledger clerk employé(e) aux écritures (du grand livre des achats)

bounce (v) *[cheque]* (chèque) sans provision

box number numéro (m) de boîte postale

boxed set (présentation sous) coffret (m)

boycott (n) boycott (m) *ou* boycottage (m)

boycott (v) boycotter

bracket (n) *[tax]* tranche (f)

bracket (v) together grouper *ou* réunir *[les éléments d'une liste]*

branch (n) succursale (f); agence (f) *[d'une banque]*

branch manager *[company]* directeur (-trice) de succursale

branch manager *[bank]* directeur (-trice) d'agence

branch office succursale (f); agence (f) *[d'une banque]*

brand (n) marque (f) *ou* nom (m)

brand image image (f) de marque *ou* réputation (f)

brand loyalty fidélité (f) à la marque

brand name marque de fabrique *ou* nom de marque

brand new tout neuf (toute neuve)

breach of contract non respect (m) *ou* rupture (f) de contrat

breach of warranty non respect (m) *ou* rupture (f) de garantie

break (n) pause (f) *ou* arrêt (m)

break (v) *[contract]* rompre (un accord *ou* un contrat)

break down (v) *[itemize]* ventiler les frais

break down (v) *[machine]* être en panne *ou* avoir une panne

break down (v) *[talks]* échouer; prendre fin

break even (v) rentrer dans ses frais

break off (v) negotiations arrêter *ou* rompre les négociations

break (v) the law enfreindre la loi

breakages (n) casse (f)

breakdown (n) *[items]* détail (m) *ou* ventilation (f)

breakdown (n) *[machine]* panne (f) *ou* défaillance (f)

breakdown (n) *[talks]* rupture (f)

breakeven point seuil (m) de rentabilité

bribe (n) pot-de-vin (m)

bribe (v) acheter *ou* corrompre quelqu'un

brief (v) informer *ou* donner des explications

briefcase (n) serviette (f) *ou* porte-documents (m)

bring (v) apporter *ou* amener

bring a civil action intenter un procès à quelqu'un

bring in *[yield]* rapporter

bring out *[launch]* produire *ou* lancer

British (adj) britannique *ou* anglais (-aise)

brochure brochure (f)

broke *[informal]* fauché(e) *ou* sans le sou

broker (n) courtier (m)

brokerage *or* **broker's commission** courtage (m) *ou* commission (f) (d'agent)

brown paper papier (m) kraft

bubble pack blister (m)

budget (n) *[government]* budget (m)

budget (n) *[personal, company]* budget (m)

budget (v) budgéter *ou* budgétiser

budget account *[in bank]* compte (m) crédit

budget deficit déficit (m) budgétaire

budgetary (adj) budgétaire (adj)

budgetary control contrôle (m) budgétaire

budgetary policy politique (f) budgétaire

budgeting préparation (f) de budget; budgétisation (f)

build in (v) incorporer *ou* intégrer

building society société (f) de crédit immobilier

built-in incorporé(e) *ou* intégré(e)

bulk (n) grande quantité

bulk buying achat (m) en gros

bulk shipment expédition (f) en vrac

bulk: in bulk en gros; en vrac

bulky volumineux (-euse)

bull (n) *[Stock Exchange]* spéculateur (m) à la hausse *ou* haussier (m)

bull market marché (m) haussier *ou* à la hausse

bulletin (n) bulletin (m)

bullion (n) lingots (mpl) (d'or ou d'argent)

bureau (n) **de change** bureau (m) de change

bus (n) bus (m) *ou* autobus (m)

business (n) *[commerce]* affaires (fpl) *ou* entreprise (f)

business *[company]* entreprise (f)

business *[discussion]* question (f) *ou* point (m)

business: on business pour affaires

business address adresse (f) du bureau *ou* du lieu de travail

business call visite (f) d'affaires

business card carte (f) professionnelle

business centre centre (m) *ou* quartier (m) des affaires

business class *[travel]* classe (f) affaires

business equipment équipements (mpl) de bureau

business gift cadeau (m) d'affaires

business hours heures (fpl) d'ouverture *ou* de bureau

business letter lettre (f) d'affaires

business lunch déjeuner (m) d'affaires

business premises local (m) à usage de bureaux; locaux (mpl) commerciaux

business strategy stratégie (f) des affaires

business transaction transaction (f) *ou* opération (f)

business trip voyage (m) d'affaires

businessman *or* **businesswoman** homme d'affaires *ou* femme d'affaires

busy (adj) *[work, phone]* occupé(e)

buy (v) acheter

buy back racheter

buy for cash acheter au comptant

buy forward acheter à terme

buyer (n) *[for a store]* acheteur (-euse)

buyer *[client]* acheteur (-euse)

buyer's market marché (m) à la baisse

buying (n) achat (m)

buying department service (m) achats

by-product sous-produit (m)

Cc

cable address adresse (f) télégraphique

calculate (v) calculer; estimer

calculation (n) calcul (m)

calculator (n) calculatrice (f); calculette (f)

calendar month mois (m) civil; mois complet

calendar year année (f) civile

call (n) *[for money]* demande (f) (de remboursement d'un prêt)

call (n) *[phone]* appel (m) *ou* communication (f) (téléphonique)

call (n) *[Stock Exchange]* appel (m) de fonds

call (n) *[visit]* visite (f)

call (v) *or* **make a call** *[phone]* téléphoner à *ou* appeler (quelqu'un)

call (v) **a meeting** convoquer une réunion *ou* une assemblée

call off (v) **a deal** annuler un contrat

call off a strike annuler un ordre de grève

call on (v) *[visit]* visiter

call rate (n) fréquence (f) des visites (d'un représentant)

callable bond obligation (f) remboursable par anticipation

campaign (n) campagne (f)

cancel (v) annuler; décommander (un rendez-vous)

cancel a cheque annuler un chèque

cancel a contract annuler *ou* résilier un contrat

cancellation (n) annulation (f); résiliation (f) *[contrat]*

cancellation clause clause (f) résolutoire

cancellation of an appointment annulation (f) d'un rendez-vous

candidate (n) candidat(e)

canvass (v) prospecter *ou* faire du porte-à-porte

canvasser (n) démarcheur (m) qui fait du porte-à-porte

canvassing (n) démarchage (m) *ou* prospection (f)

canvassing techniques techniques (fpl) de démarchage

capable of capable de

capacity (n) *[ability]* don (m) *ou* capacité (f)

capacity *[production]* capacité (f) *ou* rendement (m)

capacity *[space]* capacité (f) *ou* volume (m)

capacity utilization utilisation (f) de la capacité

capital (n) capital (m) *ou* capitaux (mpl)

capital account compte (m) de capital

capital assets actif (m) immobilisé *ou* immobilisations (fpl)

capital equipment biens (mpl) d'équipement

capital expenditure (coût d') acquisition (f) d'immobilisations

capital gains plus-value (f)

capital gains tax impôt (m) sur les plus-values

capital goods biens (mpl) d'équipement

capital loss moins-value (f)

capital-intensive industry industrie à fort coefficient de capital

capitalization (n) capitalisation (f)

capitalization of reserves capitalisation des réserves

capitalize (v) doter en capital *ou* capitaliser

capitalize on profiter de *ou* exploiter

captive market marché (m) captif

capture (v) prendre le contrôle (de)

capture 10% of the market accaparer 10% du marché

carbon copy copie (f) carbone

carbon paper (papier) carbone (m)

carbonless (adj) sans carbone *ou* autocopiant(e)

card (n) *[business card]* carte (f) (professionnelle)

card *[material]* carton (m)

card *[membership]* carte (f) de membre

card *[postcard]* carte postale

card index (n) fichier (m)

card phone téléphone (m) à carte

card-index (v) mettre sur fiches

card-index file fichier (m)

card-indexing (n) mise (f) sur fiches

cardboard (n) carton (m) *[matériau]*

cardboard box boîte (f) en carton *ou* carton (m)

care of (c/o) aux bons soins de *ou* chez

cargo (n) cargaison (f)

cargo ship cargo (m)

carnet *[international document]* carnet (m) ATA

carriage transport (m) *ou* port (m)

carriage forward port dû *ou* en port dû

carriage free franco de port *ou* franc de port

carriage paid port payé *ou* en port payé

carrier *[company]* transporteur (m) *ou* entreprise (f) de transports

carrier *[vehicle]* camion (m); *[ship]* navire (m)

carry (v) *[approve in a vote]* adopter *ou* voter

carry *[have in stock]* avoir en stock

carry *[produce interest]* produire (un intérêt)

carry *[transport]* transporter; acheminer

carry a line of goods suivre une ligne de produits

carry forward reporter

carry on a business diriger une entreprise

carry over a balance reporter un solde

cartel cartel (m)

carton *[box]* boîte (f) en carton *ou* carton (m)

carton *[material]* carton (m)

case (n) *[box]* caisse (f)

case (n) *[suitcase]* valise (f)

case (v) *[put in boxes]* emballer *ou* mettre dans une boîte

cash (adv) (payer) (au) comptant *ou* (payer) cash

cash (n) *[money]* argent (m) comptant *ou* espèces (fpl) *ou* liquide (m) *ou* cash (m)

cash (v) a cheque encaisser un chèque *ou* remettre un chèque à l'encaissement

cash account compte (m) de caisse

cash (n) advance avance (f) de caisse

cash and carry libre-service (m) de gros *ou* cash and carry (m)

cash balance solde (m) de trésorerie

cash book livre (m) de caisse

cash card carte (f) de retrait

cash deal vente (f) au comptant

cash deposit dépôt (m) en espèces

cash desk caisse (f)

cash discount escompte (m) de caisse

cash dispenser distributeur (m) automatique de billets (DAB) *ou* billetterie (f)

cash float encaisse (f) *ou* caisse (f)

cash flow marge (f) brute d'auto-financement (MBA); flux (m) de trésorerie

cash flow forecast prévisions (fpl) de trésorerie

cash flow statement plan (m) de trésorerie

cash in hand avoir (m) en caisse

cash offer offre (f) en espèces *ou* offre au comptant

cash on delivery (c.o.d.) livraison (f) contre remboursement

cash payment paiement (au) comptant

cash price prix (m) du comptant

cash purchase achat (m) (au) comptant

cash register *[till]* caisse (f) (enregistreuse)

cash reserves réserves (fpl) de trésorerie

cash sale vente (f) au comptant

cash terms paiement (m) comptant

cash transaction opération (f) au comptant

cash voucher bon (m) de caisse

cashable (adj) encaissable *ou* qui peut être encaissé(e)

cashier (n) caissier (-ière)

cashier's check *[US]* chèque (m) de banque

casting vote (n) voix (f) prépondérante

casual work (n) travail (m) temporaire

casual worker travailleur (-euse) *ou* employé(e) temporaire

catalogue catalogue (m)

catalogue price prix (m) catalogue

category catégorie (f)

cater for (v) fournir

caveat emptor aux risques de l'acheteur

ceiling (n) plafond (m)

ceiling price prix (m) plafond

cellular telephone téléphone (m) cellulaire

central (adj) central(e)

central bank banque (f) centrale

central purchasing achats (mpl) centralisés

centralization (n) centralisation (f)

centralize (v) centraliser

centre *[important town]* centre (m)

CEO (chief executive officer) directeur (m) général

certificate (n) certificat (m)

certificate of approval certificat d'homologation

certificate of deposit certificat de dépôt *ou* bon (m) de caisse

certificate of guarantee certificat de garantie

certificate of origin certificat d'origine

certificate of registration certificat d'enregistrement

certificated (adj) certifié(e)

certificated bankrupt failli (m) concordataire

certified accountant expert-comptable (m) (diplômé)

certified cheque chèque certifié

certified copy copie certifiée conforme

certify (v) certifier

cession (n) cession (f)

chain (n) *[of stores]* chaîne (f) de magasins

chain store magasin (m) à succursales multiples

chairman *[of committee]* président(e)

chairman *[of company]* président(e)

chairman and managing director président-directeur général (PDG)

Chamber of Commerce Chambre (f) de commerce et d'industrie

change (n) *[cash]* monnaie (f)

change (n) *[difference]* changement (m)

change (v) *[become different]* changer

change (v) *[money]* changer (de l'argent)

change hands changer de propriétaire

change machine distributeur (m) de monnaie

channel (n) canal (m)

channel (v) canaliser

channels of distribution canaux (mpl) de distribution

charge (n) *[in court]* inculpation (f) *ou* accusation (f)

charge (n) *[money]* prix (m) *ou* droit (m) *ou* frais (mpl)

charge (n) *[on account]* débit (m); imputation (f)

charge (v) **(in court]** inculper *ou* accuser quelqu'un

charge (v) *[money]* demander *ou* faire payer *ou* facturer

charge a purchase mettre (un achat) sur un compte

charge account compte (m) d'achat

charge card carte (f) accréditive

chargeable (adj) imputable *ou* à la charge de

charges forward en port dû *ou* frais à payer

charter (n) affrètement (m) *ou* nolisage (m)

charter (v) affréter *ou* noliser

charter an aircraft affréter *ou* noliser un avion

charter flight vol (m) charter

charter plane avion (m) charter

charterer (n) affréteur (m)

chartering (n) affrètement (m) *ou* nolisage (m)

chase (v) *[an order]* relancer *ou* activer (le travail)

chase (v) *[follow]* poursuivre

cheap bon marché

cheap labour main-d'oeuvre (f) bon marché

cheap money argent (m) bon marché

cheap rate tarif (m) réduit

check (n) *[examination]* contrôle (m) *ou* vérification (f)

check (n) *[stop]* arrêt (m) *ou* interruption (f)

check (v) *[examine]* contrôler *ou* vérifier

check (v) *[stop]* arrêter *ou* interrompre

check in *[at airport]* se présenter à l'enregistrement

check in *[at hotel]* arriver à l'hôtel; s'inscrire à l'arrivée (à l'hôtel)

check-in (n) *[at airport]* enregistrement (m)

check-in counter enregistrement (m)

check-in time heure (f) d'enregistrement

check out *[of hotel]* quitter l'hôtel; régler la note d'hôtel au départ

checkout *[in supermarket]* caisse (f)

check sample échantillon-témoin (m)

cheque (n) chèque (m)

cheque (guarantee) card carte (de garantie) bancaire

cheque account; checking account *[US]* compte (m) de chèques

cheque book carnet (m) de chèques *ou* chéquier (m)

cheque number numéro (m) de chèque

cheque stub talon (m) de chèque

cheque to bearer chèque (m) au porteur

chief (adj) principal(e)

chief clerk chef (m) de bureau

chief executive (officer) président-directeur (m) général (PDG)

choice (adj) de choix *ou* de qualité

choice (n) *[choosing]* choix (m)

choice (n) *[items to choose from]* choix (m)

choice (n) *[thing chosen]* choix (m)

choose (v) choisir

Christmas bonus treizième mois

chronic (adj) chronique (adj)

chronological order ordre (m) chronologique

c.i.f. (cost, insurance and freight) CAF (coût, assurance, fret)

circular (n) circulaire (f)

circular letter circulaire (f)

circular letter of credit lettre (f) de crédit circulaire

circulation (n) *[money]* circulation (f)

circulation *[newspaper]* tirage (m)

civil law code (m) civil *ou* droit (m) civil

claim (n) réclamation (f) *ou* revendication (f) *ou* demande (f)

claim (v) *[insurance]* réclamer (des dommages-intérêts)

claim (v) *[right]* réclamer

claim (v) *[suggest]* prétendre

claimant (n) requérant(e)

claims department service (m) des réclamations

claims manager chef (m) du service des réclamations

class (n) classe (f) *ou* catégorie (f)

classification (n) classification (f)

classified ads annonces classées *ou* petites annonces

classified advertisements annonces classées *ou* petites annonces

classified directory répertoire (m) d'adresses par professions

classify (v) classer

clause (n) clause (f) *ou* article (m)

clawback (n) récupération (f) *ou* reprise (f)

clear (adj) *[complete]* entier (-ière) *ou* complet (-ète)

clear (adj) *[easy to understand]* clair(e)

clear (v) *[stock]* liquider

clear: to clear en solde

clear (v) a cheque compenser un chèque

clear (v) a debt rembourser une dette

clear (adj) profit bénéfice (m) net

clearance certificate *[customs]* certificat (m) de passage en douane *ou* de dédouanement

clearance of a cheque compensation (f) d'un chèque

clearance sale soldes (m&fpl)

clearing (n) *[paying]* acquittement (m) (d'une dette)

clearing bank banque (f) de compensation

clerical error erreur (f) d'écriture

clerical staff personnel (m) de bureau

clerical work travail (m) de bureau

clerk (n) employé(e) de bureau

client (n) client(e)

clientele (n) clientèle (f)

climb (v) grimper

clinch (v) (a deal) conclure (un marché)

clipping service agence (f) de coupures de presse

close (n) *[end]* fin (f) *ou* clôture (f)

close (v) *[after work]* fermer (après le travail)

close a bank account fermer un compte en banque

close a meeting lever la séance

close an account fermer *ou* clôturer un compte

close down fermer (un magasin *ou* une usine)

close to (adj) près de

closed fermé(e)

closed circuit TV télévision (f) en circuit fermé

closed market marché d'exclusivité

closing (adj) final(e) *ou* dernier (-ière)

closing (n) fermeture (f)

closing balance bilan (m) de fin d'exercice

closing bid dernière enchère (f)

closing date date (f) limite

closing price prix (m) *ou* cours (m) de clôture

closing stock stock (m) en fin d'exercice

closing time heure (f) de fermeture

closing-down sale liquidation (f) du stock

closure (n) fermeture (f)

c/o (care of) aux bons soins de *ou* chez

co-creditor cocréancier (-ière)

co-director codirecteur (-trice)

co-insurance coassurance (f)

co-operate (v) collaborer *ou* coopérer

co-operation (n) coopération (f)

co-operative (adj) coopératif (-ive)

co-operative (n) coopérative (f) *[société]*

co-opt (v) someone coopter quelqu'un

co-owner (n) copropriétaire (mf)

co-ownership (n) copropriété (f)

c.o.d. *or* **COD (cash on delivery)** livraison (f) contre remboursement

code (n) code (m)

code of practice politique (f) générale (de l'entreprise)

coding (n) codage (m) *ou* chiffrage (m)

coin (n) pièce (f) de monnaie

cold call (n) visite (f) impromptue (d'un représentant)

cold start (n) démarrage (m) à *ou* de zéro

cold storage (n) conservation (f) en chambre froide

cold store (n) chambre (f) froide *ou* entrepôt (m) frigorifique

collaborate (v) collaborer

collaboration (n) collaboration (f)

collapse (n) effondrement (m)

collapse (v) s'effondrer *ou* s'écrouler

collateral (adj) en nantissement

collateral (n) garantie (f) *ou* nantissement (m)

collect (v) *[fetch]* aller chercher

collect (v) *[money]* percevoir

collect (v) a debt recouvrer une créance

collect call *[US]* appel (m) en PCV

collection (n) *[of goods]* enlèvement (m)

collection *[of money]* recouvrement (m) *ou* perception (f)

collection *[postal]* levée (f)

collection charges *or* **collection rates** frais (mpl) d'enlèvement

collective (adj) collectif (-ive)

collective ownership propriété (f) collective

collective wage agreement convention (f) collective sur les salaires

collector (n) percepteur (m) *ou* receveur (m)

commerce (n) commerce (m)

commercial (adj) commercial(e)

commercial (n) *[TV]* publicité (f) *ou* pub (f) *ou* message (m) publicitaire *[à la télévision]*

commercial attaché attaché(e) commercial(e)

commercial college école (f) supérieure de commerce

commercial course cours (m) de commerce

commercial directory répertoire (m) d'entreprises

commercial district quartier (m) commerçant

commercial failure faillite (f) *ou* banqueroute (f)

commercial law droit (m) commercial

commercial traveller représentant(e) de commerce *ou* délégué(e) commercial(e) *ou* VRP (m)

commercial undertaking entreprise (f) commerciale

commercialization (n) commercialisation (f)

commercialize (v) commercialiser

commercials (n) *[TV]* la publicité *[à la télévision]*

commission (n) *[committee]* commission (f) (d'enquête)

commission *[money]* commission (f)

commission agent agent (m) à la commission

commission rep représentant (m) à la commission

commit (v) *[crime]* commettre

commit funds to a project affecter une somme à un projet

commitments (n) engagements (mpl) financiers

commodity (n) marchandise (f) *ou* denrée (f)

commodity exchange bourse (f) de commerce *ou* des matières premières

commodity futures opérations (fpl) à terme sur les matières premières

commodity market marché (m) des matières premières

common *[frequent]* courant(e) *ou* commun(e)

common *[belonging to more than one]* commun(e)

common carrier entreprise (f) de transports publics

Common Market Marché (m) Commun

common ownership propriété (f) collective

common pricing fixation (f) concertée des prix

communicate (v) communiquer

communication (n) *[general]*
communication (f)

communication *[message]* message
(m) *ou* communication (f)

communications communications (fpl)

community (n) communauté (f) *ou*
collectivité (f)

commute (v) *[exchange]* échanger

commute (v) *[travel]* voyager (chaque
jour) entre son domicile et son lieu
de travail

commuter (n) banlieusard (m) *[qui
fait le trajet quotidien de son
domicile à son lieu de travail]*

companies' register (n) registre (m)
du commerce et des sociétés (RCS)

company (n) société (f) *ou* compagnie
(f)

company director directeur (-trice);
administrateur (-trice)

company law droit (m) des sociétés

company secretary secrétaire (mf)
général(e)

comparability (n) comparabilité (f)

comparable (adj) comparable

compare (v) comparer

compare with (v) être comparable à

comparison (n) comparaison (f)

compensate (v) dédommager *ou*
indemniser

compensation (n) compensation (f)

compensation for damage
dédommagement (m) *ou*
indemnisation (f)

compete (v) with someone *or* **with a
company** faire concurrence à *ou*
concurrencer quelqu'un *ou* une société

competing (adj) concurrentiel (-elle) *ou*
en concurrence

competing firms entreprises (fpl)
concurrentes

competing products produits (mpl)
concurrentiels

competition (n) concurrence (f)

competitive (adj) concurrentiel (-elle)
ou compétitif (-ive)

competitive price prix (m)
concurrentiel *ou* prix compétitif

competitive pricing fixation (f) de prix
compétitifs

competitive products produits (mpl)
concurrentiels

competitively priced à (un) prix
compétitif

competitiveness (n) compétitivité (f)

competitor (n) concurrent(e)

complain (v) (about) se plaindre (de)

complaint (n) réclamation (f)

complaints department service (m)
des réclamations

complementary (adj) complémentaire

complete (adj) complet (-ète) *ou*
achevé(e)

complete (v) exécuter *ou* terminer

completion exécution (f) *ou*
achèvement (m) (de travaux, etc.)

completion date date (f) d'achèvement
(de travaux)

completion of a contract signature (f)
d'un contrat

compliance (n) acceptation (f)

complimentary (adj) de faveur

complimentary ticket billet (m) gratuit
ou billet de faveur

compliments slip carte (f)
professionnelle (qui accompagne un
envoi)

comply with (v) se conformer à

composition (n) *[with creditors]*
accommodement (m)

compound interest intérêts (mpl)
composés

comprehensive (adj) global(e) *ou*
général(e)

comprehensive insurance assurance
(f) tous risques

compromise (n) compromis (m)

compromise (v) arriver à un
compromis

compulsory (adj) obligatoire; forcé(e)

compulsory liquidation liquidation (f)
forcée

compulsory purchase *[of property]*
expropriation (f)

computer (n) ordinateur (m)

computer bureau société (f) de
services et d'ingénierie informatique
(SSII)

computer department service (m)
informatique

computer error erreur (f) d'ordinateur

computer file fichier (m)
(informatique)

computer language langage (m) de programmation

computer listing listing (m) *ou* sortie (f) d'imprimante

computer printer imprimante (f) (d'ordinateur)

computer printout sortie (f) d'imprimante *ou* listing (m)

computer program programme (m) *ou* logiciel (m)

computer programmer programmeur (-euse) *ou* informaticien (-ienne)

computer programming programmation (f)

computer services services (mpl) informatiques

computer system système (m) informatique

computer terminal terminal (m) d'ordinateur

computer time temps (m) d'ordinateur

computer-readable en langage machine

computer-readable codes codes (mpl) en langage machine

computerize (v) informatiser

computerized (adj) informatisé(e)

concealment (n) of assets dissimulation (f) d'actif

concern (n) *[business]* entreprise (f) *ou* firme (f)

concern (n) *[worry]* préoccupation (f)

concern (v) concerner

concession (n) *[reduction]* réduction (f)

concession *[right]* concession (f) *ou* droit (m) exclusif de vente

concessionaire (n) concessionnaire (mf)

conciliation (n) conciliation (f)

conclude (v) *[agreement]* conclure

condition (n) *[state]* condition (f) *ou* état (m)

condition *[terms]* condition (f)

condition: on condition that à (la) condition que *ou* sous réserve de

conditional (adj) conditionnel (-elle)

conditions of employment conditions (fpl) d'emploi

conditions of sale conditions (fpl) de vente

conduct (v) negotiations mener des négociations

conference (n) *[large]* congrès (m)

conference *[small]* conférence (f)

conference phone téléphone (m) de conférence

conference room salle (f) de conférences *ou* de réunion

confidence (n) confiance (f)

confidential (adj) confidentiel (-elle)

confidential report rapport (m) confidentiel

confidentiality (n) confidentialité (f)

confirm (v) confirmer

confirm a booking confirmer une réservation

confirm by letter envoyer une lettre de confirmation

confirm someone in a job confirmer une embauche

confirmation confirmation (f)

conflict (n) of interest conflit (m) d'intérêts

conglomerate (n) conglomérat (m)

connect (v) lier *ou* relier

connecting flight correspondance (f)

connection lien (m) *ou* relation (f)

consider (v) examiner *ou* étudier

consign (v) consigner

consignee (n) destinataire (mf) *ou* consignataire (mf)

consignment (n) *[sending]* expédition (f) *ou* envoi (m)

consignment (n) *[things sent, received]* envoi (m); arrivage (m)

consignment note bordereau (m) d'expédition

consignor (n) expéditeur (m)

consist of (v) consister en *ou* comprendre

consolidate (v) consolider

consolidate *[shipments]* grouper

consolidated consolidé(e)

consolidated shipment envoi (m) groupé

consolidation (n) groupage (m) (d'envois)

consortium (n) consortium (m)

constant (adj) constant(e)

consult (v) consulter

consultancy assistance (f)

consultancy firm cabinet-conseil (m)

consultant (n) expert (m) *ou* consultant (m)

consulting engineer ingénieur conseil (m)

consumables (n) produits (mpl) de consommation

consumer (n) consommateur (-trice)

consumer credit crédits (mpl) à la consommation

consumer durables biens (mpl) de consommation durables

consumer goods biens (mpl) de consommation

consumer panel panel (m) de consommateurs

consumer price index indice (m) des prix à la consommation

consumer protection protection (f) du consommateur

consumer research recherche (f) des besoins des consommateurs

consumer spending dépenses (fpl) des consommateurs

consumption (n) consommation (f)

contact (n) *[general]* contact (m)

contact (n) *[person]* relation (f) *ou* contact (m)

contact (v) contacter *ou* joindre

contain (v) contenir

container (n) *[box, tin]* contenant (m)

container (n) *[for shipping]* conteneur (m)

container port port (m) pour porte-conteneurs

container ship porte-conteneurs (m)

container terminal terminal (m) maritime (pour porte-conteneurs)

containerization (n) *[putting into containers]* conteneurisation (f) *ou* mise (f) en conteneurs

containerization *[shipping in containers]* transport (m) par conteneurs

containerize (v) *[put into containers]* conteneuriser *ou* mettre (des marchandises) en conteneurs

containerize *[ship in containers]* expédier (des marchandises) par conteneurs

content (n) contenu (m) *ou* teneur (f)

contents (n) *[things contained]* contenu (m)

contested takeover rachat (m) contesté

contingency (n) imprévu (m) *ou* éventualité (f)

contingency fund fonds (m) de prévoyance

contingency plan plan (m) d'urgence

continual (adj) continuel (-elle)

continually (adv) continuellement *ou* sans cesse

continuation (n) continuation (f) *ou* poursuite (f)

continue (v) continuer

continuous (adj) continu(e)

continuous feed *[paper]* alimentation (f) en continu

continuous stationery papier (m) en continu *ou* papier listing

contra account compte (m) de contrepartie

contra an entry contrepasser une écriture

contra entry écriture (f) de contrepartie *ou* contrepassation (f)

contract (n) contrat (m); engagement (m)

contract (v) contracter

contract law droit (m) des contrats et des obligations

contract note avis (m) d'exécution

contract of employment contrat (m) de travail

contract work travail (m) contractuel

contracting party partie (f) contractante

contractor (n) entrepreneur (m)

contractual (adj) contractuel (-elle)

contractual liability responsabilité (f) contractuelle

contractually (adv) conformément à un contrat

contrary (n) contraire (m)

contrast (n) contraste (m)

contribute (v) contribuer (une somme) *ou* cotiser

contribution contribution (f)

contribution of capital versement (m) au capital

contributor (n) *[of money]* donateur (-trice)

contributor (n) *[of work, etc.]* collaborateur (-trice)

control (n) *[check]* contrôle (m) *ou* vérification (f) *ou* surveillance (f)

control (n) *[power]* contrôle (m) *ou* maîtrise (f)

control (v) *[check]* contrôler *ou* vérifier *ou* surveiller

control (v) *[have power]* contrôler *ou* maîtriser

control (v) a business diriger une entreprise

control (n) key *[computer keyboard]* touche (f) de contrôle

control systems tests (mpl) et diagnostics

controlled economy économie (f) dirigée

controller *[US]* chef comptable (m)

controller *[who checks]* contrôleur (m) *ou* vérificateur (m)

controlling (adj) qui contrôle

convene (v) convoquer

convenient (adj) pratique *ou* commode

conversion (n) conversion (f)

conversion of funds *[embezzlement]* détournement (m) de fonds

conversion price *or* **conversion rate** taux (m) de conversion

convert (v) changer de l'argent

convertibility (n) convertibilité (f)

convertible currency monnaie (f) convertible

convertible loan stock valeurs (f) convertibles

conveyance (n) acte (m) de cession

conveyancer (n) notaire (mf) (qui rédige un acte de cession)

conveyancing (n) rédaction (f) d'un acte de cession

cooling off period (after purchase) délai (m) de réflexion

cooperative society société (f) coopérative *ou* coopérative (f)

copartner (n) coassocié(e)

copartnership (n) coparticipation (f)

cope (v) se débrouiller *ou* s'en tirer

copier (n) photocopieur (m) *ou* photocopieuse (f)

copy (n) *[book]* exemplaire (n)

copy (n) *[document]* document (m)

copy (n) *[duplicate]* copie (f)

copy (n) *[newspaper]* exemplaire (m) *ou* numéro (m)

copy (v) faire une copie *ou* reproduire

copying machine photocopieur (m) *ou* photocopieuse (f)

corner (n) *[angle]* coin (m) *ou* angle (m)

corner (n) *[monopoly]* situation (f) de monopole

corner shop magasin (m) du coin

corner (v) the market accaparer le marché

corporate (adj) image image (f) de marque (de la société)

corporate name raison (f) sociale

corporate plan plan (m) de développement de la société

corporate planning planification (f) dans l'entreprise

corporate profits bénéfices (mpl) d'une société

corporation (n) société (f)

corporation tax impôt (m) sur les bénéfices des sociétés

correct (adj) correct(e) *ou* exact(e)

correct (v) corriger

correction (n) correction (f)

correspond (v) with someone *[write]* correspondre avec quelqu'un

correspond with something *[fit]* correspondre à quelque chose

correspondence (n) correspondance (f)

correspondent (n) *[journalist]* correspondant(e) *ou* journaliste (mf)

correspondent (n) *[who writes letters]* correspondant(e)

cost (n) coût (m) *ou* frais (mpl) *ou* prix (m)

cost (v) coûter; valoir

cost accountant responsable (mf) de la comptabilité analytique

cost accounting comptabilité (f) analytique

cost analysis analyse (f) des coûts

cost centre centre (m) de coût

cost factor facteur (m) (de) coût

cost of living coût (m) de la vie

cost of sales coût (m) de revient (des marchandises vendues)

cost plus coût (m) majoré

cost price prix (m) coûtant

cost, insurance and freight (c.i.f.) coût, assurance, fret (CAF)

cost-benefit analysis étude (f) du rapport coût-bénéfice

cost-cutting (n) réduction (f) des frais

cost-effective (adj) rentable

cost-effectiveness (n) rentabilité (f)

cost-of-living allowance indemnité (f) de vie chère

cost-of-living bonus prime (f) de vie chère

cost-of-living increase augmentation (f) indexée sur le coût de la vie

cost-of-living index indice (m) du coût de la vie

cost-push inflation inflation (f) par les coûts

costing (n) calcul (m) du prix de revient

costly (adj) cher (chère) *ou* onéreux (-euse)

costs (n) frais (mpl) *[de procès]*

counsel (n) avocat-conseil (m)

count (v) *[add]* compter

count (v) *[include]* inclure

counter (n) comptoir (m); rayon (m)

counter staff vendeurs (-euses) *ou* préposé(e)s au(x) comptoir(s)

counter-claim (n) demande (f) reconventionnelle

counter-claim (v) opposer une demande reconventionnelle

counter-offer contre-proposition (f)

counterbid (n) surenchère (f)

counterfeit (adj) faux (fausse)

counterfeit (v) contrefaire

counterfoil (n) talon (m) *ou* souche (f) *[chéquier, etc.]*

countermand (v) annuler *[rendez-vous, réunion]*

countersign (v) contresigner

country (n) *[not town]* campagne (f); province (f); région (f)

country *[state]* pays (m)

country of origin pays (m) d'origine

coupon bon (m)

coupon ad publicité (f) avec coupon-réponse

courier (n) *[guide]* accompagnateur (-trice)

courier *[messenger]* coursier (m)

court (n) cour (f) *ou* tribunal (m)

court case procès (m)

covenant (n) engagement (m) contractuel

covenant (v) s'engager (à verser une somme d'argent déterminée)

cover (n) *[insurance]* garantie (f) *ou* couverture (f)

cover (n) *[protective cover]* housse (f)

cover (v) *[expenses]* couvrir (ses dépenses)

cover (v) *[put on top]* couvrir *ou* recouvrir

cover (v) costs couvrir les coûts de production

cover (v) a risk être assuré contre un risque

cover charge (n) *[in restaurant]* couvert (m)

cover note (n) attestation (f) provisoire d'assurance

covering letter *or* **note** lettre (f) d'accompagnement

crash (n) *[accident]* accident (m)

crash (n) *[financial]* crise (f) (financière); krach (m)

crash (v) *[fail]* faire faillite *ou* s'effondrer

crash (v) *[hit]* s'écraser contre

crate (n) caisse (f)

crate (v) mettre (des marchandises) en caisse(s)

credit (n) crédit (m)

credit: in credit *[account]* créditeur (-trice) (adj)

credit: on credit à crédit

credit (v) (an account) créditer (un compte)

credit account *[in shop]* compte (m) d'achat

credit agency agence (f) de notation financière

credit balance solde (m) créditeur

credit bank banque (f) de crédit

credit card carte (f) de crédit

credit card sale vente (f) réglée avec (une) carte de crédit

credit ceiling plafond (m) de crédit

credit column colonne (f) des crédits

credit control contrôle (m) de crédit *ou* encadrement (m) du crédit

credit entry écriture (f) au crédit

credit facilities facilités (fpl) de crédit

credit freeze restriction (f) *ou* encadrement (m) du crédit

credit limit plafond (m) *ou* limite (f) de crédit

credit note facture (f) d'avoir *ou* note (f) de crédit

credit policy politique (f) en matière de crédit

credit rating notation (f) *ou* note (f) financière

credit side colonne (f) des crédits *ou* côté (m) crédit

credit-worthy (adj) solvable

creditor (n) créancier (m)

cross (v) a cheque barrer un chèque

cross off (v) radier (quelque chose d'une liste)

cross out (v) barrer

cross rate taux (m) (de change) croisé

crossed cheque chèque (m) barré

cubic (adj) cube

cubic measure mesure (f) de volume

cum avec

cum coupon coupon attaché

cum dividend avec dividende

cumulative (adj) cumulatif (-ive)

cumulative interest intérêts (mpl) composés

cumulative preference share action (f) privilégiée cumulative

currency (n) devise (f) (étrangère)

currency conversion conversion (f) en devises étrangères

currency note billet (m) de banque

currency reserves réserves (fpl) de devises

current (adj) courant(e)

current account compte (m) courant

current assets actif (m) circulant

current cost accounting méthode (f) des coûts courants

current liabilities dettes (fpl) à court terme *ou* passif (m) exigible

current price prix (m) courant *ou* actuel

current rate of exchange taux (m) de change en vigueur

current yield rendement (m) courant *ou* taux (m) de rendement (d'une action)

curriculum vitae (CV) curriculum (m) vitae (CV)

curve courbe (f)

custom (n) clientèle (f)

custom-built *or* **custom-made** (fait) sur mesure *ou* sur commande

customer (n) client(e)

customer appeal facteur (m) de séduction du client

customer loyalty fidélité (f) de la clientèle

customer satisfaction satisfaction (f) du client

customer service department service (m) clients

customs douane (f)

Customs and Excise Administration (f) des douanes

customs barrier barrière (f) douanière

customs broker agent (m) en douane

customs clearance dédouanement (m)

customs declaration déclaration (f) en douane

customs declaration form formulaire (m) de déclaration en douane

customs duty droit (m) de douane

customs entry point poste (m) frontière

customs examination contrôle (m) douanier

customs formalities formalités (fpl) de douane *ou* formalités douanières

customs officer *or* **customs official** douanier (m)

customs receipt récépissé (m) des douanes

customs seal plomb (m) de la douane

customs tariff tarif (m) douanier

customs union union (f) douanière

cut (n) réduction (f)

cut (v) réduire *ou* diminuer *ou* supprimer

cut down on expenses réduire les dépenses

cut price (n) prix (m) réduit

cut-price (adj) à prix réduit *ou* au rabais

cut-price goods marchandises à prix sacrifiés

cut-price petrol essence à prix réduit

cut-price store magasin à prix réduits *ou* de discount

cut-throat competition concurrence (f) féroce

CV (curriculum vitae) curriculum (m) vitae (CV)

cycle cycle (m)

cyclical (adj) cyclique

cyclical factors facteurs (mpl) conjoncturels

Dd

daily journalier (-ière) *ou* quotidien (-ienne)

daisy-wheel printer imprimante (f) à marguerite

damage (n) dommage (m) *ou* dégâts (mpl)

damage (v) abîmer *ou* endommager

damage survey expertise (f) des dégâts

damage to property dommages (mpl) matériels

damaged endommagé(e) *ou* abîmé(e)

damages dommages-intérêts (mpl) *ou* dommages et intérêts

data (n) données (fpl)

data processing traitement (m) de données *ou* informatique (f)

data retrieval recherche (f) d'information

database base (f) de données

date (n) date (f)

date (v) dater

date of receipt date (f) de réception

date stamp *[device]* timbre (m) dateur

dated (adj) daté(e) (de)

day (n) *[24 hours]* jour (m)

day *[working day]* jour (m) *ou* journée (f) (de travail)

day shift équipe (f) de jour

day-to-day ordinaire *ou* courant(e) *ou* au jour le jour

dead (adj) *[person]* mort(e) *ou* décédé(e)

dead account compte (m) oisif *ou* compte qui dort

dead loss perte (f) sèche

deadline (n) date (f) limite

deadlock (n) impasse (f)

deadlock (v) arriver à une impasse

deadweight charge (f) en lourd

deadweight cargo port (m) en lourd

deadweight tonnage charge (f) en lourd

deal (n) marché (m) *ou* accord (m) *ou* contrat (m)

deal in (v) faire le commerce de

deal with (v) an order s'occuper d'une commande *ou* exécuter une commande

deal with someone faire affaire *ou* traiter avec quelqu'un

dealer (n) négociant(e) *ou* marchand(e)

dealing (n) *[commerce]* commerce (m)

dealing *[Stock Exchange]* opération (f) boursière *ou* de Bourse

dear (adj) *[costly]* cher (chère) *ou* coûteux (-euse)

dear (adj) *[starting a letter]* cher (chère)

Dear Madam; Dear Sir Madame; Monsieur

debenture (n) obligation (f) (émise par une société)

debenture holder obligataire (mf)

debit (n) débit (m)

debit (v) an account débiter un compte

debit balance solde (m) débiteur

debit column colonne (f) des débits

debit entry écriture (f) au débit

debit note note (f) de débit

debits and credits débit et crédit *ou* passif et actif

debt (n) dette (f)

debt collection recouvrement (m) de créances

debt collection agency agence (f) de recouvrement (de créances)

debt collector agent (m) de recouvrement (de créances)

debtor (n) débiteur (m)

debtor side colonne (f) des débits

debts due créances (fpl) exigibles

decentralization (n) décentralisation (f)

decentralize (v) décentraliser

decide (v) décider de; se décider à

decide on a course of action arrêter un plan d'action

deciding (adj) décisif (-ive)

deciding factor facteur (m) décisif

decimal (n) décimale (f)

decimal (adj) point virgule (f) (décimale)

decision (n) décision (f)

decision maker décideur (m)

decision making prise (f) de décision

decision-making processes processus (m) de prise de décision

deck (n) *[ship]* pont (m) (d'un navire)

deck cargo pontée (f)

declaration (n) déclaration (f)

declaration of bankruptcy jugement (m) déclaratif de faillite

declaration of income déclaration (f) de revenus

declare (v) déclarer

declare goods to customs déclarer des marchandises à la douane

declare someone bankrupt déclarer quelqu'un en faillite

declared déclaré(e)

declared value valeur (f) déclarée

decline (n) baisse (f) *ou* ralentissement (m)

decline (v) *[fall]* être en baisse *ou* diminuer

decontrol (v) libérer

decrease (n) baisse (f) *ou* diminution (f)

decrease (v) baisser *ou* diminuer

decrease (n) in price baisse (f) de prix

decrease (n) in value diminution (f) *ou* perte (f) de valeur

decreasing (adj) décroissant(e) *ou* en baisse

deduct (v) déduire *ou* retenir

deductible (adj) déductible

deduction (n) déduction (f) *ou* retenue (f)

deed (n) acte (m)

deed of assignment acte (m) de cession (de créance)

deed of covenant engagement (m) contractuel (à verser une somme déterminée)

deed of partnership contrat (m) d'association

deed of transfer acte (m) de cession (de propriété)

deeds (of a house) acte (m) de propriété

default (n) manquement (m) *ou* défaillance (f)

default (v) ne pas faire face à ses engagements

default on payments se trouver en cessation de paiements

defaulter (n) témoin (m) défaillant; partie (f) défaillante

defect (n) défaut (m) *ou* vice (m) de fabrication

defective *[faulty]* défectueux (-euse)

defective *[not valid]* non valable *ou* non valide

defence (n) *[legal]* défense (f)

defence *[protection]* défense (f)

defence counsel avocat (m) de la défense

defend (v) défendre

defend a lawsuit se défendre en justice

defendant (n) défendeur (défenderesse) *ou* accusé(e) *ou* prévenu(e)

defer (v) différer *ou* remettre

defer payment différer le paiement

deferment (n) ajournement (m) *ou* remise (f)

deferment of payment délai (m) de paiement

deferred reporté(e) *ou* différé(e)

deferred creditor créancier (m) différé

deferred payment paiement (m) différé

deficit (n) déficit (m)

deficit financing financement (m) du déficit budgétaire

deflation (n) déflation (f)

deflationary (adj) déflationniste

defray (v) *[costs]* défrayer *ou* couvrir des frais

defray someone's expenses rembourser les frais de quelqu'un

del credere ducroire

del credere agent commissionnaire (m) ducroire

delay (n) retard (m)

delay (v) être en retard *ou* retarder

delegate (n) délégué(e)

delegate (v) déléguer

delegation (n) *[action]* délégation (f) (de pouvoirs)

delegation *[people]* délégation (f)

delete (v) rayer *ou* supprimer

deliver (v) livrer

delivered price prix tout compris *[port et emballage inclus]*

delivery (n) *[goods]* livraison (f) *ou* envoi (m)

delivery date date (f) de livraison

delivery note bulletin (m) de livraison

delivery of a bill of exchange transfert (m) *ou* cession (f) d'une traite

delivery of goods livraison (f) de marchandises

delivery order instructions (fpl) pour la livraison

delivery time délai (m) de livraison

delivery van camion (m) *ou* camionnette (f) de livraison

deliveryman (n) livreur (m)

demand (n) *[for payment]* demande (f) *ou* réclamation (f)

demand (n) *[need]* demande (f)

demand: on demand à vue *ou* à présentation

demand (v) réclamer

demand bill traite (f) à vue

demand deposit dépôt (m) à vue

demand-led inflation inflation (f) liée à la demande

demerge (v) effectuer une (opération de) scission

demerger (n) scission (f)

demonstrate (v) faire une démonstration

demonstration (n) démonstration (f)

demonstration model modèle (m) *ou* appareil (m) de démonstration

demonstrator (n) démonstrateur (-trice)

demurrage (n) surestarie (f)

department (n) *[in government]* ministère (m)

department *[in office]* service (m) *ou* bureau (m)

department *[in shop]* rayon (m)

department store grand magasin

departmental (adj) départemental(e)

departmental manager *[shop]* chef (m) de rayon *[d'un magasin]*

departure (n) *[going away]* départ (m)

departure *[new venture]* nouveau départ *ou* nouvelle orientation

departure lounge *[airport]* salle (f) d'embarquement

departures (n) *[at airport, etc.]* départs (mpl)

depend on (v) dépendre de *ou* compter sur

depending on suivant *ou* en fonction de

deposit (n) *[in bank]* dépôt (m)

deposit (n) *[paid in advance]* acompte (m) *ou* provision (f) *ou* arrhes (fpl)

deposit (v) verser de l'argent (sur un compte)

deposit account compte (m) de dépôt(s) *ou* compte sur livret

deposit slip *[bank]* bordereau (m) de versement

depositor (n) déposant(e)

depository (n) *[place]* dépôt (m)

depot (n) dépôt (m) *ou* entrepôt (m)

depreciate (v) *[amortize]* amortir

depreciate *[lose value]* diminuer de valeur *ou* se déprécier

depreciation (n) *[amortizing]* amortissement (m) *ou* dépréciation (f)

depreciation *[loss of value]* moins-value (f) *ou* dévaluation (f)

depreciation rate taux (m) d'amortissement

depression (n) dépression (f)

dept (= department)

deputize (v) for someone assurer l'intérim de quelqu'un

deputy (n) suppléant(e) *ou* adjoint(e)

deputy manager directeur (-trice) adjoint(e)

deputy managing director directeur général adjoint *ou* directrice générale adjointe

deregulation (n) déréglementation (f)

describe (v) décrire

description (n) description (f)

design (n) conception (f) *ou* étude (f) *ou* design (m)

design (v) dessiner *ou* concevoir

design department bureau (m) d'études

desk (n) bureau (m)

desk diary agenda (m) de bureau

desk-top publishing (DTP) publication (f) assistée par ordinateur (PAO)

despatch (= dispatch)

destination (n) destination (f)

detail (n) détail (m) *ou* précision (f)

detail (v) détailler

detailed détaillé(e)

detailed account compte (m) détaillé

determine (v) déterminer *ou* fixer

Deutschmark (n) mark (m) (allemand) *ou* Deutschemark (m)

devaluation (n) dévaluation (f)

devalue (v) dévaluer

develop (v) *[build]* aménager

develop *[plan]* développer *ou* mettre au point

developing country pays (m) en développement (PED)

development (n) développement (m)

device (n) dispositif (m) *ou* système (m)

diagram (n) diagramme (m) *ou* schéma (m) *ou* graphique (m)

dial (v) faire *ou* composer un numéro

dial (v) a number composer un numéro (de téléphone)

dial (v) direct appeler en direct

dialling (n) composition (f) d'un numéro (de téléphone)

dialling code indicatif (m) (téléphonique)

dialling tone tonalité (f) (du téléphone)

diary (n) agenda (m)

dictate (v) dicter

dictating machine Dictaphone (m)

dictation (n) dictée (f)

differ (v) différer

difference (n) différence (f)

differences in price différences (fpl) de prix

different (adj) différent(e)

differential (adj) différentiel (-ielle)

differential tariffs tarifs (mpl) différentiels

digit (n) chiffre (m)

dilution of equity dilution (f) du capital

direct (adj) direct(e)

direct (adv) directement

direct (v) diriger *ou* mener

direct cost coût (m) direct

direct debit prélèvement (m) automatique

direct mail publicité (f) directe *ou* publipostage (m)

direct selling vente (f) par correspondance

direct tax impôt (m) direct

direct taxation impôt(s) direct(s) *ou* imposition (f) directe

direct-mail advertising publicité (f) directe *ou* publipostage (m)

direction (n) direction (f)

directions for use mode (m) d'emploi

directive (n) directive (f)

director (n) administrateur (-trice); directeur (-trice)

directorship (n) directorat (m) *ou* poste (m) de directeur

directory (n) *[addresses]* répertoire (m) d'adresses

directory *[telephone]* annuaire (m) (des téléphones)

disburse (v) débourser

discharge (n) *[of debt]* règlement (m) d'une dette

discharge (v) *[employee]* renvoyer *ou* congédier

discharge (v) a debt régler *ou* acquitter une dette

disclaimer (n) déni (m) de responsabilité

disclose (v) révéler *ou* divulguer

disclose a piece of information divulguer un renseignement

disclosure (n) révélation (f) *ou* divulgation (f)

discontinue (v) cesser (la fabrication *ou* la vente d'un produit)

discount (n) réduction (f) *ou* remise (f) *ou* escompte (m) *ou* rabais (m)

discount (v) vendre au rabais

discount house *[bank]* banque (f) d'escompte

discount house *[shop]* magasin (m) de discount *ou* discounter (m)

discount price prix (de) discount

discount rate *[bank]* taux d'escompte

discount store magasin (m) de discount *ou* discounter (m)

discountable (adj) escomptable

discounted cash flow (DCF) cash-flow (m) actualisé

discounted value valeur (f) actualisée

discounter (n) magasin (m) de discount *ou* discounter (m)

discrepancy (n) erreur (f) *ou* écart (m)

discuss (v) discuter

discussion (n) discussion (f)

diseconomies (n) of scale déséconomies (fpl) d'échelle

dishonour (v) a bill ne pas honorer une traite

disinflation (n) désinflation (f)

disinvest (v) désinvestir

disinvestment (n) désinvestissement (m)

disk (n) disque (m)

disk drive lecteur (m) de disques *ou* de disquettes

diskette (n) disquette (f)

dismiss (v) (an employee) licencier (un employé)

dismissal (n) licenciement (m)

dispatch (n) *[goods sent]* envoi (m)

dispatch (n) *[sending]* envoi (m) *ou* expédition (f)

dispatch (v) *[send]* expédier (des marchandises)

dispatch department service (m) des livraisons *ou* service des expéditions

dispatch note bordereau (m) d'expédition

display (n) présentation (f) *ou* étalage (m)

display (v) présenter

display case vitrine (f)

display material matériel (m) publicitaire

display pack emballage (m) de présentation; conditionnement (m)

display stand présentoir (m) *ou* étalage (m)

display unit présentoir (m); gondole (f)

disposable (adj) à jeter après usage

disposal (n) *[sale]* vente (f)

dispose (v) of excess stock *[sell]* écouler le surplus de stock

dissolve (v) dissoudre

dissolve a partnership dissoudre une association

distress merchandise marchandises vendues en catastrophe *ou* à tout prix

distress sale vente (f) forcée

distributable profit bénéfice (m) distribuable

distribute (v) *[goods]* distribuer (des marchandises)

distribute *[share]* distribuer

distribution (n) distribution (f); *[books]* diffusion (f)

distribution channels canaux (mpl) de distribution

distribution costs frais (mpl) de distribution *ou* de diffusion

distribution manager responsable (mf) de la distribution *ou* de la diffusion

distribution network réseau (m) de distribution

distributor (n) distributeur (m); concessionnaire (m); *[books]* diffuseur (m)

distributorship (n) concession (f) *[pour la distribution de certains produits]*

diversification (n) diversification (f)

diversify (v) diversifier *ou* varier

dividend (n) dividende (m)

dividend cover couverture (f) des dividendes

dividend warrant chèque (m) de dividende

dividend yield taux (m) de rendement d'une action

division (n) *[part of a company]* division (f) *ou* secteur (m)

division *[part of a group]* division (f)

dock (n) bassin (m)

dock (v) *[remove money]* retenir (une somme)

dock (v) *[ship]* arriver à quai *ou* accoster

docket (n) fiche (f) (de contenu)

doctor's certificate certificat (m) médical

document (n) document (m)

documentary (adj) documentaire

documentary evidence *or* **proof** (document) justificatif (m) *ou* pièce (f) justificative

documentation (n) documentation (f)

documents documents (mpl); dossier (m)

dole (n) indemnité (f) de chômage

dollar (n) *[American]* dollar (m) (américain) *ou* le billet vert

dollar area zone (f) dollar

dollar balance balance (f) commerciale en dollars

dollar crisis crise (f) du dollar

dollar stocks actions (fpl) en dollars

domestic (adj) intérieur(e) *ou* domestique *ou* national(e)

domestic market marché (m) intérieur

domestic production production (f) intérieure

domestic sales ventes (fpl) intérieures

domestic trade commerce (m) intérieur

domicile domicile (m)

door (n) porte (f)

door-to-door porte-à-porte (m)

door-to-door salesman démarcheur (m)

door-to-door selling *[canvassing]* démarchage (m) *ou* porte-à-porte (m)

dormant account compte (m) oisif *ou* qui dort

dossier (n) dossier (m)

dot-matrix printer imprimante (f) matricielle

double (adj) double

double (v) doubler

double taxation double imposition (f)

double taxation agreement convention (f) entre deux pays sur la double imposition

double-book (v) surréserver *ou* faire du surbooking

double-booking (n) surréservation (f) *ou* surbooking (m)

down en bas *ou* vers le bas

down payment acompte (m)

down time temps (m) d'arrêt *ou* temps improductif

down-market bas de gamme

downside factor facteur (m) pessimiste *ou* négatif

downtown (adv) au centre de la ville

downtown (n) centre(-)ville (m)

downturn (n) repli (m) *ou* baisse (f) *ou* recul (m)

downward vers le bas *ou* en baisse

dozen (n) douzaine (f)

drachma (n) *[Greek currency]* drachme (f)

draft (n) *[money]* traite (f) *ou* lettre (f) de change

draft (n) *[rough plan]* esquisse (f) *ou* ébauche (f) *ou* avant-projet (m)

draft (v) esquisser *ou* ébaucher

draft a contract faire une ébauche de contrat

draft a letter faire un brouillon de lettre

draft plan *or* **draft project** esquisse (f) *ou* ébauche (f) *ou* avant-projet (m)

draw (v) *[a cheque]* tirer un chèque *[sur une banque]*

draw *[money]* tirer *ou* retirer *[de l'argent]*

draw up (v) rédiger

draw up a contract rédiger un contrat

drawee (n) tiré (m)

drawer (n) tireur (m)

drawing account compte (m) courant

drive (n) *[campaign]* campagne (f)

drive (n) *[energy]* energie (f)

drive (n) *[part of machine]* commande (f)

drive (v) *[a car]* conduire (une voiture)

driver (n) conducteur (-trice)

drop (n) chute (f) *ou* baisse (f)

drop (v) chuter *ou* baisser

drop in sales chute (f) des ventes

dud (adj) cheque chèque (m) sans provision

due (adj) *[awaited]* attendu(e)

due (adj) *[owing]* dû (due)

dues (n) *[orders of items not yet on the market]* commandes (fpl) en attente *ou* anticipées

duly *[in time]* en temps voulu

duly *[legally]* dûment

dummy (n) maquette (f)

dummy pack emballage (m) factice *ou* boîte (f) factice

dump bin (n) présentoir (m) de produits en vrac

dump (v) goods on a market faire du dumping

dumping (n) dumping (m)

duplicate (n) double (m) *ou* duplicata (m) *ou* copie (f)

duplicate (v) copier *ou* faire une copie; polycopier

duplicate (v) a letter faire une copie d'une lettre

duplicate receipt *or* **duplicate of a receipt** duplicata (m) d'une quittance

duplication (n) reproduction (f)

durable goods biens (mpl) durables

duty (n) *[tax]* taxe (f) *ou* droit (m)

duty-free *[article]* hors taxe *ou* exempt(e) de droits

duty-free shop boutique (f) hors taxe

duty-paid goods marchandises (fpl) dédouanées

Ee

e. & o.e. (errors and omissions excepted) sauf erreur ou omission

early (adj & adv) tôt *ou* de bonne heure

earmark (v) funds for a project affecter des fonds à un projet

earn (v) *[interest]* rapporter; être rémunéré

earn *[money]* gagner

earning capacity niveau (m) de salaire possible

earnings *[profit]* bénéfice (m)

earnings *[salary]* salaire (m) *ou* revenu (m)

earnings per share *or* **earnings yield** rendement (m) *ou* revenu (m) d'une action

earnings-related pension retraite (f) proportionnelle (au salaire)

easy (adj) facile

easy terms facilités (fpl) de paiement

ECGD (Export Credit Guarantee Department) bureau (m) d'assurance crédit à l'exportation

economic (adj) *[general]* économique

economic *[profitable]* rentable

Economic and Monetary Union (EMU) Union (f) économique et monétaire (UEM)

economic cycle cycle (m) économique

economic development développement (m) économique

economic growth croissance (f) économique

economic indicators indicateurs (mpl) économiques

economic model modèle (m) économique

economic planning planification (f) économique

economic trends tendances (fpl) économiques *ou* conjoncture (f) économique

economical (adj) économique; avantageux (-euse)

economics (n) *[profitability]* côté (m) économique *ou* rentabilité (f)

economics *[study]* économie (f) (politique)

economies of scale économies (fpl) d'échelle

economist (n) économiste (mf)

economize (v) économiser *ou* faire des économies

economy (n) *[saving]* économie (f)

economy *[system]* économie (f) *ou* régime (m) économique

economy class *[travel]* classe (f) touriste

economy size format (m) économique

ecu *or* **ECU (European currency unit)** écu *ou* ECU (m)

effect (n) résultat (m) *ou* effet (m)

effect (v) effectuer

effective (adj) efficace

effective date date (f) d'entrée en vigueur

effective demand demande (f) effective

effective yield rendement (m) effectif

effectiveness (n) efficacité (f)

efficiency (n) efficacité (f) *ou* performance (f)

efficient (adj) efficace *ou* performant(e); compétent(e) *[personne]*

effort (n) effort (m)

elasticity (n) élasticité (f)

elect (v) élire *ou* choisir

election (n) élection (f)

electronic mail *or* **email** courrier (m) électronique

electronic point of sale (EPOS) point (m) de vente électronique

elevator (n) *[goods]* monte-charge (m)

elevator *[grain]* silo (m)

email (electronic mail) courrier (m) électronique

embargo (n) embargo (m)

embargo (v) mettre l'embargo sur

embark (v) embarquer *ou* monter à bord (d'un navire)

embark on (v) entreprendre

embarkation (n) embarquement (m)

embarkation card carte (f) d'embarquement

embezzle (v) détourner des fonds

embezzlement (n) détournement (m) de fonds

embezzler (n) escroc (m)

emergency (n) urgence (f); situation (f) critique

emergency reserves réserves (fpl) de secours *ou* fonds (m) de secours

employ (v) employer

employed (adj) *[in job]* employé(e)

employed (adj) *[money]* investi(e)

employed (adj) *[used]* employé(e) *ou* utilisé(e)

employee (n) employé(e) *ou* salarié(e)

employer (n) employeur (m)

employment (n) emploi (m)

employment agency agence (f) *ou* bureau (m) de placement

empty (adj) vide

empty (v) vider

EMS (European Monetary System) SME (système monétaire européen)

encash (v) toucher un chèque *ou* encaisser un chèque

encashment (n) encaissement (m)

enclose (v) joindre

enclosure (n) (encl. *or* **enc.)** pièce (f) jointe (p.j.)

end (n) fin (f)

end (v) prendre fin *ou* finir *ou* se terminer

end of season sale vente (f) de fin de saison

end product produit (m) fini

end user utilisateur (m) (final) *ou* consommateur (m)

endorse (v) a cheque endosser un chèque

endorsee (n) endossataire (mf)

endorsement (n) *[action]* endossement (m)

endorsement *[on insurance]* avenant (m)

endorser (n) endosseur (m)

energy (n) *[electricity]* énergie (f)

energy *[human]* énergie (f) *ou* dynamisme (m)

energy-saving (adj) qui économise l'énergie

enforce (v) faire exécuter *ou* faire observer

enforcement (n) application (f) *ou* mise (f) en vigueur

engage (v) employer *ou* embaucher

engaged (adj) *[telephone]* occupé(e)

engaged tone tonalité 'occupé'

enquire se renseigner

enquiry demande (f) (officielle)

enter (v) *[go in]* entrer

enter *[write in]* inscrire *ou* enregistrer *ou* noter

enter into *[discussion]* entamer (des discussions)

enterprise (n) entreprise (f)

entertainment allowance indemnité (f) de représentation

entitle (v) (someone to) autoriser (quelqu'un) *ou* donner le droit (à quelqu'un de)

entitlement (n) droit (m)

entrepot port (port) entrepôt (m)

entrepreneur (n) entrepreneur (m)

entrepreneurial (adj) d'entrepreneur; dynamique mais risqué

entrust (v) confier

entry (n) *[going in]* entrée (f)

entry *[writing]* écriture (f)

entry visa visa (m) d'entrée

envelope (n) enveloppe (f)

epos *or* **EPOS (electronic point of sale)** point (m) de vente électronique

equal (adj) égal(e) *ou* même

equal (v) égaler

equalization (n) égalisation (f)

equip (v) équiper

equipment (n) équipement (m) *ou* matériel (m)

equities (n) actions (fpl) ordinaires

equity (n) droit (m) de participation

equity *or* **shareholders' equity** capitaux (mpl) propres

equity capital capital (m) social

ERM (Exchange Rate Mechanism) mécanisme (m) de change (du SME)

erode (v) éroder *ou* réduire

error (n) erreur (f)

error rate taux (m) d'erreur

errors and omissions excepted (e. & o.e.) sauf erreur ou omission

escalate (v) monter rapidement

escape clause clause (f) échappatoire

escrow account compte (m) bloqué

escrow: in escrow à la garde d'un tiers

escudo *[Portuguese currency]* escudo (m)

essential (adj) essentiel (-elle)

establish (v) établir *ou* ouvrir *ou* fonder

establishment (n) *[business]* établissement (m) *ou* maison (f) de commerce

establishment *[staff]* personnel (m)

estimate (n) *[calculation]* évaluation (f) *ou* estimation (f)

estimate (n) *[quote]* devis (m)

estimate (v) estimer

estimated (adj) estimé(e) *ou* estimatif (-ive)

estimated figure chiffre (m) estimatif

estimated sales estimation (f) des ventes

estimation (n) estimation (f)

EU (European Union) UE (Union européenne)

Eurocheque (n) eurochèque (m)

Eurocurrency (n) eurodevise (f)

Eurodollar (n) eurodollar (m)

Euromarket (n) Euromarché (m)

European (adj) européen (-éenne)

European Investment Bank (EIB) Banque Européenne d'Investissement (BEI)

European Monetary System (EMS) système monétaire européen (SME)

European Union (EU) Union européenne (UE)

evade (v) se soustraire à *ou* échapper à

evade tax frauder le fisc

evaluate (v) évaluer

evaluate costs évaluer les coûts

evaluation (n) évaluation (f)

evasion (n) évasion (f)

ex coupon coupon détaché

ex dividend ex-dividende

ex-directory *[telephone]* sur la liste rouge

exact (adj) exact(e)

exactly exactement

examination (n) *[inspection]* examen (m) *ou* contrôle (m)

examination *[test]* examen (m)

examine (v) examiner

exceed (v) excéder *ou* dépasser

excellent (adj) excellent(e)

except excepté *ou* sauf *ou* à l'exception de

exceptional (adj) exceptionnel (-elle)

exceptional items postes (mpl) exceptionnels

excess (n) excédent (m) *ou* surplus (m)

excess baggage excédent (m) de bagages

excess capacity surcapacité (f)

excess profits bénéfices (mpl) exceptionnels

excessive (adj) excessif (-ive) *ou* démesuré(e)

excessive costs frais (mpl) excessifs

exchange (n) *[currency]* change (m)

exchange (v) *[currency]* changer de l'argent

exchange (v) *[one thing for another]* échanger

exchange control contrôle (m) des changes

exchange rate taux (m) de change

exchangeable (adj) échangeable

Exchequer Ministère (m) des Finances

excise (v) *[cut out]* supprimer

excise duty droits (mpl) de régie

Excise officer receveur (m) des contributions indirectes

exclude (v) exclure

excluding à l'exception de

exclusion (n) exclusion (f)

exclusion clause clause (f) d'exclusion

exclusive agreement contrat (m) d'exclusivité

exclusive of non compris(e)

exclusive of tax hors taxe

exclusivity (n) exclusivité (f)

execute (v) exécuter

execution (n) exécution (f)

executive (adj) exécutif (-ive)

executive (n) directeur (-trice) *ou* dirigeant (m) *ou* cadre (m)

executive director administrateur (m) dirigeant; cadre (m) supérieur

exempt (adj) exempté(e) *ou* exonéré(e)

exempt (v) exempter *ou* exonérer

exempt from tax exonéré(e) d'impôt

exemption (n) exemption (f) *ou* dispense (f)

exemption from tax exonération (f) d'impôt

exercise (n) exercice (m)

exercise (v) exercer

exercise an option lever une option

exercise of an option levée (f) d'une option

exhibit (v) exposer

exhibition (n) exposition (f)

exhibition hall hall (m) *ou* pavillon (m) d'exposition

exhibitor (n) exposant(e)

expand (v) augmenter *ou* développer; se développer

expansion (n) croissance (f) *ou* développement (m)

expenditure (n) dépense (f)

expense (n) dépense (f) *ou* frais (mpl)

expense account note (f) de frais; frais (mpl) de représentation

expenses (n) dépenses (fpl) *ou* frais (mpl)

expensive (adj) cher (chère) *ou* coûteux (-euse)

experienced (n) expérimenté(e) *ou* compétent(e)

expertise (n) compétence (f)

expiration (n) expiration (f)

expire (v) expirer *ou* prendre fin *ou* venir à expiration

expiry (n) terminaison (f) *ou* expiration (f)

expiry date date (f) d'expiration

explain (v) expliquer *ou* donner une raison

explanation (n) explication (f) *ou* raison (f)

exploit (v) exploiter

explore (v) explorer *ou* étudier *ou* examiner

export (n) exportation (f) *ou* export (m)

export (v) exporter

Export Credit Guarantee Department (ECGD) bureau (m) d'assurance-crédit à l'exportation

export department service (m) des exportations *ou* service export

export duty taxe (f) à l'exportation *ou* droit (m) de sortie

export house maison (f) d'exportation

export licence *or* **export permit** licence (f) *ou* permis (m) d'exportation

export manager chef du service export

export trade commerce (m) d'exportation

exporter (n) exportateur (m) *ou* société (f) exportatrice

exporting (adj) qui exporte *ou* exportateur (-trice)

exports (n) exportations (fpl) *ou* marchandises (fpl) exportées

exposure (n) *[risk]* risque (m)

express (adj) *[fast]* rapide *ou* express

express (adj) *[stated clearly]* explicite *ou* exprès (-esse)

express (v) *[send fast]* expédier rapidement *ou* par exprès

express (v) *[state]* exprimer

express delivery livraison (f) exprès

express letter lettre (f) exprès *ou* prioritaire

extend (v) *[grant]* accorder

extend *[make longer]* prolonger

extended credit crédit (m) à long terme

extension (n) *[making longer]* prolongation (f)

extension *[telephone]* poste (m) (téléphonique)

external (adj) *[foreign]* extérieur(e) *ou* étranger (-ère)

external *[outside a company]* externe

external account *[bank]* compte (m) extérieur *ou* compte de non-résident

external audit audit (m) externe

external auditor auditeur (m) externe

external growth croissance (f) externe

external trade commerce (m) extérieur

extra (adj) en plus *ou* en sus *ou* supplémentaire

extra charges supplément (m) *ou* frais (mpl) supplémentaires

extraordinary (adj) extraordinaire

extraordinary items postes (mpl) exceptionnels

extras (n) frais (mpl) supplémentaires

Ff

face value valeur (f) nominale

facilities (n) installations (fpl); locaux (mpl)

facility [building] bâtiment (m)

facility [ease] facilité (f)

fact-finding mission mission (f) d'enquête

factor (n) [influence] facteur (m)

factor (n) [person, company] factor (m) ou société (f) d'affacturage ou de factoring

factor (v) faire de l'affacturage

factoring affacturage (m) ou factoring (m)

factoring charges commission (f) d'affacturage

factors of production facteurs (mpl) de production

factory (n) usine (f) ou fabrique (f)

factory inspector inspecteur (m) du travail

factory outlet magasin (m) d'usine

factory price prix (m) départ usine

fail (v) [go bust] faire faillite

fail [not to do something] omettre de

fail [not to succeed] échouer

failing that à défaut ou sinon

failure (n) [lack of success] échec (m)

failure (n) [machine] panne (f) ou arrêt (m) ou défaillance (f)

failure to pay non-paiement (m) (d'une facture)

fair (adj) honnête ou correct(e)

fair dealing or trading transactions (fpl) honnêtes

fair price prix (m) raisonnable ou équitable

fair trade accord (m) de réprocité (internationale)

fair wear and tear usure (f) normale

fake (n) faux (m)

fake (v) falsifier

faked documents documents (mpl) ou papiers falsifiés

fall (n) chute (f) ou baisse (f) ou effondrement (m)

fall (v) [go lower] baisser ou diminuer

fall (v) [on a date] avoir lieu ou tomber

fall behind [be in a worse position] se laisser distancer

fall behind [be late] être en retard ou prendre du retard

fall due venir à échéance

fall off diminuer ou chuter

fall through échouer ou ne pas avoir lieu

falling (adj) en baisse

false (adj) faux (fausse) ou incorrect(e)

false description description (f) mensongère

false pretences moyens (mpl) frauduleux

false weight faux poids (m) ou poids inexact

falsification (n) falsification (f)

falsify (v) falsifier ou truquer

family company société (f) familiale

FAO (= for the attention of) à l'attention de

fare (n) prix (m) du billet

farm out (v) work sous-traiter

fast (adj) rapide

fast (adv) rapidement

fast-selling items articles qui se vendent rapidement

fault (n) [blame] faute (f)

fault [mechanical] défaut (m)

faulty equipment matériel (m) défectueux

favourable (adj) avantageux (-euse)

favourable balance of trade balance (f) commerciale bénéficiaire ou excédentaire

fax (n) fax (m) ou télécopie (f)

fax (n) (machine) fax (m) ou télécopieur (m)

fax (v) faxer ou envoyer par fax ou par télécopie

feasibility (n) faisabilité (f)

feasibility report rapport (m) de faisabilité

fee (n) [admission] droit (m) d'entrée

fee *[for services]* honoraires (mpl) *ou* rémunération (f)

feedback (n) information (f) (en retour) *ou* réaction (f)

ferry (n) ferry (m)

fiddle (n) combine (f)

fiddle (v) trafiquer

field (n) champ (m)

field sales manager responsable (mf) d'une équipe de représentants régionaux

field work enquête (f) sur le terrain

FIFO (first in first out) PEPS (premier entré, premier sorti)

figure (n) chiffre (m); montant (m)

figures chiffres (mpl); résultat (m) (quantitatif)

file (n) *[computer]* fichier (m)

file (n) *[documents]* dossier (m)

file (v) *[request]* déposer une requête

file (v) a patent application déposer une demande de brevet

file (v) documents classer (des documents)

filing (n) *[action]* classement (m)

filing cabinet classeur (m)

filing card fiche (f)

fill (v) a gap combler un manque

final (adj) final(e) *ou* dernier (-ière)

final demand dernier rappel

final discharge paiement (m) libératoire

final dividend dernier dividende *ou* solde (m) de dividende

final result *[accounts]* résultat (m) net

finalize (v) mettre au point

finance (n) finance (f)

finance (v) financer

finance an operation financer une opération

finance company société (f) de crédit *ou* de financement

finance director directeur financier

finances (n) *[funds]* finances (fpl)

financial (adj) financier (-ière)

financial adviser conseiller financier

financial asset actif (m) financier

financial crisis crise (f) financière

financial institution institution (f) financière

financial position position (f) *ou* situation (f) financière

financial resources ressources (fpl) financières

financial risk risque (m) financier

financial statement état (m) financier

financial year exercice (m) financier

financially financièrement

financing (n) financement (m)

fine (adj) *[very good]* très bien

fine (adj) *[very small]* fin(e)

fine (n) amende (f)

fine (v) condamner quelqu'un à une amende

fine tuning réglage (m) plus fin *ou* plus précis (de l'économie)

finished (adj) fini(e)

finished goods produits (mpl) finis

fire (n) feu (m) *ou* incendie (m)

fire damage dégâts (mpl) causés par le feu

fire insurance assurance (f) incendie *ou* assurance contre l'incendie

fire regulations consignes (fpl) en cas d'incendie

fire risk risque (m) d'incendie

fire-damaged goods marchandises (fpl) abîmées au cours d'un incendie

firm (adj) ferme *ou* définitif (-ive) *ou* soutenu(e)

firm (n) firme (f) *ou* maison (f) *ou* société (f) *ou* entreprise (f)

firm (v) se maintenir

firm price prix (m) ferme

first (adj) premier (-ière)

first in first out (FIFO) premier entré, premier sorti (PEPS)

first option en première option

first quarter premier trimestre (m)

first-class de première qualité

fiscal (adj) fiscal(e)

fiscal measures mesures (fpl) fiscales

fittings (n) accessoires (mpl); équipement (m)

fix (v) *[arrange]* fixer *ou* établir

fix (v) *[mend]* réparer

fix a meeting for 3 p.m. fixer une réunion à 15h

fixed (adj) fixe *ou* établi(e)

fixed assets actif (m) immobilisé

fixed costs coûts (mpl) fixes

fixed deposit dépôt (m) à terme fixe

fixed exchange rate taux (m) de change fixe

fixed income revenu (m) fixe

fixed interest intérêt (m) fixe

fixed scale of charges barème (m) fixe *ou* échelle (f) de prix fixe

fixed-interest investments investissements (mpl) à intérêt fixe

fixed-price agreement contrat (m) forfaitaire

fixing (n) détermination (f) *ou* fixation (f)

flat (adj) *[dull]* terne

flat (adj) *[fixed]* fixe

flat (n) appartement (m)

flat rate taux (m) fixe *ou* forfait (m)

flexibility (n) souplesse (f) *ou* flexibilité (f)

flexible (adj) souple *ou* adaptable *ou* flexible

flexible prices prix (mpl) flexibles

flexible pricing policy politique (f) de fixation souple des prix

flight (n) *[of money]* fuite (f) (d'argent)

flight *[of plane]* vol (m)

flight of capital fuite (f) de capitaux

flip chart tableau (m) à feuilles mobiles

float (n) *[cash]* avance (f) (de caisse)

float (n) *[of company]* lancement (m) d'une société (en Bourse)

float (v) *[a currency]* laisser flotter une devise

float (v) a company lancer une société (en Bourse)

floating (adj) flottant(e)

floating exchange rates taux (m) de change flottants

floating (n) of a company lancement (m) d'une société (en Bourse)

flood (n) inondation (f)

flood (v) inonder

floor (n) *[level]* étage (m)

floor *[surface]* sol (m) *ou* plancher (m)

floor manager chef (m) de rayon

floor plan plan (m) d'ensemble

floor space surface (f) au sol

flop (n) échec (m) *ou* ratage (m) *ou* fiasco (m)

flop (v) échouer *ou* rater

flotation (n) lancement (m) d'une société en Bourse

flourish (v) prospérer

flourishing (adj) prospère *ou* florissant(e)

flourishing trade commerce (m) prospère

flow (n) flux (m) *ou* mouvement (m)

flow (v) s'écouler

flow chart *or* **flow diagram** graphique (m) d'évolution

fluctuate (v) fluctuer *ou* osciller

fluctuating (adj) variable *ou* qui fluctue

fluctuation (n) fluctuation (f)

FOB *or* **f.o.b. (free on board)** franco à bord (FAB)

follow (v) suivre

follow up (v) *[examine further]* suivre *ou* poursuivre *ou* exploiter

follow-up letter lettre (f) de relance

for sale à vendre

forbid (v) défendre *ou* interdire

force majeure force (f) majeure

force (v) prices down faire baisser les prix

force prices up faire monter les prix

forced (adj) forcé(e)

forced sale liquidation (f) forcée *ou* vente (f) forcée

forecast (n) prévisions (fpl)

forecast (v) prévoir

forecasting (n) prévision (f) *ou* estimation (f)

foreign (adj) étranger (-ère)

foreign currency devises (fpl) (étrangères)

foreign exchange *[currency]* change (m)

foreign exchange *[rate of exchange]* (cours du) change (m)

foreign exchange broker cambiste (mf)

foreign exchange dealing opération (f) de change

foreign exchange market marché (m) des changes

foreign investments investissements (mpl) à l'étranger

foreign money order mandat (m) international

foreign trade commerce (m) extérieur

forfeit (n) confiscation (f)

forfeit (v) perdre par confiscation

forfeit a deposit perdre des arrhes

forfeiture (n) confiscation (f) (d'un bien)

forge (v) falsifier *ou* contrefaire

forgery (n) *[action]* falsification (f)

forgery *[copy]* contrefaçon (f)

fork-lift truck chariot (m) élévateur

form (n)*[paper]* formulaire (m)

form (v) former *ou* constituer *ou* créer

formal (adj) officiel (-elle)

formality (n) formalité (f)

forward à l'avance *ou* à terme

forward buying achat (m) à terme

forward dealing opération (f) à terme

forward market marché (m) à terme

forward rate taux (m) de change à terme

forward sales ventes (fpl) à terme

forwarding (n) acheminement (m) *ou* expédition (f)

forwarding address adresse (f) de réexpédition

forwarding agent transitaire (m)

forwarding instructions instructions (fpl) relatives à l'expédition

fourth quarter quatrième trimestre (m)

fragile (adj) fragile

franc (n) *[French, Belgian, Swiss currency]* franc (m)

franchise (n) franchise (f)

franchise (v) accorder une franchise *ou* franchiser

franchisee (n) franchisé (m)

franchiser (n) franchiseur (m)

franchising (n) franchisage (m)

franco (adv) franco

frank (v) affranchir (une lettre)

franking machine machine (f) à affranchir

fraud (n) fraude (f)

fraudulent (adj) frauduleux (-euse)

fraudulent transaction transaction frauduleuse

fraudulently frauduleusement

free (adj) *[no payment]* gratuit(e)

free (adj) *[no restrictions]* libre

free (adj) *[not busy]* libre

free (adj) *[not occupied]* libre

free (adv) *[no payment]* gratuitement *ou* sans payer

free (v) libérer

free delivery livraison gratuite *ou* colis expédié franc de port

free gift prime (f)

freelance (adj) freelance

freelance (n) *or* **freelancer** collaborateur (-trice) indépendant(e)

free market economy économie (f) de marché *ou* économie libérale

free of charge gratuit(e); gratuitement

free of duty exempt(e) de taxe *ou* hors taxe

free of tax exonéré(e) d'impôt

free on board (f.o.b.) franco à bord (FAB)

free on rail franco wagon

free port port (m) franc

free sample échantillon (m) gratuit

free trade libre-échange (m)

free trade agreement accord (m) de libre-échange

free trade area zone (f) de libre-échange

free trade zone zone franche

free trial essai (m) gratuit

free zone zone (f) franche

freeze (n) gel (m) *ou* blocage (m)

freeze (v) *[prices]* bloquer *ou* geler

freeze (v) credits geler *ou* limiter les crédits

freeze wages and prices bloquer les salaires et les prix

freight (n) *[carriage]* fret (m) *ou* prix (m) du transport

freight car wagon (m) de marchandises

freight costs port (m) *ou* frais (mpl) de transport

freight depot dépôt (m) *ou* entrepôt (m) de marchandises

freight forward (en) port dû

freight plane avion-cargo (m)

freight rates tarifs (mpl) d'expédition

freight train train (m) de marchandises

freightage (n) frais (mpl) de transport

freighter (n) *[plane]* avion-cargo (m)

freighter *[ship]* cargo (m)

freightliner (n) train (m) de marchandises en conteneurs

frequent (adj) fréquent(e)

frozen (adj) gelé(e)

frozen account compte (m) gelé

frozen assets actifs (mpl) gelés *ou* fonds (mpl) bloqués

frozen credits crédits (mpl) gelés

fulfil (v) an order exécuter une commande

fulfilment (n) exécution (f)

full (adj) plein(e) *ou* complet (-ète)

full discharge of a debt pour acquit

full payment règlement (m) total

full price prix (m) fort

full refund remboursement (m) total

full-scale (adj) total(e) *ou* complet (-ète)

full-time (adj) à temps complet *ou* à plein temps

full-time employment travail (m) à plein temps

fund (n) fonds (mpl)

fund (v) financer

funding (n) *[financing]* financement (m)

funding *[of debt]* consolidation (f) (d'une dette)

further to suite à *ou* en réponse à

future delivery livraison (f) future

futures (n) opérations (fpl) à terme *[en Bourse]*

Gg

gain (n) *[getting bigger]* accroissement (m) *ou* augmentation (f)

gain (n) *[increase in value]* augmentation (f) (de valeur)

gain (v) *[become bigger]* augmenter; gagner

gain (v) *[get]* acquérir *ou* obtenir

gap (n) vide (m)

gap in the market créneau (m) sur le marché

GDP (gross domestic product) PIB (produit intérieur brut)

gear adapter *ou* ajuster

gearing (n) effet (m) de levier *ou* ratio (m) d'endettement

general (adj) général(e)

general audit vérification (f) générale des comptes

general average avarie (f) commune

general insurance assurance (f) multirisque

general manager directeur (-trice) général(e)

general meeting assemblée (f) générale

general office siège (m) social

general post office poste (f) centrale

general strike grève (f) générale

gentleman's agreement gentleman's agreement (m)

genuine (adj) véritable *ou* authentique

genuine purchaser acheteur (m) sérieux

get (v) recevoir

get along se débrouiller

get back *[something lost]* récupérer

get into debt s'endetter

get rid of something se débarrasser de quelque chose

get round (a problem) éviter *ou* contourner (une difficulté)

get the sack être renvoyé *ou* licencié *ou* mis à la porte

get through to *[telephone]* joindre *[au téléphone]*

gift (n) cadeau (m)

gift coupon bon (m) d'achat

gift shop boutique (f) de souvenirs

gift voucher chèque-cadeau (m)

gilt-edged securities (n) *or* **gilts (n)** titres (mpl) d'état *ou* obligations (fpl) d'état

giro account compte (m) de virement (à la Girobank)

giro cheque chèque (m) de virement

giro system système (m) de virement bancaire

give (v) *[as gift]* offrir

give *[pass]* donner

give away *[free]* offrir (en prime)

giveaway (n) cadeau (m) (publicitaire) gratuit

giveaway price prix défiant toute concurrence

glut (n) surplus (m) *ou* surabondance (f)

glut (v) surcharger *ou* encombrer

GNP (gross national product) PNB (produit national brut)

go (v) aller

go into business se lancer dans les affaires

go-ahead (adj) dynamique *ou* entreprenant(e)

go-slow (n) grève (f) du zèle *ou* grève perlée

going (adj) *[rate, price]* actuel (-elle) *ou* courant(e)

going rate tarif en vigueur

good (adj) bon (bonne)

good buy bonne affaire

good management bonne gestion

good quality bonne qualité

good value (for money) aubaine (f); rapport qualité/prix excellent

goods (n) marchandises (fpl)

goods depot dépôt (m) *ou* entrepôt (m)

goods in transit marchandises (fpl) en transit

goods train train (m) de marchandises

goodwill goodwill (m)

government (n) gouvernement (m) *ou* Etat (m)

government (adj) gouvernemental(e) *ou* du gouvernement *ou* de l'Etat

government bonds bons (mpl) du Trésor

government contractor fournisseur (m) du gouvernement

government stock titres (mpl) d'Etat

government-backed avec l'aval du gouvernement

government-controlled contrôlé(e) par l'Etat; d'Etat

government-regulated réglementé(e) par l'Etat

government-sponsored subventionné(e) par l'Etat

graded advertising rates tarifs (mpl) publicitaires dégressifs

graded hotel hôtel (m) classé

graded tax impôt (m) progressif

gradual (adj) progressif (-ive)

graduate trainee stagiaire (mf) diplômé(e)

graduated (adj) progressif (-ive)

graduated income tax impôt (m) progressif

gram *or* **gramme (n)** gramme (m)

grand total total (m) général *ou* somme (f) globale

grant (n) subvention (f); bourse (f)

grant (v) accorder *ou* octroyer

gratis gratis *ou* gratuitement

grid (n) grille (f)

grid structure structure (f) en grille

gross (adj) brut(e) *ou* sans déductions

gross (n) (= 144) douze douzaines *ou* grosse (f)

gross (v) rapporter brut *ou* faire un profit brut

gross domestic product (GDP) produit (m) intérieur brut (PIB)

gross earnings revenu (m) brut

gross income salaire (m) brut

gross margin marge (f) brute

gross national product (GNP) produit (m) national brut (PNB)

gross profit bénéfice (m) brut

gross salary salaire (m) brut

gross tonnage jauge (f) brute

gross weight poids (m) brut

gross yield rendement (m) brut

group (n) *[of businesses]* groupe (m) (industriel)

group *[of people]* groupe (m)

growth (n) croissance (f)

growth index indice (m) de croissance

growth rate taux (m) de croissance

guarantee (n) garantie (f)

guarantee (v) garantir

guarantee a bill of exchange avaliser une traite

guarantee a debt se porter garant d'une dette

guarantee : go guarantee for someone se porter garant de quelqu'un

guaranteed for six months *[product]* garanti(e) six mois

guaranteed minimum wage salaire (m) minimum garanti

guarantor (n) avaliste (m) *ou* garant (m)

guideline (n) ligne (f) de conduite *ou* directive (f)

guild guilde (f) *ou* corporation (f)

guilder *[Dutch currency]* florin (m)

Hh

haggle (v) marchander

half (adj) demi(e)

half (n) moitié (f) *ou* demie (f)

half a dozen *or* **a half-dozen** demi-douzaine (f)

half-price sale solde (m) à moitié prix

half-year semestre (m) (comptable)

half-yearly accounts comptes (mpl) semestriels

half-yearly payment paiement (m) semestriel

half-yearly statement relevé (m) semestriel

hand in (v) remettre

hand luggage bagages (mpl) à main

hand over (v) remettre

handle (v) *[deal with]* s'occuper de *ou* traiter

handle (v) *[sell]* vendre

handling (n) manutention (f)

handling charge frais (mpl) de manutention

handwriting (n) écriture (f)

handwritten (adj) écrit(e) à la main *ou* manuscrit(e)

handy (adj) pratique

harbour (n) port (m)

harbour dues droits (mpl) de port

harbour facilities installations (fpl) portuaires

hard bargain affaire (f) difficile

hard bargaining tractations (fpl) difficiles

hard copy copie (f) (sur) papier *ou* imprimé (m)

hard currency devise (f) forte

hard disk disque (m) dur

hard sell (n) vente (n) agressive

hard selling (politique de) vente (f) agressive

harmonization (n) *[of prices, etc.]* harmonisation (f)

haulage (n) transport (m) routier

haulage contractor entrepreneur (m) de transports routiers

haulage costs *or* **haulage rates** frais (mpl) de transport (routier)

head (n) of department chef (m) de service

head office siège (m) social *ou* bureau (m) central

headquarters (HQ) siège (m) social

heads of agreement protocole (m) d'accord

health (n) santé (f)

health insurance assurance (f) maladie

healthy profit bénéfice (m) substantiel

heavy (adj) *[important]* lourd(e) *ou* important(e) *ou* massif (-ive)

heavy *[weight]* lourd(e)

heavy costs *or* **heavy expenditure** frais (mpl) importants

heavy equipment matériel (m) lourd

heavy goods vehicle (HGV) poids lourd (m)

heavy industry industrie (f) lourde

heavy machinery installations (fpl) lourdes *ou* matériel (m) lourd

hectare (n) hectare (m)

hedge (n) couverture (f)

hedging (n) opérations (fpl) de couverture

HGV (heavy goods vehicle) poids lourd (m)

hidden asset bien (m) masqué

hidden reserves caisse (f) noire *ou* réserves (fpl) occultes

high interest intérêt (m) élevé

high rent loyer (m) élevé

high taxation taux (m) d'imposition élevé

high-quality (adj) de première qualité

high-quality goods marchandises (fpl) de première qualité

highest bidder le plus offrant

highly motivated sales staff personnel (m) de vente très motivé

highly qualified hautement qualifié(e)

highly-geared company société qui a un fort coefficient d'endettement

highly-paid qui perçoit un salaire élevé

highly-priced onéreux (-euse) *ou* coûteux (-euse)

hire (n) location (f)

hire (v) a car louer une voiture

hire car voiture de location

hire purchase (HP) achat (m) à crédit *ou* à tempérament

hire (v) staff embaucher du personnel

hire-purchase company société (f) de crédit

historic(al) cost prix (m) d'origine *ou* coût (m) historique

historical figures chiffres (mpl) d'origine

hive off (v) décentraliser

hoard (v) faire des réserves *ou* amasser

hoarding (n) *[for posters]* panneau (m) d'affichage

hoarding *[of goods]* accumulation (f) de provisions

hold (n) *[ship, plane]* cale (f) (d'un navire); soute (f) (d'un avion)

hold (v) *[contain]* contenir

hold (v) *[keep]* détenir *ou* garder

hold a meeting *or* **a discussion** tenir une réunion *ou* une discussion

hold out for maintenir sa position

hold over remettre *ou* ajourner

hold the line please *or* **please hold** *[phone]* ne quittez pas, s'il vous plaît!

hold up (v) *[delay]* retarder

hold-up (n) *[delay]* retard (m)

holder (n) *[person]* titulaire (mf) *ou* détenteur (-trice)

holder *[thing]* support (m); étui (m)

holding (n) portefeuille (m) d'actions

holding company holding (m)

holiday pay salaire (m) payé pendant les vacances

home address adresse (f) personnelle

home consumption consommation (f) domestique

home market marché (m) intérieur

home sales ventes (fpl) intérieures

homeward freight fret (m) de retour

homeward journey voyage (m) de retour

homeworker (n) travailleur (-euse) *ou* ouvrier (-ière) à domicile

honorarium (n) honoraires (mpl)

honour (v) a bill honorer *ou* acquitter une traite

honour one's signature honorer sa signature

horizontal (adj) communication communication (f) horizontale

horizontal integration intégration (f) horizontale

hotel (n) hôtel (m)

hotel accommodation chambre (f) d'hôtel

hotel bill note (f) d'hôtel

hotelier (n) hôtelier (m)

hotel manager directeur (-trice) d'hôtel

hotel staff personnel (m) hôtelier

hour heure (f)

hourly (adv) à l'heure *ou* horaire

hourly rate tarif (m) horaire

hourly wage salaire (m) horaire

hourly-paid workers ouvriers payés à l'heure

house (n) *[company]* maison (f) *ou* firme (f) *ou* entreprise (f)

house *[for family]* maison (f); résidence (f)

house insurance assurance-habitation (f)

house magazine journal (m) de l'entreprise

house-to-house porte-à-porte (m)

house-to-house selling vente (f) à domicile *ou* porte-à-porte (m) *ou* démarchage (m)

HP (= hire purchase) achat (m) à crédit *ou* à tempérament

HQ (= headquarters) siège (m) social

human resources ressources (fpl) humaines

hurry up (v) *[order]* activer *ou* accélérer *[une commande]*

hype (n) publicité (f) excessive

hype (v) lancer (un produit) à grand renfort de publicité

hypermarket (n) hypermarché (m) *[grande surface]*

Ii

illegal (adj) illégal(e)

illegality (n) illégalité (f)

illegally (adv) illégalement

illicit (adj) illicite

ILO (International Labour Organization) OIT (Organisation Internationale du Travail)

IMF (International Monetary Fund) FMI (Fonds Monétaire International)

imitation (n) imitation (f)

immediate (adj) immédiat(e)

immediately tout de suite *ou* immédiatement

imperfect (adj) défectueux (-euse); imparfait(e); de second choix

imperfection (n) imperfection (f)

implement (n) outil (m) *ou* instrument (m)

implement (v) appliquer *ou* mettre en pratique; exécuter

implement (v) an agreement appliquer un accord

implementation (n) exécution (f) *ou* application (f)

import (n) importation (f) *ou* import (m)

import (v) importer

import ban interdiction (f) d'importer

import duty *or* **import levy** taxe (f) à l'importation

import licence *or* **import permit** licence (f) d'importation

import quota quota (m) d'importation

import restrictions limitations (fpl) des importations

import surcharge surtaxe (f) à l'importation

import-export (n & adj) (d') import-export (m)

importance (n) importance (f)

important (adj) important(e)

importation (n) importation (f)

importer (n) importateur (-trice)

importing (adj) importateur (-trice)

importing (n) importation (f)

imports importations (fpl)

impose (v) imposer

impulse buyer acheteur impulsif

impulse purchase achat (m) impulsif *ou* achat d'impulsion

in-house dans l'entreprise *ou* dans la maison

in-house training formation (f) dans l'entreprise

incentive (n) incitation (f)

incentive bonus *or* **incentive payment** prime (f) d'incitation au travail

incidental (adj) expenses faux frais (mpl)

include (v) inclure *ou* comprendre

inclusive (adj) inclus(e) *ou* compris(e)

inclusive charge tarif (m) tout compris

inclusive of tax taxe (f) comprise *ou* toutes taxes comprises (TTC)

income (n) revenu (m)

income tax impôt (m) sur le revenu

incoming call *[phone]* appel (m) venant de l'extérieur

incoming mail courrier (m) à l'arrivée

incompetent (adj) incompétent(e)

incorporate (v) incorporer *ou* intégrer

incorporate *[a company]* constituer; immatriculer (une société)

incorporation (n) constitution (f); immatriculation (f) d'une société

incorrect (adj) incorrect(e)

incorrectly incorrectement

increase (n) augmentation (f) *ou* hausse (f)

increase (n) *[higher salary]* augmentation (f) (de salaire)

increase (v) augmenter *[le prix d'un article]*

increase (v) in price augmenter de prix *ou* coûter plus cher

increasing (adj) en augmentation *ou* de plus en plus grand

increment (n) augmentation (f) de salaire automatique

incremental (adj) qui augmente régulièrement

incremental cost coût (m) marginal

incremental scale échelle (f) mobile des salaires

incur (v) *[costs]* engager (des dépenses)

incur (v) *[risk]* courir (le risque de)

incur debts contracter des dettes

indebted (adj) qui a une dette *ou* qui doit de l'argent

indebtedness (n) endettement (m)

indemnification (n) indemnisation (f) *ou* dédommagement (m)

indemnify (v) indemniser *ou* dédommager

indemnify someone for a loss indemniser quelqu'un d'une perte

indemnity (n) indemnité (f)

independent (adj) indépendant(e)

independent company société (f) indépendante

index (n) *[alphabetical]* index (m)

index (n) *[of prices]* indice (m) (des prix)

index (v) indexer

index card fiche (f) *[de fichier]*

index number numéro (m) de référence; indice (m)

index-linked (adj) indexé(e) (sur l'indice du coût de la vie)

indexation (n) indexation (f)

indicator (n) indicateur (m)

indirect indirect(e)

indirect labour costs charges (fpl) indirectes

indirect tax impôt (m) indirect

indirect taxation imposition (f) indirecte *ou* impôts (mpl) indirects

induction (n) initiation (f)

induction courses *or* **induction training** cours (mpl) d'initiation

industrial (adj) industriel (-elle)

industrial accident accident (m) du travail

industrial (arbitration) tribunal conseil (m) de prud'hommes

industrial capacity capacité (f) industrielle

industrial centre centre (m) industriel

industrial design esthétique (f) industrielle *ou* dessin (m) industriel

industrial disputes conflits (mpl) du travail

industrial espionage espionnage (m) industriel

industrial estate zone (f) industrielle

industrial expansion développement (m) industriel

industrial processes procédés (mpl) industriels

industrial relations relations (fpl) entre employeurs et employés

industrialist (n) industriel (m)

industrialization (n) industrialisation (f)

industrialize (v) industrialiser

industrialized societies pays (mpl) industrialisés

industry (n) *[companies]* industrie (f)

industry *[general]* industrie (f)

inefficiency (n) inefficacité (f); incompétence (f) *[personne]*

inefficient (adj) inefficace; incompétent(e) *[personne]*

inexpensive (adj) bon marché; peu *ou* pas cher (chère)

inflated currency monnaie (f) inflationniste

inflated prices prix (mpl) gonflés (artificiellement)

inflation (n) inflation (f)

inflationary (adj) inflationniste

influence (n) influence (f)

influence (v) influencer

inform (v) informer *ou* renseigner

information (n) renseignement(s) (m(pl))

information bureau bureau (m) de renseignements

information officer responsable (mf) de l'information

infrastructure (n) infrastructure (f)

infringe (v) transgresser

infringe a patent contrefaire un produit protégé par un brevet

infringement (n) of customs regulations non respect (m) des formalités douanières

infringement of patent contrefaçon (f) (d'un produit breveté)

initial (adj) initial(e)

initial (v) parapher *ou* signer de ses initiales

initial capital capital (m) initial *ou* capital d'investissement

initials (n) *[letters]* initiales (fpl)

initiate (v) commencer

initiate discussions entamer des discussions

initiative (n) initiative (f)

inland (adj) intérieur(e)

Inland Revenue le fisc

innovate (v) innover

innovation (n) innovation (f)

innovative (adj) innovateur (-trice)

innovator (n) innovateur (-trice)

input (v) information saisir *ou* introduire des données

input tax TVA exigible (sur biens et services)

inquire (v) se renseigner

inquiry (n) demande (f) (de reseignement(s))

insider (n) initié(e)

insider dealing *or* **trading** délit (m) d'initié(s)

insolvency (n) insolvabilité (f)

insolvent (adj) insolvable

inspect (v) inspecter *ou* vérifier *ou* contrôler

inspection (n) inspection (f) *ou* vérification (f) *ou* contrôle (m)

instalment (n) versement (m)

instant (adj) *[current]* courant *ou* de ce mois

instant (adj) *[immediate]* instantané(e) *ou* immédiat(e)

instant credit crédit (m) immédiat

institute (n) institut (m)

institute (v) instituer *ou* engager

institution (n) institution (f)

institutional (adj) institutionnel (-elle)

institutional investors investisseurs (mpl) institutionnels

instruction (n) ordre (m) *ou* instruction (f)

instrument (n) *[device]* instrument (m) *ou* appareil (m)

instrument *[document]* acte (m) *ou* document (m) *ou* instrument (m)

insufficient funds *[US]* (compte) insuffisamment approvisionné

insurable (adj) assurable

insurance (n) assurance (f)

insurance agent agent (m) d'assurances

insurance broker courtier (m) d'assurances

insurance claim déclaration (f) de sinistre

insurance company compagnie (f) d'assurances

insurance contract contrat (m) d'assurance

insurance cover garantie (f) *ou* couverture (f) d'assurance

insurance policy police (f) d'assurance

insurance premium prime (f) d'assurance

insurance rates tarifs (mpl) d'assurance

insurance salesman agent (m) d'assurances

insure (v) assurer

insurer (n) assureur (m) *ou* compagnie (f) d'assurances

intangible (adj) incorporel (-elle)

intangible assets immobilisations (fpl) incorporelles

interest (n) *[investment]* participation (f)

interest (n) *[paid on investment, on loan]* intérêt (m)

interest (v) intéresser (quelqu'un)

interest charges intérêts (mpl) (à payer) *ou* frais (mpl) financiers

interest rate taux (m) d'intérêt

interest-bearing deposits dépôts (mpl) rémunérés

interest-free credit crédit (m) gratuit

interface (n) interface (f)

interface (v) connecter *ou* relier (par interface)

interim dividend dividende (m) intérimaire

interim payment paiement (m) intérimaire *ou* acompte (m)

interim report rapport (m) intérimaire

intermediary (adj) intermédiaire (m)

internal (adj) *[inside a company]* interne

internal *[inside a country]* intérieur(e)

internal audit audit (m) interne

internal auditor auditeur (m) interne

internal telephone téléphone (m) interne *ou* intérieur

international (adj) international(e)

international call *[phone]* appel (m) (téléphonique) international

international direct dialling système (m) téléphonique automatique international

International Labour Organization (ILO) Organisation (f) Internationale du Travail (OIT)

international law droit (m) international

International Monetary Fund (IMF) Fonds (m) Monétaire International (FMI)

international trade commerce (m) international

interpret (v) interpréter *ou* servir d'interprète

interpreter (n) interprète (mf)

intervention price prix (m) d'intervention

interview (n) interview (m)

interview (n) *[for a job]* entretien (m)

interview (v) interviewer

interview (v) *[for a job]* avoir un entretien avec (un candidat)

interviewee (n) interviewé(e)

interviewer (n) interviewer (m)

introduce (v) présenter

introduction (n) *[bringing into use]* introduction (f)

introduction *[letter]* lettre (f) d'introduction

introductory offer offre (f) de lancement

invalid (adj) non valable *ou* non valide; périmé(e)

invalidate (v) invalider *ou* annuler

invalidation (n) invalidation (f) *ou* annulation (f)

invalidity (n) invalidité (f)

inventory (n) *[list of contents]* inventaire (m)

inventory (n) *[US: stock]* stock (m)

inventory (v) inventorier *ou* faire l'inventaire

inventory control contrôle (m) des stocks *ou* gestion (f) des stocks

invest (v) investir *ou* placer (de l'argent)

investigate (v) enquêter *ou* examiner

investigation (n) enquête (f)

investment (n) investissement (m) *ou* placement (m)

investment income revenus (mpl) de placements

investor (n) investisseur (m)

invisible assets biens (mpl) incorporels

invisible earnings revenus (mpl) invisibles

invisible trade commerce (m) invisible

invitation (n) invitation (f)

invite (v) inviter quelqu'un à *ou* demander à quelqu'un de

invoice (n) facture (f) *ou* note (f)

invoice (v) facturer; envoyer une facture

invoice number numéro (m) de facture

invoice value montant (m) (total) de la facture

invoicing (n) facturation (f)

invoicing department service (m) de la facturation

IOU (= I owe you) reconnaissance (f) de dette

irrecoverable debt dette (f) irrécouvrable

irredeemable bond obligation (f) non remboursable

irregular (adj) irrégulier (-ière)

irregularities (n) irrégularités (fpl)

irrevocable (adj) irrévocable

irrevocable acceptance acceptation (f) irrévocable

irrevocable letter of credit lettre (f) de crédit irrévocable

issue (n) *[magazine]* numéro (m)

issue (n) *[of shares]* émission (f) d'actions nouvelles

issue (v) *[shares]* émettre (des actions)

issue a letter of credit émettre une lettre de crédit

issue instructions donner des instructions

issuing bank banque (f) émettrice *ou* banque d'émission

item (n) *[accounts]* poste (m)

item *[on agenda]* question (f) *[à l'ordre du jour]*

item *[thing for sale]* article (m)

itemize (v) détailler

itemized account compte (m) détaillé

itemized invoice facture (f) détaillée

itinerary (n) itinéraire (m)

Jj

job (n) *[employment]* emploi (m) *ou* travail (m)

job *[piece of work]* travail (m) *ou* tâche (f)

job analysis analyse (f) des tâches *ou* de la fonction

job application candidature (f) à un emploi *ou* demande (f) d'emploi

job cuts suppression (f) d'emplois

job description description (f) de la fonction *ou* profil (m) de poste

job satisfaction satisfaction (f) au travail

job security sécurité (f) de l'emploi

job specification description (f) de la fonction *ou* profil (m) de poste

job title titre (m)

join (v) joindre *ou* relier

joint (adj) commun(e) *ou* conjoint(e); mixte

joint account compte (m) joint

joint discussions discussions (fpl) collectives *[dans l'entreprise]*

joint management codirection (f) *ou* cogestion (f)

joint managing director codirecteur (-trice) général(e) *ou* directeur (-trice) général(e) adjoint(e)

joint owner copropriétaire (mf)

joint ownership copropriété (f) *ou* propriété (f) en commun

joint signatory cosignataire (mf)

joint-stock company société (f) anonyme par actions

joint venture joint-venture (f) *ou* coentreprise (f)

jointly conjointement

journal (n) *[accounts book]* journal (m) *ou* livre-journal (m)

journal *[magazine]* revue (f) *ou* journal (m)

judge (n) juge (m) *ou* magistrat (m)

judge (v) juger *ou* estimer

judgement (n) *or* **judgment** jugement (m)

judgment debtor débiteur condamné à rembourser une dette

judicial processes procédures (fpl) juridiques

jump (v) the queue resquiller dans une queue

junior (adj) subalterne; débutant(e)

junior clerk employé(e) subalterne

junior executive *or* **junior manager** cadre (m) débutant *ou* jeune cadre

junior partner simple associé(e)

junk bonds obligations (fpl) d'une société en cours d'OPA *ou* junk bonds (mpl)

junk mail prospectus (mpl) publicitaires *[par la poste]*

jurisdiction (n) juridiction (f)

Kk

keen (adj) competition compétition (f) acharnée *ou* concurrence (f) vive

keen demand demande (f) forte

keen prices prix (mpl) compétitifs

keep (v) a promise tenir une promesse

keep back (v) retenir

keep up (v) maintenir

keep up with the demand satisfaire à la demande

key (n) *[on keyboard]* touche (f)

key *[to door]* clef (f) *ou* clé (f)

key *[very important]* clé

key factor facteur (m) clé

key industry industrie (f) clé

key personnel *or* **key staff** personnel (m) clé

key post poste (m) clé

keyboard (n) clavier (m)

keyboard (v) saisir (sur clavier) *[des données]*

keyboarder (n) claviste (mf) *ou* opérateur (-trice) de saisie

keyboarding (n) saisie (f) (de données sur clavier)

kilo *or* **kilogram (n)** kilo (m) *ou* kilogramme (m)

knock down (v) *[price]* baisser (un prix)

knock off (v) *[reduce price]* baisser un prix de *ou* faire un rabais de

knock off *[stop work]* arrêter le travail *ou* débrayer

knock-on effect réaction (f) en chaîne *ou* répercussion (f)

knockdown prices prix (mpl) sacrifiés

krona (n) *[currency in Sweden and Iceland]* couronne (f)

krone (n) *[currency in Denmark and Norway]* couronne (f)

Ll

label (n) étiquette (f) *ou* label (m)

label (v) étiqueter

labelling (n) étiquetage (m)

labour (n) travail (m)

labour costs coût (m) de la main-d'oeuvre

labour disputes conflits (mpl) du travail

labour force main-d'oeuvre (f)

labour-intensive industry industrie (f) à forte densité de main-d'oeuvre

labour laws législation (f) du travail

labour relations relations (fpl) entre employeurs et employés

labour union syndicat (m) (ouvrier)

lack (n) of funds manque (m) de fonds

land (n) terre (f) *ou* terrain (m)

land (v) *[of plane]* atterrir

land (v) *[passengers, cargo]* débarquer

land goods at a port débarquer des marchandises dans un port

landed costs prix (m) à quai

landing card carte (f) de débarquement

landing charges frais (mpl) de débarquement

landlord (n) *or* **landlady (n)** propriétaire (m) *[d'un logement locatif]*

lapse (v) expirer *ou* n'être plus valide

laser printer imprimante (f) laser

last in first out (LIFO) dernier entré, premier sorti (DEPS)

last quarter dernier trimestre (m)

late (adv) en retard

late-night opening nocturne (m)

latest (adj) le dernier *ou* la dernière; le plus récent *ou* la plus récente

launch (n) lancement (m)

launch (v) lancer (un produit)

launching (n) *[action]* lancement (m)

launching costs coûts (mpl) de lancement

launching date date (f) de lancement

launder (money) blanchir (des capitaux)

law (n) *[rule]* loi (f)

law *[study]* droit (m)

law courts cour (f) de justice *ou* tribunal (m) *ou* tribunaux (mpl)

law of diminishing returns loi (f) des rendements décroissants

law of supply and demand loi (f) de l'offre et de la demande

lawful (adj) légal(e) *ou* licite *ou* légitime

lawful trade commerce (m) licite

lawsuit (n) procès (m)

lawyer (n) avocat(e)

lay off (v) workers mettre à pied *ou* licencier des ouvriers

LBO (= leveraged buyout) rachat d'une société avec des capitaux garantis par l'actif de la société

L/C (= letter of credit) lettre (f) de crédit

leader (n) *[person]* chef (m) *ou* leader (m)

lead time délai (m) de livraison *ou* d'exécution

leaflet (n) prospectus (m) *ou* feuillet (m)

leakage (n) coulage (m) *ou* fuite (f)

lease (n) bail (m) *ou* location-bail (f)

lease (v) *[of landlord, of tenant]* louer (à bail)

lease back (v) faire une opération de cession-bail

lease-back (n) cession-bail (m)

lease (v) equipment louer du matériel en crédit-bail

leasing (contrat de) location (f)

leave (n) congé (m)

leave (v) *[go away]* quitter *ou* partir

leave (v) *[resign]* démissionner *ou* partir

leave of absence autorisation (f) d'absence *ou* congé (m)

ledger (n) registre (m) *ou* grand livre

left (adj) *[not right]* gauche; de gauche

left luggage office consigne (f)

legal (adj) *[according to law]* légal(e) *ou* licite

legal *[referring to law]* légal(e) *ou* juridique

legal advice conseils (mpl) juridiques

legal adviser conseiller (m) juridique

legal costs *or* **legal charges** frais (mpl) de justice *ou* frais juridiques

legal department service (m) du contentieux

legal expenses frais (mpl) de justice *ou* frais juridiques

legal proceedings poursuites (fpl) judiciaires

legal status situation (f) légale *ou* statut légal

legal tender monnaie (f) légale

legislation (n) législation (f)

lend (v) prêter

lender (n) prêteur (-euse)

lending (n) prêt (m) *ou* crédit (m)

lending limit plafond (m) de crédit

lessee (n) locataire (mf) à bail

lessor (n) bailleur, bailleresse

let (n) (période de) location (f)

let (v) louer

let (v) an office louer un bureau *[donner à bail]*

letter (n) lettre (f)

letter of application lettre (f) de candidature *ou* de demande d'emploi

letter of appointment lettre (f) d'embauche; (lettre de) nomination (f)

letter of complaint lettre (f) de réclamation

letter of credit (L/C) lettre (f) de crédit

letter of intent lettre (f) d'intention

letter of reference lettre (f) de recommandation

letters patent brevet (m) d'invention

letting agency agence (f) immobilière *ou* de location

level (n) niveau (m)

level off *or* **level out (v)** se stabiliser

leverage (n) ratio (m) d'endettement; effet (m) de levier

leveraged buyout (LBO) rachat d'une société avec des capitaux garantis par l'actif de la société

levy (n) impôt (m) *ou* contribution (f)

levy (v) lever *ou* percevoir (un impôt)

liabilities (n) dettes (fpl) *ou* passif (m)

liability (n) responsabilité (f) *[obligation légale]*

liable for (adj) responsable de *[légalement]*

liable to (adj) passible de *ou* assujetti(e) à

licence (n) autorisation (f) *ou* permis (m)

license (v) autoriser; octroyer un permis

licensee (n) titulaire (mf) d'une licence

licensing (n) octroi (m) *ou* concession (f) de licence

lien (n) droit (m) de retention

life assurance *or* **life insurance** assurance-vie (f)

life interest jouissance (f) à vie *ou* usufruit (m)

LIFO (last in first out) DEPS (dernier entré, premier sorti)

lift (n) ascenseur (m)

lift (v) *[remove]* lever

lift (v) an embargo lever l'embargo

lift (v) credit restrictions désencadrer le crédit

limit (n) limite (f)

limit (v) limiter

limitation (n) limitation (f) *ou* limite (f)

limited (adj) limité(e)

limited (liability) company (Ltd) société (f) à responsabilité limitée (S.A.R.L.)

limited market marché (m) restreint

limited partnership société (f) en commandite simple (SCS)

line (n) ligne (f)

line management *or* **line organization** organisation (f) hiérarchique *ou* verticale

line printer imprimante (f) ligne à ligne

liquid assets disponibilités (fpl) *ou* liquidités (fpl)

liquid: go liquid réaliser son actif

liquidate (v) a company liquider une entreprise

liquidate stock liquider du stock

liquidation (n) liquidation (f) d'un société

liquidator (n) liquidateur (m)

liquidity (n) liquidité (f)

liquidity crisis crise (f) de liquidité *ou* problème (m) de trésorerie

lira (n) *[currency in Italy and Turkey]* lire (f)

list (n) liste (f)

list (n) *[catalogue]* catalogue (m)

list (v) faire *ou* dresser *ou* établir une liste

list price prix (m) catalogue

listed company société (f) cotée en Bourse

litre (n) litre (m)

Lloyd's register registre (m) maritime Lloyd

load (n) charge (f) *ou* chargement (m)

load (v) embarquer *ou* charger

load (v) *[computer program]* charger (un programme)

load a lorry *or* **a ship** charger un camion *ou* un navire

load factor coefficient (m) de remplissage *[avion]*

loading bay aire (f) de chargement

loading ramp plateforme (f) de chargement

loan (n) *[borrowing]* emprunt (m)

loan *[lending]* prêt (m)

loan (v) prêter

loan capital capital (m) d'emprunt

loan stock emprunt obligataire

lobby (n) groupe (m) de pression

local (adj) local(e)

local call *[phone]* communication (f) urbaine

local government municipalités (fpl)

local labour main-d'oeuvre (f) locale

lock (n) serrure (f)

lock (v) fermer à clé

lock up a shop *or* **an office** fermer (un magasin *ou* un bureau à la fin de la journée)

lock up capital bloquer *ou* immobiliser des capitaux

lock-up premises magasin (m) sans logement

log (v) enregistrer

log calls *[phone]* enregistrer le nombre et la durée des appels

logo (n) logo (m)

long (adj) long (longue)

long credit crédit (m) à long terme

long-dated bill effet (m) à longue échéance

long-range à longue portée *ou* à long terme

long-standing de longue date

long-standing agreement accord (m) de longue date

long-term à long terme

long-term debts dettes (fpl) à long terme

long-term forecast prévisions (fpl) à long terme

long-term liabilities dettes (fpl) à long terme

long-term loan prêt (m) *ou* emprunt (m) à long terme

long-term objectives objectifs (mpl) à long terme

long-term planning planification (f) à long terme

loophole (n) faille (f)

loose (adj) [goods] en vrac

lorry (n) camion (m)

lorry driver camionneur (m)

lorry-load charge (f) complète d'un camion

lose (v) (something) perdre

lose [fall to a lower level] chuter

lose an order perdre une commande

lose money perdre de l'argent

loss (n) [not a profit] déficit (m) *ou* perte (f)

loss [of something] perte (f)

loss of an order perte d'une commande

loss of earnings perte de salaire *ou* manque (m) à gagner

loss-leader produit (m) d'appel *ou* article-réclame (m)

lot (n) [of items] lot (m)

low (adj) bas (basse)

low (n) niveau (m) très bas

low sales ventes (fpl) médiocres

low-grade (item) de qualité inférieure

low-level de bas niveau *ou* peu important

low-quality de qualité inférieure *ou* médiocre

lower (adj) moindre *ou* moins élevé(e) *ou* inférieur(e)

lower (v) baisser *ou* diminuer

lower prices baisser les prix

lowering (n) réduction (f) *ou* diminution (f)

Ltd (limited liability company) S.A.R.L. (société à responsabilité limitée)

luggage (n) bagages (mpl)

lump sum (n) montant (m) *ou* versement (m) unique; versement forfaitaire

luxury goods *or* items articles (mpl) de luxe

Mm

machine (n) machine (f) *ou* appareil (m)

macro-economics (n) macro-économie (f)

magazine (n) revue (f) *ou* magazine (m) *ou* périodique (m)

magazine insert encart (m) publicitaire

magazine mailing envoi (m) de revues par la poste *ou* mailing (m) de revues

magnetic tape *or* mag tape bande (f) magnétique

mail (n) [letters sent or received] courrier (m)

mail (n) [postal system] poste (f)

mail (v) poster; expédier *ou* envoyer par la poste

mail shot mailing (m)

mail-order vente (f) par correspondance (VPC)

mail-order business *or* mail-order maison (f) de vente par correspondance

mail-order catalogue catalogue (m) de vente par correspondance

mailing (n) envoi (m) par la poste

mailing list fichier (m) d'adresses

mailing piece prospectus (m) *ou* imprimé (m) publicitaire *[envoyé par la poste]*

mailing shot mailing (m) *ou* publipostage (m)

main (adj) principal(e)

main building bâtiment (m) principal

main office siège (m) social

maintain (v) *[keep at same level]* maintenir *ou* conserver

maintain *[keep going]* maintenir *ou* entretenir

maintenance (n) *[keeping in working order]* entretien (m) *ou* maintenance (f)

maintenance *[keeping things going]* maintien (m)

maintenance of contacts maintien (m) *ou* entretien (m) de relations

maintenance of supplies maintien (m) du stock de fournitures

major (adj) important(e) *ou* majeur(e)

major shareholder actionnaire (m) important

majority (n) majorité (f)

majority shareholder actionnaire (m) majoritaire

make (v) faire

make good *[a defect, a loss]* compenser *ou* réparer

make money faire un gain *ou* un profit

make out *[invoice]* rédiger *ou* établir

make provision for prévoir *ou* prendre des dispositions

make-ready time temps de mise en marche d'une machine

make up for *[compensate]* compenser *ou* dédommager (une perte, etc.)

maladministration (n) mauvaise gestion (f)

man (n) *[worker]* homme (m) *ou* ouvrier (m)

man (v) assurer une permanence *[à un stand, etc.]*

man-hour heure/homme (f) *ou* heure travaillée

manage (v) gérer *ou* diriger

manage property gérer une propriété

manage to arriver à *ou* réussir à

manageable (adj) qui peut être contrôlé *ou* géré

management (n) *[action]* gestion (f) *ou* management (m) *ou* direction (f)

management *[managers]* la direction *ou* l'administration (f); les cadres (mpl)

management accounts comptes (mpl) de gestion

management buyout (MBO) rachat (m) de l'entreprise par ses salariés

management consultant conseiller (m) en gestion d'entreprise

management course cours (m) de management *ou* de gestion d'entreprise

management team équipe (f) dirigeante *ou* équipe de direction

management techniques techniques (fpl) de gestion

management trainee jeune cadre en stage

management training formation (f) en gestion d'entreprise

manager (n) *[of branch, shop]* directeur (-trice) d'agence; gérant(e)

manager *[of department]* directeur (-trice) *ou* chef (m) (de service) *ou* manager (m)

managerial (adj) de gestion

managerial staff personnel (m) de direction; les cadres (mpl)

managing director (MD) directeur (-trice) général(e)

mandate (n) mandat (m)

manifest (n) manifeste (m)

manned (adj) avec du personnel en service

manning (n) effectifs (mpl)

manning levels besoins (mpl) en effectifs

manpower (n) main-d'oeuvre (f)

manpower forecasting prévisions (fpl) des besoins en main-d'oeuvre

manpower planning planification (f) de la main-d'oeuvre

manpower requirements besoins (mpl) en main-d'oeuvre

manpower shortage pénurie (f) de main-d'oeuvre

manual (adj) manuel (-elle)

manual (n) manuel (m) *ou* livret (m)

manual work travail (m) manuel

manual worker manoeuvre (m) *ou* travailleur (m) manuel

manufacture (n) fabrication (f) *ou* usinage (m)

manufacture (v) fabriquer *ou* manufacturer *ou* usiner

manufactured goods produits (mpl) manufacturés

manufacturer (n) fabricant (m) *ou* constructeur (m)

manufacturer's recommended price (MRP) prix (m) de vente conseillé

manufacturing (n) fabrication (f); transformation (f)

manufacturing capacity capacité (f) de production

manufacturing costs coûts (mpl) *ou* frais (mpl) de fabrication

manufacturing overheads frais (mpl) de fabrication

margin *[profit]* marge (f)

margin of error marge (f) d'erreur

marginal (adj) marginal(e) *ou* faible

marginal cost coût (m) marginal

marginal pricing méthode (f) de coûts marginaux

marine (adj) maritime

marine insurance assurance (f) maritime

marine underwriter assureur (m) maritime

maritime (adj) maritime

maritime law droit (m) maritime

maritime lawyer spécialiste (mf) en droit maritime

maritime trade commerce (m) maritime

mark (n) *[stamp]* marque (f); estampille (f)

mark (n) *[currency used in Germany]* mark (m) (allemand)

mark (v) marquer *ou* noter

mark down (v) réduire (le prix d'un article) *ou* démarquer (un article)

mark-down (n) réduction (f) de prix *ou* rabais (m)

mark up (v) augmenter *ou* majorer (le prix d'un article)

mark-up (n) *[action]* augmentation (f) *ou* majoration (f) (de prix)

mark-up *[profit margin]* marge (f) bénéficiaire

marker pen marqueur (m) *ou* surligneur (m)

market (n) *[place]* marché (m)

market (n) *[possible sales]* marché (m)

market (n) *[where a product might sell]* marché (m)

market (v) vendre *ou* commercialiser

market analysis analyse (f) du marché

market analyst analyste (m) de marché

market capitalization capitalisation (f) boursière

market economist économiste (m) financier

market forces tendances (fpl) du marché

market forecast prévisions (fpl) du marché

market leader N° 1 du marché *ou* leader (m)

market opportunity créneau (m)

market penetration pénétration (f) du marché

market price prix (m) du marché

market rate cours (m) du marché

market research étude (f) de marché

market share part (f) du marché

market trends tendances (fpl) du marché

market value valeur (f) marchande

market value *[stockmarket]* valeur (f) à la cote

marketable (adj) *[product]* facile à commercialiser *ou* à vendre

marketing (n) marketing (m) *ou* commercialisation (f)

marketing agreement accord (m) de commercialisation

marketing department *or* **division** service (m) (du) marketing

marketing manager directeur (-trice) du marketing

marketing strategy stratégie (f) commerciale

marketing techniques techniques (fpl) de marketing

marketplace (n) *[in town]* place (f) du marché

marketplace *[place where something is sold]* marché (m)

mass (n) *[of people]* foule (f)

mass *[of things]* grande quantité

mass market product produit (m) grand public

mass marketing distribution (f) grand public

mass media médias (mpl)

mass production production (f) *ou* fabrication (f) en série

mass-produce (v) fabriquer en série

mass-produce cars fabriquer des voitures en série

Master's degree in Business Administration (MBA) maîtrise (f) de gestion d'entreprise

material (n) *[for building, etc.]* matériau (m)

material (n) *[furniture]* matériel (m) *ou* équipement (m)

materials control contrôle (m) des fournitures *ou* des matériaux (en magasin)

materials handling manutention (f) du matériel

maternity leave congé (m) de maternité

matter (n) *[problem]* sujet (m) *ou* problème (m)

matter (n) *[to be discussed]* point (m) *ou* question (f)

matter (v) avoir de l'importance *ou* importer

mature (v) venir *ou* arriver à échéance

mature economy maturité (f) économique

maturity date date (f) d'échéance

maximization (n) maximalisation (f)

maximize (v) maximaliser *ou* maximiser

maximum (adj) maximum *ou* maximal(e)

maximum (n) maximum (m)

maximum price prix (m) maximum

MBA (Master in Business Administration) maîtrise (f) de gestion d'entreprise

MBO (management buyout) rachat (m) de l'entreprise par ses salariés

MD (managing director) directeur (-trice) général(e)

mean (adj) moyen (-enne)

mean (n) moyenne (f)

mean annual increase augmentation annuelle moyenne

means *[money]* moyens (mpl)

means *[ways]* moyen (m) *ou* façon (f)

means test enquête (f) sur les ressources (d'une personne)

measure (n) mesure (f)

measure (v) mesurer

measurement (n) of profitability analyse (f) de la rentabilité *ou* mesure (f) du rendement

measurements (n) mesures (fpl) *ou* dimensions (fpl)

media coverage couverture (f) médiatique

median (n) médiane (f)

mediate (v) intervenir comme médiateur

mediation (n) médiation (f) *ou* intervention (f)

mediator (n) médiateur (-trice)

medium (adj) moyen (-enne)

medium (n) moyen (m)

medium-sized (adj) moyen (-enne)

medium-term à moyen terme

meet (v) *[expenses]* faire face (aux dépenses)

meet (v) *[requirements]* satisfaire *ou* convenir (à)

meet (v) *[someone]* rencontrer (quelqu'un); se rencontrer *ou* se réunir

meet a deadline respecter un délai

meet a demand satisfaire *ou* répondre à la demande

meet a target atteindre un objectif

meeting (n) réunion (f) *ou* assemblée (f)

meeting place lieu (m) de réunion

member (n) *[of a group]* membre (m)

membership (n) *[all members]* ensemble (m) des membres d'un groupe

membership *[being a member]* appartenance (f) *ou* adhésion (f) *ou* affiliation (f)

memorandum (n) *or* **memo (n)** note (f) *ou* mémorandum (m)

memory (n) *[computer]* mémoire (f)

merchandise (n) marchandise (f)

merchandize (v) commercialiser

merchandize (v) a product commercialiser un produit

merchandizer (n) spécialiste (mf) des techniques marchandes *ou* marchandiseur (m)

merchandizing (n) techniques (fpl) marchandes *ou* marchandisage (m) *ou* merchandising (m)

merchant (n) marchand(e) *ou* négociant(e)

merchant *[wholesaler]* grossiste (mf)

merchant bank banque (f) d'affaires

merchant navy marine (f) marchande

merchant ship *or* **merchant vessel** navire (m) marchand *ou* cargo (m)

merge (v) fusionner

merger (n) fusion (f)

merit (n) mérite (m)

merit award *or* **merit bonus** prime (f) d'encouragement

message (n) message (m)

messenger (n) commissionnaire (m) *ou* coursier (m)

micro-economics (n) micro-économie (f)

microcomputer (n) micro-ordinateur (m)

mid-month accounts comptes (mpl) de quinzaine

mid-week en milieu de semaine

middle management cadres (mpl) moyens

middle-sized company entreprise (f) de taille moyenne

middleman (n) intermédiaire (m)

million (n) million (m)

millionaire (n) millionnaire (m)

minimarket (n) supérette (f)

minimum (adj) minimum *ou* minimal(e)

minimum (n) minimum (m)

minimum dividend dividende (m) minimum

minimum payment paiement (m) minimum

minimum wage salaire (m) minimum (garanti)

minor shareholders petits actionnaires (mpl)

minority (n) minorité (f)

minority shareholder actionnaire (m) minoritaire

minus moins *ou* sans

minus factor facteur (m) négatif

minute (n) *[time]* minute (f)

minute (v) enregistrer *ou* prendre note de

minutes (n) *[of meeting]* procès-verbal (m)

misappropriate (v) détourner des fonds

misappropriation (n) détournement (m) de fonds

miscalculate (v) faire une erreur de calcul

miscalculation (n) erreur (f) de calcul

miscellaneous (adj) divers(e) *ou* varié(e)

miscellaneous items articles (mpl) divers

mismanage (v) mal gérer

mismanagement (n) mauvaise gestion

miss (v) *[not to hit, not to meet]* manquer *ou* rater

miss an instalment être en retard d'un versement

miss a target ne pas atteindre un objectif *ou* manquer son but

miss a train, a plane manquer *ou* rater un train, un avion

mistake (n) erreur (f) *ou* faute (f)

misunderstanding (n) malentendu (m)

mixed (adj) *[different sorts]* mixte

mixed *[neither good nor bad]* mitigé(e)

mixed economy économie (f) mixte

mobile phone téléphone (m) mobile

mobility (n) mobilité (f)

mobilize (v) mobiliser

mobilize capital mobiliser des capitaux

mock-up (n) maquette (f)

mode (n) mode (m)

mode of payment modalités (fpl) de paiement

model (n) *[person]* mannequin (m)

model *[small copy]* modèle (m) réduit *ou* maquette (f)

model *[style of product]* modèle (m)

model (v) *[clothes]* présenter des modèles de collection

model (adj) agreement accord-type (m)

modem (n) modem (m)

moderate (adj) modéré(e)

moderate (v) modérer *ou* limiter

monetary (adj) monétaire

monetary base base (f) monétaire

monetary unit unité (f) monétaire

money (n) argent (m)

money changer courtier (m) de change *ou* bureau (m) de change

money markets marchés (mpl) monétaires

money order mandat (m) postal *ou* mandat-poste (m)

money rates taux (m) d'intérêt de l'argent

money supply masse (f) monétaire

money up front avance (f) *ou* paiement (m) d'avance

money-making (adj) qui rapporte

moneylender (n) prêteur (-euse)

monitor (n) *[screen]* écran (m) (d'ordinateur)

monitor (v) contrôler *ou* vérifier

monopolization (n) monopolisation (f)

monopolize (v) monopoliser

monopoly (n) monopole (m)

month (n) mois (m)

month end fin (f) de mois

month-end accounts comptes (mpl) de fin de mois

monthly (adj) mensuel (-elle)

monthly (adv) mensuellement *ou* chaque mois

monthly payments paiements (mpl) mensuels *ou* mensualités (fpl)

monthly statement relevé (m) mensuel

moonlight (v) travailler au noir

moonlighter (n) travailleur (-euse) au noir

moonlighting (n) travail (m) au noir

more than plus de; supérieur(e) à

moratorium (n) moratoire (m)

mortgage (n) hypothèque (f) *ou* prêt (m) hypothécaire

mortgage (v) prêter sur hypothèque

mortgage payments remboursements (mpl) de prêt (hypothécaire)

mortgagee (n) prêteur (m) (sur hypothèque)

mortgager *or* **mortgagor (n)** emprunteur (m) (sur hypothèque)

most-favoured nation nation (f) la plus favorisée

motivated (adj) motivé(e)

motivation (n) motivation (f)

motor insurance assurance (f) automobile

mount up (v) augmenter *ou* monter *ou* flamber

mounting (adj) grandissant(e)

move (v) *[be sold]* se vendre

move *[house, office]* déménager

move *[propose]* déposer (une motion)

movement mouvement (m) *ou* fluctuation (f)

movements of capital mouvements (mpl) de capitaux

MRP (manufacturer's recommended price) prix (m) de vente conseillé

multicurrency operation opération (f) multidevise

multilateral (adj) multilatéral(e)

multilateral agreement accord (m) multilatéral

multilateral trade commerce (m) multilatéral

multidedia (n) multimédia

multinational (adj) multinational(e)

multinational (n) multinationale (f)

multiple (adj) multiple

multiple entry visa visa (m) permanent (bon pour plusieurs entrées)

multiple ownership propriété (f) collective

multiple store magasin (m) à succursales multiples

multiplication (n) multiplication (f)

multiply (v) multiplier

mutual (adj) commun(e) *ou* mutuel (-elle) *ou* réciproque

mutual (insurance) company mutuelle (f)

Nn

NAFTA (North American Free Trade Agreement) Aléna (Accord de libre-échange nord-américain)

national (adj) national(e)

national advertising publicité (f) à l'échelon national

nationalization (n) nationalisation (f)

nationalize (v) nationaliser

nationalized industry industrie (f) nationalisée

nationwide (adj) national(e) *ou* à l'échelon national

natural resources ressources (fpl) naturelles

natural wastage *[workers]* départs (mpl) naturels

near letter-quality (NLQ) *[printer]* qualité (f) courrier

necessary (adj) nécessaire *ou* indispensable

negative cash flow cash-flow (m) négatif *ou* trésorerie (f) négative

neglected business entreprise (f) mal gérée

neglected shares valeurs (fpl) négligées

negligence (n) négligence (f)

negligent (adj) négligent(e)

negligible (adj) négligeable

negotiable (adj) négociable

negotiable instrument effet (m) négociable

negotiate (v) négocier

negotiation (n) négociation (f)

negotiator (n) négociateur (-trice)

net (adj) net (nette)

net (v) toucher *ou* gagner net

net assets *or* **net worth** actif (m) net; valeur (f) nette

net earnings *or* **net income** profit (m) net; revenu (m) net

net income *or* **net salary** salaire (m) net

net loss perte (f) nette

net margin marge (f) nette

net price prix (m) net

net profit bénéfice (m) net *ou* gain (m) net

net receipts recettes (fpl) nettes

net sales ventes (fpl) nettes

net weight poids (m) net

net worth valeur (f) nette

net yield rendement (m) net

network (n) réseau (m)

network (v) *[computers]* connecter en réseau

news agency agence (f) de presse

newspaper (n) journal (m)

niche (n) créneau (m) (sur le marché)

night (n) nuit (f)

night rate tarif (m) de nuit *ou* tarif réduit

night shift équipe (f) de nuit

nil (noun) néant (m) *ou* zéro (m)

nil return état (m) néant

NLQ (near letter-quality) qualité (f) courrier

no-claims bonus *[insurance]* bonus (m)

no-strike agreement *or* **no-strike clause** clause (f) interdisant la grève

nominal capital capital (m) nominal

nominal ledger grand livre (m) général

nominal rent loyer (m) symbolique

nominal value valeur (f) nominale

nominee (n) personne (f) désignée

nominee account compte confié à un fondé de pouvoir

non-delivery non-livraison (f)

non-executive director administrateur (m) non dirigeant

non-feasance délit (m) par abstention

non-negotiable instrument effet (m) non négociable

non-payment (n) *[of a debt]* non-paiement (m)

non profit-making non lucratif (-ive) *ou* sans but lucratif

non-recurring items postes (mpl) exceptionnels

non-refundable deposit arrhes (fpl) non remboursables

non-returnable packing emballage (m) perdu *ou* non consigné

non-stop sans arrêt; sans escale *ou* non-stop [*vol*]

non-taxable income revenu (m) non imposable

non-voting shares actions (fpl) sans droit de vote

norm (n) norme (f)

North American Free Trade Agreement (NAFTA) Accord de libre-échange nord-américain (Aléna)

notary public notaire (mf)

note (n) avis (m) *ou* note (f)

note (v) [*write down*] noter

note (n) of hand billet (m) à ordre

notice (n) [*piece of information*] notice (f) *ou* note (f) (d'information)

notice [*that worker is leaving his job*] préavis (m)

notice [*time allowed*] préavis (m)

notification (n) notification (f) *ou* avis (m)

notify (v) notifier

null (adj) nul (nulle)

number (n) [*figure*] numéro (m)

number (v) numéroter

numbered account compte (m) numéroté

numeric or **numerical (adj)** numérique

numeric keypad [*on keyboard*] clavier (m) *ou* pavé (m) numérique

Oo

objective (adj) objectif (-ive)

objective (n) objectif (m)

obligation (n) [*debt*] dette (f)

obligation [*duty*] obligation (f)

obsolescence (n) obsolescence (f)

obsolescent (adj) obsolescent(e)

obsolete (adj) obsolète *ou* qui n'est plus en usage

obtain (v) obtenir *ou* se procurer

obtainable (adj) disponible *ou* qu'on peut se procurer

occupancy (n) occupation (f)

occupancy rate taux (m) d'occupation

occupant (n) occupant (m)

occupational (adj) professionnel (-elle)

occupational accident accident (m) du travail

odd (adj) [*not a pair*] dépareillé(e)

odd [*not even*] impair(e)

odd numbers nombres (mpl) impairs

off [*away from work*] absent(e)

off [*cancelled*] annulé(e)

off [*reduced by*] avec réduction

off-peak en dehors des heures de pointe

off-season morte-saison (f)

off the record officieusement *ou* en privé

off-the-job training formation (f) professionnelle dans un centre spécialisé

offer (n) offre (f)

offer (v) [*to buy*] offrir *ou* proposer

offer (v) [*to sell*] mettre en vente

offer for sale offre (f) publique de vente (OPV)

offer price [*shares*] prix (m) d'émission (d'une action)

office (n) bureau (m)

office equipment équipement (m) *ou* matériel (m) de bureau

office furniture meubles (mpl) de bureaux

office hours heures (fpl) de bureau

office security mesures (fpl) de sécurité dans les bureaux

office space local (m) pour bureaux

office staff personnel (m) de bureau

office stationery fournitures (fpl) de bureau

offices to let bureaux (mpl) à louer

official (adj) officiel (-elle)

official (n) fonctionnaire (m)

official receiver administrateur (m) judiciaire

official return déclaration (f) officielle

officialese (n) jargon (m) administratif

offset (v) losses against tax déduire ses pertes des impôts

off-shore (adj) offshore

off-shore bank banque (f) offshore

off-shore fund placement (m) dans un paradis fiscal

oil *[petroleum]* pétrole (m)

oil price prix (m) du pétrole

oil-exporting countries pays (mpl) exportateurs de pétrole

old (adj) vieux, vieil (vieille)

old-established (adj) établi(e) depuis longtemps

old-fashioned (adj) démodé(e)

ombudsman (n) médiateur (m) *ou* ombudsman (m)

omission (n) omission (f)

omit (v) oublier *ou* omettre (de faire quelque chose)

on a short-term basis à court terme

on account en acompte

on agreed terms aux termes le l'accord

on an annual basis chaque année *ou* sur une base annuelle

on average en moyenne

on approval à l'essai *ou* à condition

on behalf of au nom de

on board à bord

on business pour affaires

on condition that à (la) condition que *ou* sous réserve de

on credit à crédit

on demand à vue *ou* à présentation

on duty de service

on favourable terms à des conditions avantageuses *ou* exceptionnelles

on line *or* **online** en ligne

on request sur demande

on sale en vente

on the increase qui va en augmentant

on time à l'heure

on-the-job training formation (f) dans l'entreprise *ou* sur le tas *ou* sur le terrain

one-off isolé(e) *ou* unique

one-off item article (m) unique *ou* non suivi

one-sided (adj) unilatéral(e)

one-sided agreement accord (m) unilatéral

one-way fare tarif (m) d'un aller simple

one-way trade commerce (m) unilatéral

OPEC (Organization of Petroleum Exporting Countries) OPEP (Organisation des pays exportateurs de pétrole)

open (adj) *[not closed]* ouvert(e)

open (v) *[begin]* démarrer *ou* entamer

open (v) *[start new business]* ouvrir

open a bank account ouvrir un compte en banque

open a line of credit autoriser *ou* ouvrir une ligne de crédit

open a meeting ouvrir la séance

open (adj) account compte (m) ouvert

open (v) an account ouvrir un compte

open cheque chèque (m) non barré

open credit découvert (m) autorisé *ou* crédit (m) à découvert

open market marché (m) libre

open (v) negotiations entamer des négociations

open (adj) ticket billet (m) open

open (adj) to offers ouvert à toute proposition

open-ended agreement accord (m) flexible *ou* non limité

open-plan office bureau (m) à modules *ou* bureau paysager

opening (adj) initial(e)

opening (n) ouverture (f)

opening balance bilan (m) initial

opening bid offre (f) d'ouverture *ou* première mise (f)

opening hours heures (fpl) d'ouverture

opening price *[auction]* mise (f) à prix

opening price *[shares]* prix (m) *ou* cours (m) d'ouverture

opening stock stock (m) initial *ou* stock d'ouverture

opening time heure(s) (f(pl)) d'ouverture

operate (v) être en vigueur

operate (v) *[machine]* (faire) fonctionner

operating budget budget (m) opérationnel

operating costs *or* **operating expenses**
coûts (mpl) opérationnels *ou* coûts
d'exploitation

operating manual manuel (m)
d'utilisation

operating profit bénéfice (m)
commercial

operating system système (m)
d'exploitation

operation (n) *[business]* exploitation
(f) *ou* opération (f)

operation (n) *[dealing]* opération (f)
(boursière)

operational (adj) opérationnel (-elle)

operational budget budget (m)
opérationnel

operational costs coûts (mpl)
opérationnels

operative (adj) en vigueur;
opérationnel (-elle)

operative (n) opérateur (-trice) *[d'une
machine]*

operator (n) opérateur (-trice) *[d'une
machine]*

operator (n) *[telephone]* standardiste
(mf) *ou* opératrice (f)

opinion poll sondage (m) d'opinion

opportunity (n) opportunité (f) *ou*
occasion (f)

option to purchase option (f) d'achat

optional (adj) facultatif (-ive) *ou* en
option *ou* optionnel (-elle)

optional extras accessoires (mpl) en
option

order (n) *[certain way]* ordre (m)

order (n) *[for goods]* commande (f)

order (n) *[instruction]* ordre (m) *ou*
instruction (f)

order (n) *[money]* mandat (m)

order (v) *[goods]* commander

order (v) *[put in order]* classer *ou*
ordonner

order (n) book carnet (m) de
commandes

order fulfilment exécution (f) de
commande(s)

order number numéro (m) de
commande

order picking sélection (f) des
différents éléments d'une commande

order processing traitement (m) de
commande(s)

order: on order commandé *ou* en
commande

ordinary (adj) ordinaire

ordinary shares actions (fpl) ordinaires

organization (n) *[institution]*
organisation (f)

organization *[way of arranging]*
organisation (f)

organization and methods
organisation et méthodes

organization chart organigramme (m)

**Organization of Petroleum Exporting
Countries (OPEC)** Organisation des
pays exportateurs de pétrole (OPEP)

organizational (adj) relatif à
l'organisation *ou* à la structure

organize (v) organiser

origin (n) origine (f) *ou* provenance (f)

original (adj) original(e) *ou* d'origine

original (n) original (m)

OS (= outsize) grande taille (f)

out of date démodé(e) *ou* dépassé(e)

out-of-pocket expenses débours (mpl)

out of pocket: be out of pocket en être
de sa poche

out of stock épuisé(e) *[article]*

out of stock en rupture de stock
[marchand]

out of work au *ou* en chômage

outbid (v) surenchérir

outgoing (adj) sortant(e)

outgoing mail courrier (m) au départ

outgoings (n) sorties (fpl) *ou* dépenses
(fpl)

outlay (n) dépense (f)

outlet (n) point (m) de vente

output (n) *[computer]* sortie (f) *ou*
données (fpl) de sortie

output (n) *[goods]* production (f) *ou*
rendement (m)

output (v) *[computer]* sortir

output tax TVA sur les prestations de
service

outright (adv) *[completely]*
complètement *ou* totalement

outright (adj) *[purchase]* au comptant

outside (adj) extérieur(e) *ou* à
l'extérieur

outside director administrateur (m)
externe

outside line *[phone]* ligne (f) (téléphonique) extérieure

outside office hours en dehors des heures de bureau

outsize (OS) grande taille (f)

outstanding (adj) *[exceptional]* exceptionnel (-elle)

outstanding *[unpaid]* à payer; impayé(e)

outstanding debts dettes (fpl) à payer; les impayés (mpl)

outstanding orders commandes (fpl) en attente

overall (adj) global(e) *ou* général(e)

overall plan plan (m) global

overbook (v) surréserver *ou* faire un surbooking

overbooking (n) surréservation (f) *ou* surbooking (m)

overbought (market) marché (m) surévalué

overcapacity (n) surcapacité (f)

overcharge (n) trop-perçu (m)

overcharge (v) faire payer trop cher

overdraft (n) découvert (m)

overdraft facility autorisation (f) de découvert

overdraw (v) tirer à découvert

overdrawn account compte (m) à découvert

overdue (adj) en retard

overestimate (v) surestimer

overhead budget budget (m) des frais généraux

overheads (n) *or* **overhead costs** frais (mpl) généraux *ou* d'administration générale

overmanning (n) excédent (m) de personnel

overpayment (n) trop-perçu (m)

overproduce (v) produire en excédent *ou* surproduire

overproduction (n) surproduction (f)

overseas (adj) à l'étranger *ou* outre-mer

overseas (n) l'étranger *ou* les pays étrangers

overseas markets marchés (mpl) étrangers

overseas trade commerce (m) extérieur

overspend (v) trop dépenser

overspend one's budget dépasser son budget

overstock (v) avoir un excédent de stock

overstocks (n) excédents (m) de stock

overtime (n) heures (f) supplémentaires

overtime ban refus (m) de faire des heures supplémentaires

overtime pay tarif (m) des heures supplémentaires

overvalue (v) surévaluer

overweight: to be overweight être trop lourd

owe (v) devoir

owing (adj) dû (due)

owing to en raison de *ou* à cause de

own (v) posséder *ou* détenir

own brand goods *or* **own label goods** produits (mpl) à marque du distributeur

owner (n) propriétaire (mf)

ownership (n) propriété (f)

Pp

p & p (postage and packing) frais (mpl) de port et d'emballage

PA (personal assistant) secrétaire (f) *ou* assistante de direction

pack (n) paquet (m)

pack (v) emballer *ou* empaqueter

pack (v) goods into cartons emballer des marchandises dans des cartons

pack (n) of envelopes paquet (m) d'enveloppes

package (n) *[of goods]* paquet (m) *ou* colis (m)

package *[of services]* contrat (m) global

package deal contrat (m) global; forfait (m)

package holiday forfait-vacances (m); voyage (m) organisé

packaging (m) *[action]* emballage (m) *ou* conditionnement (m)

packaging (material) emballage (m) *ou* conditionnement (m)

packer (n) emballeur (-euse)

packet (n) paquet (m)

packet of cigarettes paquet (m) de cigarettes

packing (n) *[action]* emballage (m)

packing (material) emballage (m)

packing case caisse (f)

packing charges frais (mpl) d'emballage

packing list *or* **packing slip** liste (f) de colisage

paid (adj) *[for work]* payé(e) *ou* rémunéré(e)

paid *[invoice]* payé(e) *ou* réglé(e)

pallet (n) palette (f)

palletize (v) mettre sur palette(s)

panel (n) panneau (m)

panel (n) (of experts) groupe (m) (d'experts)

panic buying achat (m) de précaution

paper bag sac (m) *ou* pochette (f) en papier

paper feed alimentation (f) en papier

paper loss *[accounts]* perte (f) théorique

paper profit *[accounts]* bénéfice (m) théorique *ou* gain (m) théorique

paperclip (n) trombone (m)

papers (n) documents (mpl)

paperwork (n) paperasserie (f)

par (adj) au pair *ou* à la parité

par value valeur (f) nominale *ou* valeur au pair

parcel (n) paquet (m) *ou* colis (m)

parcel (v) empaqueter

parcel post service (m) colis (postaux)

parent company maison (f) mère *ou* société (f) mère

parity (n) parité (f) *ou* égalité (f)

part (n) part (f) *ou* partie (f)

part exchange reprise (f) (contre achat)

part-owner copropriétaire (mf)

part-ownership copropriété (f)

part-time (adj & adv) temps (m) partiel *ou* mi-temps (m)

part-time work *or* **part-time employment** travail (m) à temps partiel *ou* à mi-temps

part-timer (n) employé(e) à temps partiel *ou* à mi-temps

partial loss sinistre (m) partiel

partial payment acompte (m)

particulars (n) détails (mpl) *ou* coordonnées (fpl)

partner (n) associé(e)

partnership (n) association (f) *ou* société (f)

party (n) partie (f) *[juridique]*

patent (n) brevet (m)

patent agent agent (m) en brevets

patent (v) an invention faire breveter une invention

patent applied for *or* **patent pending** demande (f) de brevet déposée

patented (adj) breveté(e)

pay (n) *[salary]* salaire (m) *ou* paie (f) *ou* traitement (m) *ou* rémunération (f)

pay (v) *[bill]* payer *ou* verser (de l'argent)

pay (v) *[worker]* payer *ou* rémunérer

pay a bill régler *ou* payer une note

pay a dividend verser un dividende

pay an invoice régler une facture

pay back rembourser

pay by cheque régler *ou* payer par chèque

pay by credit card régler *ou* payer avec une carte de crédit

pay cash payer comptant

pay (n) cheque chèque (m) de salaire

pay desk caisse (f)

pay (v) in advance payer d'avance

pay in instalments payer par versements échelonnés

pay interest verser un intérêt

pay money down verser un acompte *ou* une provision

pay off (v) *[debt]* rembourser

pay off *[worker]* congédier *ou* licencier (avec paie)

pay out (v) verser de l'argent

pay phone téléphone (m) public

pay (n) rise augmentation (f) de salaire

pay (n) slip bulletin (m) de salaire *ou* feuille (f) de paie

pay the bill *[at restaurant]* payer l'addition

pay up (v) régler une dette

payable (adj) payable

payable at sixty days payable à soixante jours

payable in advance payable à l'avance

payable on delivery payable à la livraison *ou* livraison contre remboursement

payable on demand payable à vue *ou* sur présentation

payables (n) comptes (mpl) fournisseurs

payback (n) remboursement (m)

payback clause clause (f) de remboursement (d'un prêt)

payback period délai (m) de remboursement *ou* d'amortissement

payee (n) bénéficiaire (mf)

payer (n) payeur (m)

paying (adj) qui rapporte *ou* lucratif (-ive) *ou* rentable

paying (n) paiement (m)

paying-in slip bordereau (m) de versement

payload (n) *[lorry]* charge (f) utile

payment (n) paiement (m) *ou* règlement (m); versement (m)

payment by cheque règlement (m) par chèque

payment by credit card règlement avec carte de crédit

payment by results paiement (m) au rendement *ou* salaire (m) au rendement

payment in cash paiement (m) en espèces *ou* au comptant *ou* cash

payment in kind paiement (m) en nature

payment on account acompte (m)

PC (personal computer) ordinateur (m) personnel

P/E ratio (price/earnings ratio) PER (m) (coefficient de capitalisation des résultats)

peak (n) maximum (m) *ou* record (m)

peak (v) culminer; atteindre un record *ou* un niveau élevé

peak output production (f) record

peak period heures (fpl) de pointe

peg (v) prices bloquer les prix

penalize (v) pénaliser *ou* sanctionner

penalty (n) amende (f) *ou* pénalité (f) *ou* sanction (f)

penalty clause clause (f) pénale

pending (adj) en attente

penetrate (v) a market pénétrer un marché *ou* s'implanter sur un marché

pension (n) pension (f) de retraite

pension fund caisse (f) de retraite

pension scheme régime (m) de retraite

per par *ou* pour

per annum *or* **per year** par année

per capita par personne *ou* par tête

per cent *[%]* pour cent *[%]*

per day par jour

per head par personne *ou* par tête

per hour (de) l'heure; à l'heure

per week par semaine

per year par année

percentage (n) pourcentage (m); taux (m)

percentage discount pourcentage (m) de remise

percentage increase taux (m) d'augmentation

percentage point un pour cent

performance (n) performance (f)

performance rating évaluation (f) du rendement

period (n) période (f) *ou* durée (f)

period of notice délai (m) de préavis *ou* délai-congé (m)

period of validity durée (f) *ou* période (f) de validité

periodic *or* **periodical (adj)** périodique

periodical (n) périodique (m) *ou* revue (f)

peripherals (n) *[computer]* périphériques (mpl) (d'ordinateur)

perishable (adj) périssable

perishable goods *or* **perishables (n)** denrées (fpl) périssables

permission (n) permission (f) *ou* autorisation (f)

permit (n) permis (m)

permit (v) autoriser quelqu'un à faire quelque chose

personal (adj) privé(e) *ou* personnel (-elle)

personal allowances *[income tax]* abattement (m); revenu (m) exonéré d'impôt

personal assets biens (mpl) meubles

personal assistant (PA) secrétaire (f) *ou* assistante de direction

personal computer (PC) ordinateur (m) personnel

personalized (adj) personnalisé(e)

personalized cheques chèques personnalisés

personnel (n) *[staff]* personnel (m)

personnel department service (m) du personnel

personnel management gestion (f) du personnel

personnel manager chef (m) du personnel

peseta (n) *[Spanish currency]* peseta (f) (espagnole)

petty (adj) peu important

petty cash petite caisse (f)

petty cash box caisse (f)

petty expenses petites *ou* menues dépenses (fpl)

phase in (v) introduire graduellement

phase out (v) mettre fin graduellement (à)

phone (n) téléphone (m)

phone (v) téléphoner *ou* appeler

phone back (v) rappeler

phone call appel (m) (téléphonique) *ou* coup (m) de fil

phone card télécarte (f)

phone for (something) demander *ou* commander par téléphone

phone number numéro (m) de téléphone

photocopier photocopieur (m)

photocopy (n) photocopie (f)

photocopy (v) photocopier

photocopying (n) (action de faire des) photocopies (fpl)

photocopying bureau service (m) de reproduction

picking list inventaire (m) de position

pie chart (n) diagramme (m) circulaire *ou* camembert (m)

piece (n) pièce (f)

piece rate *[rate of pay]* tarif (m) unitaire

piecework (n) travail (m) à la pièce *ou* aux pièces

pilferage *or* **pilfering (n)** chapardage (m)

pilot (adj) pilote *ou* modèle

pilot (n) *[person]* pilote (m)

pilot scheme programme (m) pilote

pioneer (n) pionnier (m) *ou* novateur (-trice)

pioneer (v) innover

place (n) *[in a competition]* place (f) *ou* rang (m)

place (n) *[job]* poste (m) *ou* emploi (m)

place (n) *[situation]* endroit (m) *ou* lieu (m)

place (v) placer

place an order passer une commande

place (n) of work lieu (m) de travail

plaintiff (n) partie (f) plaignante

plan (n) *[drawing]* plan (m)

plan (n) *[project]* plan (m) *ou* projet (m)

plan (v) planifier; projeter

plan (v) investments faire des plans d'investissement

plane (n) avion (m)

planner (n) planificateur (-trice)

planning (n) planification (f)

plant (n) *[factory]* usine (f)

plant (n) *[machinery]* machines (fpl)

plant-hire firm société (f) de location de matériel

platform (n) *[railway station]* quai (m) (de la gare)

PLC *or* **plc (Public Limited Company)** Société anonyme (S.A.) *[cotée en Bourse]*

plug (n) *[electric]* fiche (f)

plug (v) *[block]* arrêter

plug (v) *[publicize]* faire de la publicité

plummet (v) chuter

plus plus

plus factor atout (m)

pocket (n) poche (f)

pocket (v) gagner (net) *ou* empocher

pocket calculator calculatrice (f) de poche

point (n) point (m)

point of sale (p.o.s. *or* **POS)** point (m) de vente

point of sale material (POS material) matériel (m) de publicité sur le lieu de vente (PLV)

policy (n) politique (f)

pool (n) pool (m)

pool (v) resources mettre les ressources en commun

poor (adj) *[not rich]* pauvre

poor quality qualité (f) inférieure

poor service service (m) médiocre

popular (adj) populaire

popular prices prix (mpl) à la portée de tous

port (n) *[computer]* port (m)

port (n) *[harbour]* port (m)

port authority autorités (fpl) portuaires

port charges *or* **port dues** droits (mpl) de bassin

port of call port (m) d'escale

port of embarkation port (m) d'embarquement

port of registry port (m) d'attache *[d'un navire]*

portable (adj) portatif (-ive) *ou* portable

portfolio (n) portefeuille (f) (d'actions)

portfolio management gestion (f) de portefeuilles

POS *or* **p.o.s. (point of sale)** point (m) de vente

POS material (point of sale material) matériel (m) de publicité sur le lieu de vente (PLV)

position (n) *[job]* poste (m)

position *[state of affairs]* position (f)

positive (adj) positif (-ive)

positive cash flow trésorerie (f) positive

possess (v) posséder

possibility (n) possibilité (f)

possible (adj) possible

post (n) *[job]* poste (m) *ou* emploi (m)

post (n) *[letters]* courrier (m)

post (n) *[postal system]* poste (f) *ou* service (m) postal

post (v) poster *ou* mettre à la poste

post (v) an entry passer une écriture

post (n) free franco de port *ou* franc de port

postage (n) tarif (m) postal; affranchissement (m)

postage and packing (p & p) frais (mpl) de port et d'emballage

postage paid port (m) payé

postage stamp timbre-poste (m) *ou* timbre (m)

postal (adj) postal(e)

postal charges *or* **postal rates** tarifs (mpl) postaux

postal order mandat-poste (m)

postcode (n) code (m) postal

postdate (v) postdater

poste restante poste restante

postmark (n) cachet (m) de la poste

postmarked (adj) timbré(e) (de)

postpaid (adj) port (m) payé

postpone (v) remettre à plus tard *ou* reporter

postponement renvoi (m) *ou* remise (f) à plus tard

potential (adj) potentiel (-elle) *ou* possible

potential (n) potentiel (m)

potential customers clients (mpl) potentiels *ou* prospects (mpl)

potential market marché (m) potentiel

pound (n) *[currency]* livre (f) (sterling)

pound (n) *[weight: 0.45kg]* livre (f)

pound sterling livre (f) sterling

power of attorney procuration (f)

PR (public relations) relations (fpl) publiques

pre-empt (v) devancer *ou* prévenir

pre-financing (n) préfinancement (m)

prefer (v) préférer

preference (n) préférence (f) *ou* priorité (f)

preference shares actions (fpl) privilégiées

preferential (adj) privilégié(e) *ou* prioritaire

preferential creditor créancier (m) prioritaire

preferential duty *or* **preferential tariff** tarif (m) privilégié

preferred creditor créancier (m) prioritaire

premises (n) locaux (mpl)

premises: on the premises sur place

premium (n) *[extra charge]* plus-value (f) *[du change]*

premium *[insurance]* prime (f) (d'assurance)

premium *[on lease]* reprise (f)

premium offer prime (f) *ou* cadeau (m)

premium quality première qualité *ou* qualité (f) extra

premium: at a premium *[shares, etc.]* au-dessus du pair

prepack (v) *or* **prepackage (v)** préemballer *ou* conditionner

prepaid (adj) payé(e) d'avance

prepay (v) payer d'avance

prepayment (n) paiement (m) d'avance

present (adj) *[being there]* présent(e)

present (adj) *[now]* actuel (-elle)

present (n) *[gift]* cadeau (m)

present (v) *[give]* offrir

present (v) *[show a document]* présenter

present a bill for acceptance présenter une traite à l'acceptation

present a bill for payment présenter une traite au recouvrement

present (adj) value valeur (f) actuelle

presentation (n) *[exhibition]* présentation (f)

presentation *[showing a document]* présentation (f)

press (n) presse (f)

press conference conférence (f) de presse

press release communiqué (m) de presse

prestige (n) prestige (m)

prestige product produit (m) de luxe

pretax profit bénéfice (m) avant impôts

prevent (v) empêcher

prevention (n) prévention (f)

preventive (adj) préventif (-ive)

previous (adj) antérieur(e) *ou* précédent(e)

price (n) prix (m)

price (v) fixer *ou* déterminer un prix

price ceiling plafond (m) des prix

price control contrôle (m) des prix

price differential écart (m) de prix

price/earnings ratio (P/E ratio) coefficient (m) de capitalisation des résultats *ou* PER (m)

price ex quay prix (m) à quai *ou* franco à quai

price ex warehouse prix ex-entrepôt

price ex works prix départ usine

price label étiquette (f) de prix

price list catalogue (m) *ou* tarif (m) *ou* liste (f) de prix

price range fourchette (f) de prix

price reduction réduction (f) de prix *ou* rabais (m)

price-sensitive product produit (m) sensible aux changements de prix

price stability stabilité (f) des prix

price tag *or* **price ticket** étiquette (f) de prix *ou* ticket (m) de prix

price war *or* **price-cutting war** guerre (f) des prix

pricing (n) fixation (f) d'un prix

pricing policy politique (f) (de fixation) des prix

primary (adj) de base

primary industry industrie (f) de base *ou* secteur (m) primaire

prime (adj) de base

prime cost prix (m) coûtant de base

prime rate taux (m) de base bancaire

principal (adj) principal(e)

principal (n) *[money]* capital (m)

principal (n) *[person]* chef (m) *ou* directeur (-trice)

principle (n) principe (m)

print (v) imprimer

print out (v) imprimer

printer (n) *[company]* imprimeur (m)

printer *[machine]* imprimante (f)

printout (n) sortie (f) d'imprimante

prior (adj) antérieur(e) *ou* préalable

private (adj) privé(e); privatif (-ive)

private enterprise entreprise (f) privée

private limited company société (f) anonyme (S.A.) *[ordinaire]*

private ownership propriété (f) privée

private property propriété (f) privée

private sector secteur (m) privé *ou* le privé

privatization (n) privatisation (f)

privatize (v) privatiser

pro forma (n) (invoice) facture (f) pro forma

pro rata (adj & adv) au prorata

probation (n) période (f) d'essai

probationary (adj) à l'essai *ou* d'essai

problem (n) problème (m)

problem area secteur (m) difficile

problem solving solution (f) de problèmes

procedure (n) procédure (f) *ou* méthode (f)

proceed (v) (se) poursuivre *ou* continuer

process (n) procédé (m)

process (v) *[deal with]* traiter *ou* exécuter

process (v) *[raw materials]* traiter

process figures analyser des chiffres

processing (n) of information *or* **of statistics** traitement (m) de données *ou* de statistiques

produce (n) *[food]* produits (mpl) maraîchers

produce (v) *[bring out]* produire *ou* présenter

produce (v) *[interest]* rapporter

produce (v) *[make]* produire *ou* fabriquer

producer (n) producteur (-trice)

product (n) produit (m)

product advertising publicité (f) de produit

product design conception (f) de produit

product development développement (m) de nouveau(x) produit(s)

product engineer ingénieur (m) produit

product line gamme (f) *ou* ligne (f) de produits

product mix éventail (m) *ou* gamme (f) de produits

production (n) *[making]* fabrication (f) *ou* production (f)

production *[showing]* présentation (f)

production cost coût (m) de production *ou* prix (m) de revient

production department service (m) de la production *ou* de la fabrication

production line chaîne (f) de production

production manager directeur de la production *ou* chef (m) de la fabrication

production standards niveau (m) de qualité de production

production targets objectifs (mpl) de production

production unit unité (f) *ou* centre (m) de production

productive (adj) productif (-ive)

productive discussions discussions (fpl) productives

productivity (n) productivité (f) *ou* rendement (m)

productivity agreement contrat (m) de productivité

productivity bonus prime (f) de rendement

professional (adj) *[expert]* professionnel (-elle)

professional (n) *[expert]* spécialiste (m) *ou* expert (m)

professional qualifications qualifications (fpl) professionnelles

profit (n) profit (m) *ou* bénéfice (m) *ou* gain (m)

profit after tax bénéfice (m) après impôts

profit and loss account compte (m) de résultat; compte de pertes et profits

profit before tax bénéfice (m) avant impôts

profit centre centre (m) de profit

profit margin marge (f) bénéficiaire

profit-making (adj) rentable

profit-oriented company société (f) à but lucratif

profit-sharing (scheme) intéressement (m) *ou* participation (f) aux bénéfices

profitability (n) *[making a profit]* rentabilité (f)

profitability *[ratio of profit to cost]* coefficient (m) de rentabilité

profitable (adj) rentable

program (v) a computer programmer un ordinateur

programme (n) *[plan]* programme (m)

programme (n) *or* **program (n)** *[computer]* programme (m) *ou* logiciel (m)

programming (n) *[computer]* programmation (f)

programming language langage (m) de programmation

progress (n) progrès (m) *ou* avancement (m)

progress (v) avancer *ou* se dérouler

progress chaser responsable (mf) de suivi

progress payments acomptes (mpl) échelonnés

progress report rapport (m) d'avancement (du travail)

progressive (adj) progressif (-ive)

progressive taxation imposition (f) progressive

prohibitive (adj) exorbitant(e) *ou* inabordable

project (n) *[plan]* projet (m) *ou* plan (m)

project analysis analyse (f) de projet

project manager chef (m) de projet

projected (adj) prévu(e)

projected sales ventes (fpl) prévues

promise (n) promesse (f)

promise (v) promettre

promissory note billet (m) à ordre

promote (v) *[advertise]* faire de la publicité

promote (v) *[give better job]* donner de l'avancement *ou* promouvoir

promote a corporate image promouvoir l'image d'une société

promote a new product lancer un nouveau produit

promotion (n) *[publicity]* promotion (f)

promotion (n) *[to better job]* promotion (f)

promotion budget budget (m) promotionnel

promotion of a product promotion (f) d'un produit

promotional (adj) promotionnel (-elle)

promotional budget budget (m) promotionnel

prompt (adj) prompt(e) *ou* rapide

prompt payment paiement (m) immédiat

prompt service service (m) rapide

proof (n) preuve (f)

proportion (n) part (f) *ou* partie (f)

proportional (adj) proportionnel (-elle)

proposal (n) proposition (f)

proposal (n) *[insurance]* proposition (f) d'assurance

propose (v) *[a motion]* proposer

propose to (v) *[do something]* proposer de

proprietary company *[US]* holding (m)

proprietor (n) propriétaire (mf)

proprietress (nf) propriétaire (f)

prosecute (v) poursuivre en justice

prosecution (n) *[legal action]* poursuites (fpl) judiciaires

prosecution *[party in legal action]* la partie plaignante *ou* l'accusation (f)

prosecution counsel procureur (m) général

prospective (adj) probable *ou* possible

prospective buyer acheteur (m) potentiel *ou* prospect (m)

prospects (n) perspectives (fpl)

prospectus (n) prospectus (m)

protective (adj) protecteur (-trice)

protective tariff tarif (m) protectionniste

protest (n) *[against something]* protestation (f)

protest (n) *[official document]* protêt (m) (pour non-paiement)

protest (v) *[against something]* protester contre quelque chose

protest a bill dresser un protêt

protest strike grève (f) de protestation

provide (v) constituer une provision

provide for (v) tenir compte de *ou* prévoir

provided that *or* **providing** à condition (que *ou* de) *ou* pourvu que

provision (n) *[condition]* stipulation (f) *ou* clause (f)

provision *[money put aside]* provision (f) *ou* réserve (f)

provisional (adj) provisoire

provisional budget budget (m) provisoire

provisional forecast of sales chiffres (mpl) provisoires des ventes

proviso (n) condition (f)

proxy (n) *[deed]* procuration (f)

proxy (n) *[person]* fondé (m) de pouvoir

proxy vote vote (m) par procuration

public (adj) public (publique)

public finance finances (fpl) publiques

public funds fonds (mpl) publics

public holiday jour (m) férié

public image image (m) de marque

Public Limited Company (Plc) société (f) anonyme (S.A.) *[cotée en Bourse]*

public opinion opinion (f) publique

public relations (PR) relations (fpl) publiques

public relations department service (m) des relations publiques

public relations officer chargé(e) des relations publiques

public sector secteur (m) public

public transport transports (mpl) en commun

publicity (n) publicité (f)

publicity budget budget (m) publicitaire

publicity campaign campagne (f) publicitaire

publicity department service (m) de publicité

publicity expenditure dépenses (fpl) de publicité

publicity manager chef (m) *ou* responsable (mf) (du service) de la publicité

publicize (v) faire de la publicité (pour)

punt *[Irish currency]* livre (f) (irlandaise)

purchase (n) achat (m) *ou* acquisition (f)

purchase (v) acheter *ou* acquérir

purchase ledger grand livre (m) des achats

purchase order commande (f) *ou* ordre (m) d'achat

purchase price prix (m) coûtant

purchase tax taxe (f) à l'achat

purchaser (n) acheteur (m) *ou* acquéreur (m)

purchasing (n) achat (m)

purchasing department service (m) des achats

purchasing manager directeur (-trice) du service des achats

purchasing power pouvoir (m) d'achat

put (v) *[in a place]* mettre *ou* fixer

put back (v) *[later]* reporter *ou* remettre (à plus tard)

put in writing mettre par écrit *ou* rédiger

put money down verser un acompte

pyramid (n) selling vente (f) pyramidale

Qq

qty (= quantity) quantité (f)

qualified (adj) *[skilled]* qualifié(e)

qualified *[with reservations]* sous réserve

qualify (v) (as) se spécialiser *ou* faire des études spécialisées

quality (n) qualité (f)

quality control contrôle (m) de qualité

quality controller responsable (mf) du contrôle de qualité

quality label label (m) de qualité

quantity (n) (qty) quantité (f)

quantity discount remise (f) sur quantité

quarter (n) *[25%]* quart (m)

quarter *[three months]* trimestre (m)

quarter day jour (m) de règlement trimestriel

quarterly (adj) trimestriel (-elle)

quarterly (adv) trimestriellement *ou* tous les trois mois

quay (n) quai (m)

quorum (n) quorum (m)

quorum: have a quorum atteindre le quorum

quota (n) quota (m) *ou* contingent (m)

quotation (n) *[estimate of cost]* devis (m)

quote (n) *[estimate of cost]* devis (m)

quote (v) *[a reference number]* rappeler une référence

quote (v) *[estimate costs]* citer *ou* donner un prix

quoted (adj) *[company, shares]* coté(e) en Bourse

Rr

R&D (research and development) R et D (Recherche et développement)

racketeer (n) racketteur (m)

racketeering (n) racket (m)

rail (n) chemin (m) de fer

rail transport transport (m) par chemin de fer

railway *[GB] or* **railroad** *[US]* chemin (m) de fer

railway station gare (f) (de chemin de fer)

raise (v) *[increase]* augmenter

raise (v) *[obtain money]* se procurer des fonds *ou* des capitaux

raise an invoice rédiger une facture

raise (v) (a question) soulever (une question)

rally (n) reprise (f)

rally (v) remonter *ou* se redresser

random (adj) aléatoire

random check contrôle (m) aléatoire

random error erreur (f) aléatoire

random sample échantillon (m) aléatoire

random sampling échantillonnage (m) aléatoire

range (n) *[series of items]* gamme (f) *ou* variété (f)

range (n) *[variation]* éventail (m)

range (v) from ... to ... aller de ... à ... *ou* s'étendre de ... à ...

rate (n) *[amount]* taux (m)

rate (n) *[price]* tarif (m) *ou* prix (m)

rate of exchange taux (m) de change

rate of inflation taux (m) d'inflation

rate of production taux (m) de production

rate of return taux (m) de rendement

ratification (n) ratification (f)

ratify (v) ratifier

rating (n) *[credit]* notation (f) *ou* note (f) financière (d'une société)

ratio (n) ratio (m) *ou* rapport (m); taux (m)

rationalization (n) rationalisation (f)

rationalize (v) rationaliser

raw materials matières (fpl) premières

reach (v) *[arrive]* atteindre

reach *[come to]* arriver à

reach a decision prendre une décision

reach an agreement arriver à un accord

readjust (v) rajuster *ou* réajuster

readjustment (n) rajustement (m) *ou* réajustement (m)

ready (adj) prêt(e)

ready cash argent (m) comptant; cash

ready-to-wear clothes confection (f) *ou* prêt-à-porter (m)

real (adj) vrai(e) *ou* véritable

real estate biens (mpl) immobiliers

real estate agent *[US]* agent (m) immobilier

real income *or* **real wages** revenu (m) net *ou* salaire (m) net

real-time system *[computer]* système (m) en temps réel

realizable assets actif (m) réalisable

realization of assets réalisation (f) d'actif

realize (v) *[sell for money]* réaliser *[des biens, etc.]*

realize (v) *[understand]* comprendre *ou* se rendre compte de

realize (v) a project *or* **a plan** réaliser un projet *ou* un plan

realize property *or* **assets** réaliser une propriété *ou* des biens

reapply (v) poser sa candidature une deuxième fois

reappoint (v) désigner de nouveau

reappointment (n) renouvellement (m) de mandat

reassess (v) réévaluer

reassessment (n) réévaluation (f)

rebate (n) *[money back]* remboursement (m) *[d'un trop-perçu]*

rebate *[price reduction]* remise (f) *ou* ristourne (f)

receipt (n) *[paper]* reçu (m) *ou* quittance (f)

receipt *[receiving]* réception (f)

receipt book carnet (m) de quittances

receipts (n) and expenditure recettes (fpl) et dépenses

receivable (adj) à recevoir

receivables (n) comptes (mpl) clients *ou* créances (fpl)

receive (v) recevoir; réceptionner *[marchandises]*

receiver (n) destinataire (mf)

receiver *[liquidator]* administrateur (m) judiciaire

receiving (n) réception (f)

reception (n) réception (f)

reception clerk réceptionniste (mf) *ou* préposé(e) à la réception

reception desk bureau (m) de la réception; bureau d'accueil

receptionist (n) réceptionniste (mf) *ou* préposé(e) à la réception

recession (n) récession (f)

reciprocal (adj) réciproque; bilatéral(e)

reciprocal agreement accord (m) réciproque

reciprocal trade commerce (m) bilatéral

reciprocity (n) réciprocité (f)

recognition (n) reconnaissance (f)

recognize (v) a union reconnaître officiellement un syndicat

recommend (v) *[say something is good]* recommander *[un produit, etc.]*

recommend *[suggest action]* recommander *ou* conseiller *[de faire quelque chose]*

recommendation (n) recommandation (f) *ou* conseil (m)

reconcile (v) rapprocher *ou* faire concorder *[comptes]*

reconciliation (n) réconciliation (f) *ou* rapprochement (m)

reconciliation of accounts rapprochement (m) de comptes

reconciliation statement état (m) de rapprochement (bancaire)

record (n) *[better than before]* record (m)

record (n) *[for personnel]* état (m) de service (d'un employé)

record (n) *[of what has happened]* rapport (m); registre (m)

record (v) noter *ou* consigner *ou* enregistrer

record sales *or* **record losses** *or* **record profits** ventes record *ou* pertes record *ou* profits record

record: for the record pour mémoire

record: off the record en privé *ou* officieusement

record: on record publiquement *ou* officiellement

record-breaking record *ou* qui bat tous les records

recorded delivery envoi (m) recommandé

records (n) archives (fpl); dossiers (mpl)

recoup (v) one's losses récupérer son argent *ou* se dédommager de ses pertes

recover (v) *[get better]* se remettre; se reprendre

recover *[get something back]* récupérer *ou* recouvrer *ou* retrouver

recoverable (adj) récupérable *ou* recouvrable

recovery (n) *[getting better]* reprise (f) *ou* relance (f) *[de l'économie]*

recovery (n) *[getting something back]* recouvrement (m) *ou* récupération (f)

rectification (n) rectification (f)

rectify (v) rectifier

recurrent (adj) qui revient; périodique

recycle (v) recycler; se recycler *[personne]*

recycled paper papier (m) recyclé

red: in the red dans le rouge; (compte) débiteur

red tape paperasserie (f) administrative

redeem (v) rembourser *ou* amortir

redeem a bond demander le remboursement d'une obligation

redeem a debt rembourser une dette

redeem a pledge retirer un gage

redeemable (adj) remboursable

redemption (n) *[of a loan]* remboursement (m) *ou* amortissement (m) *[d'une dette]*

redemption date date (f) d'échéance du remboursement

redevelop (v) réaménager

redevelopment (n) réaménagement (m) *[d'une zone]*

redistribute (v) redistribuer

reduce (v) réduire *ou* diminuer

reduce a price baisser un prix

reduce expenditure réduire les dépenses

reduced (adj) *[on sale]* en solde

reduced (adj) rate tarif (m) réduit

reduction (n) réduction (f)

redundancy (n) licenciement (m) (économique)

redundant (adj) (employé(e)) licencié(e)

re-elect (v) réélire

re-election (n) réélection (f)

re-employ (v) réembaucher *ou* réemployer *ou* réengager

re-employment (n) réemploi (m)

re-export (n) réexportation (f)

re-export (v) réexporter

refer (v) *[pass to someone]* soumettre *ou* transmettre

refer to (v) *[go to]* se reporter à *ou* se référer à

refer to (v) *[mention]* mentionner

reference (n) *[dealing with]* référence (f)

reference *[person who reports]* répondant (m)

reference *[report on person]* référence (f) *ou* recommandation (f)

reference number numéro (m) de référence (f)

refinancing (n) of a loan refinancement (m) d'un prêt

refitting (n) *[of shop]* rénovation (f) *ou* réaménagement (m)

refresher course cours (m) *ou* stage (m) de recyclage

refund (n) remboursement (m)

refund (v) rembourser

refundable (adj) remboursable

refundable deposit avance (f) remboursable

refunding of a loan remboursement (m) d'un prêt

refusal (n) refus (m)

refuse (v) refuser

regarding concernant

regardless of malgré *ou* sans considération de

regional (adj) régional(e)

register (n) *[large book]* registre (m)

register (n) *[official list]* registre (m) *ou* état (m) *ou* liste (f)

register (v) *[at hotel]* se faire enregistrer *ou* s'inscrire

register (v) *[in official list]* enregistrer *ou* inscrire *ou* immatriculer

register (v) *[letter]* recommander (une lettre)

register (v) a company immatriculer une société

register a property inscrire une propriété au cadastre

register a trademark déposer une marque de commerce

register (n) of directors registre (m) des administrateurs d'une société

register of shareholders registre (m) des actionnaires

registered (adj) enregistré(e)

registered design modèle déposé

registered letter lettre (f) recommandée

registered office siège (m) social

registered trademark marque (f) déposée

registrar (n) officier (m) de l'état civil

Registrar of Companies greffier (m) du tribunal de commerce

registration (n) enregistrement (m)

registration fee droit (m) d'enregistrement *ou* droit d'inscription

registration form formulaire (m) d'inscription

registration number numéro (m) d'enregistrement *ou* d'immatriculation

registry (n) bureau (m) d'enregistrement

registry office *[births, marriages, deaths]* bureau (m) de l'état civil

regular (adj) *[always at same time]* régulier (-ière) *ou* habituel (-elle)

regular *[ordinary]* ordinaire *ou* normal(e)

regular customer client(e) fidèle

regular income salaire régulier

regular size taille normale

regular staff personnel régulier

regulate (v) *[adjust]* régler *ou* ajuster

regulate (v) *[by law]* réglementer

regulation (n) réglementation (f)

regulations (n) règlements (mpl)

reimbursement (n) remboursement (m)

reimbursement of expenses
remboursement (m) des frais

reimport (n) *[action]* réimportation (f)

reimport (n) *[goods]* marchandise (f)
réimportée

reimport (v) réimporter

reimportation (n) réimportation (f)

reinsurance (n) réassurance (f)

reinsure (v) réassurer

reinsurer (n) compagnie (f) de
réassurance

reinvest (v) réinvestir

reinvestment (n) réinvestissement (m)

reject (n) article imparfait; article (m)
de rebut

reject (v) rejeter *ou* refuser

rejection (n) refus (m)

relating to *or* **in relation to** se
rapportant à *ou* relatif (-ive) à

relations (n) relations (fpl)

release (v) *[free]* libérer

release (v) *[make public]* publier

release (v) *[put on the market]* mettre
en vente

release dues liquider les commandes
en attente

relevant (adj) approprié(e)

reliability (n) fiabilité (f)

reliable (adj) honnête *ou* fiable *ou* sûr(e)

remain (v) *[be left]* rester

remain *[stay]* demeurer

remainder (n) *[things left]* reste (m) *ou*
reliquat (m)

remind (v) rappeler à

reminder (n) lettre (f) de rappel

remit (n) compétence (f)

remit (v) régler

remit by cheque régler par chèque

remittance (n) règlement (m)

remote control télécommande (f)

removal (n) *[sacking someone]* renvoi
(m)

removal *[to new house]*
déménagement (m)

remove (v) enlever *ou* supprimer

remunerate (v) rémunérer *ou* rétribuer

remuneration (n) rémunération (f)

render (v) an account présenter un
compte *ou* facturer

renew (v) renouveler

renew a bill of exchange prolonger
une traite

renew a lease renouveler un bail

renew a subscription renouveler un
abonnement

renewal (n) renouvellement (m)

renewal notice avis (m) de
renouvellement

renewal of a bill prolongation (f) d'une
traite

renewal of a lease renouvellement
d'un bail

renewal of a subscription
renouvellement d'un abonnement

renewal premium prime (f) de
renouvellement

rent (n) loyer (m)

rent (v) *[pay money for]* louer
[prendre en location]

rent collector receveur (m) des loyers

rent control contrôle (m) des loyers

rent tribunal commission (f) du
logement

rent-free sans payer de loyer

rental (n) loyer (m) *ou* prix (m) de
location

rental income revenu (m) locatif

renunciation (n) abandon (m)
(d'actions)

reorder (n) commande (f) de
réapprovisionnement

reorder (v) renouveler une commande
ou se réapprovisionner

reorder level niveau (m) de
réapprovisionnement

reorganization réorganisation (f)

reorganize (v) réorganiser

rep (representative) délégué(e)
commercial(e) *ou* représentant(e) *ou*
VRP (mf)

repair (n) réparation (f)

repair (v) réparer *ou* remettre en état

repay (v) rembourser

repayable (adj) remboursable

repayment (n) remboursement (m)

repeat (v) répéter

repeat an order renouveler une
commande

repeat order nouvelle commande (f) *ou*
commande de réapprovisionnement

replace (v) remplacer

replacement (n) *[item]* remplacement (m)

replacement *[person]* remplaçant(e)

replacement value valeur (f) de remplacement

reply (n) réponse (f)

reply (v) répondre

reply coupon coupon-réponse (m)

report (n) rapport (m)

report (v) signaler; faire un rapport

report (v) *[go to a place]* se présenter

report a loss annoncer un déficit

report for an interview se présenter à un entretien

report on (v) the progress of the work rendre compte de l'avancement du travail

report to someone relever (directement) de quelqu'un

repossess (v) saisir *[un article non payé]*

repossession (n) saisie (f)

represent (v) représenter; faire de la représentation

representative (adj) représentatif (-tive)

representative (n) *[company]* représentant (m)

representative (n) *[person]* délégué(e) commercial(e) *ou* représentant(e) *ou* VRP (mf)

repudiate (v) rejeter *ou* refuser

repudiate an agreement refuser d'honorer un accord

request (n) demande (f) *ou* requête (f)

request (v) demander *ou* solliciter

request: on request sur demande

require (v) *[demand]* demander *ou* réclamer *ou* exiger

require (v) *[need]* nécessiter

requirements (n) besoins (mpl)

resale (n) revente (f)

resale price prix (m) de revente

resale price maintenance régime (m) *ou* politique (f) des prix imposés

rescind (v) annuler *ou* résilier *[un contrat]*

research (n) recherche (f) *ou* étude (f)

research (v) faire une étude *ou* faire des recherches (sur)

research and development (R & D) Recherche et développement (R et D)

research programme programme (m) de recherche

researcher (n) chercheur (-euse)

reservation (n) réservation (f)

reserve (n) *[money]* réserve (f)

reserve (n) *[supplies]* réserves (fpl) *ou* provisions (fpl)

reserve (v) *[book]* réserver *ou* retenir

reserve a room *or* **a table** *or* **a seat** retenir une chambre *ou* réserver une table *ou* réserver une place

reserve currency monnaie (f) de réserve

reserve price prix (m) minimum fixé; mise (f) à prix

reserves (n) *[kept in case of need]* réserves (fpl)

residence (n) *[staying]* résidence (f) *ou* séjour (m)

residence permit carte (f) de séjour

resident (adj) résident(e)

resident (n) résident(e)

resign (v) démissionner

resignation (n) démission (f)

resolution (n) résolution (f)

resolve (v) décider

resources (n) ressources (fpl)

respect (v) respecter

response (n) réaction (f)

responsibilities (n) responsabilités (fpl)

responsibility (n) responsabilité (f)

responsible (for) (adj) responsable de

responsible to someone relever (directement) de quelqu'un

restock (v) se réapprovisionner

restocking (n) réapprovisionnement (m)

restraint (n) contrôle (m) *ou* restriction (f)

restraint of trade limitation (f) à la liberté du commerce

restrict (v) limiter

restrict credit limiter le crédit

restriction (n) restriction (f) *ou* limitation (f)

restrictive (adj) restrictif (-ive)

restrictive practices pratiques (fpl) restrictives

restructure (v) restructurer *ou* réorganiser

restructuring (n) restructuration (f) *ou* réorganisation (f)

restructuring of a loan reconfiguration (f) d'un emprunt

restructuring of the company restructuration (f) d'une société

result (n) *[general]* résultat (m)

result from (v) découler de *ou* provenir de

result in (v) avoir pour résultat de *ou* aboutir à

results (n) *[company's profit or loss]* résultats (mpl)

resume (v) recommencer *ou* reprendre

resume negotiations reprendre les négociations

retail (n) détail (m) *ou* vente (f) au détail

retail (v) *[goods]* vendre des marchandises au détail

retail (v) *[sell for a price]* se vendre à

retail dealer détaillant(e); revendeur (m)

retail (v) goods vendre des marchandises au détail

retail (n) outlets magasins (mpl) (de détail)

retail price prix (m) de détail

retail price index indice (m) des prix à la consommation

retailer (n) détaillant(e)

retailing (n) détail (m) *ou* vente (f) au détail

retire (v) *[from one's job]* prendre sa retraite *ou* partir à la retraite

retirement (n) retraite (f)

retirement age âge (m) de la retraite

retiring (adj) *[at end of elected term]* sortant(e)

retrain (v) recycler quelqu'un; se recycler

retraining (n) recyclage (m)

retrenchment (n) compression (f) des dépenses

retrieval (n) recherche (f)

retrieval system système (m) de recherche (de données)

retrieve (v) retrouver; extraire (des données)

retroactive (adj) rétroactif (-ive)

retroactive pay rise rappel (m) (de salaire)

return (n) *[declaration]* déclaration (f)

return (n) *[going back]* retour (m)

return (n) *[profit]* revenu (m) *ou* rendement (m)

return (n) *[sending back]* retour (m)

return (v) *[declare]* déclarer

return (v) *[send back]* renvoyer *ou* retourner

return a letter to sender renvoyer une lettre à l'expéditeur; retour à l'envoyeur

return address adresse (f) de retour *ou* de l'expéditeur

return on investment (ROI) rentabilité (f) d'un investissement

returnable (adj) consigné(e)

returned empties bouteilles (fpl) consignées

returns (n) *[profits]* recettes (fpl) *ou* rentrées (fpl)

returns (n) *[unsold goods]* invendus (mpl)

revaluation (n) réévaluation (f)

revalue (v) réévaluer

revenue (n) recette (f) *ou* rentrée (f); revenu (m)

revenue accounts compte (m) de produits

revenue from advertising recettes (fpl) publicitaires

reversal (n) revers (m)

reverse (adj) inverse

reverse (v) inverser *ou* faire marche arrière

reverse charge call *[phone]* appel (m) en PCV

reverse takeover contre-OPA (f)

reverse (v) the charges appeler en PCV

revise (v) réviser

revoke (v) révoquer *ou* annuler

revolving credit crédit (m) permanent *ou* renouvelable

rider clause (f) supplémentaire *ou* avenant (m)

right (adj) *[not left]* droit(e); de droite

right (adj) *[not wrong]* correct(e); exact(e) *ou* juste

right (n) *[legal title]* droit (m)

right of veto droit (m) de veto

right of way *[on land]* servitude (f)

rightful (adj) légal(e) *ou* légitime

rightful claimant ayant droit (m)

rightful owner propriétaire (mf) légitime

right-hand man bras (m) droit

rights issue *[shares]* émission (f) prioritaire

rise (n) *[increase]* augmentation (f)

rise (n) *[salary]* augmentation (f) (de salaire)

rise (v) augmenter

risk (n) risque (m)

risk (v) *[money]* risquer

risk capital capital-risque (m)

risk premium prime (f) de risques

risk-free investment placement (m) sûr

risky (adj) risqué(e) *ou* hasardeux (-euse)

rival company société (f) concurrente

road (n) route (f)

road haulage transports (mpl) routiers

road haulier entreprise (f) de transports routiers

road tax taxe (f) différentielle sur les véhicules (à moteur)

road transport transports (mpl) routiers

rock-bottom prices prix (mpl) les plus bas

ROI (return on investment) rentabilité (f) d'un investissement

roll on/roll off ferry ferry (m) *ou* car-ferry (m)

roll over (v) credit *or* **a debt** reconduire un crédit *ou* une dette

rolling plan plan (m) continu

room (n) *[general]* pièce (f) *ou* salle (f)

room *[hotel]* chambre (f) d'hôtel

room *[space]* place (f)

room reservations bureau (m) de réservation des chambres

room service service (m) des chambres

rough (adj) approximatif (-ive) *ou* sommaire

rough calculation calcul (m) approximatif

rough draft brouillon (m)

rough estimate estimation (f) approximative

round down (v) arrondir au chiffre inférieur

round up (v) arrondir au chiffre supérieur

routine (adj) de routine *ou* routinier (-ière)

routine (n) routine (f); de routine

royalty (n) royalties (fpl) *ou* redevances (fpl) *[d'auteur, etc.]*

rubber check *[US]* chèque (m) en bois *ou* sans provision

rule (n) règle (f)

rule (v) *[be in force]* être en vigueur

rule (v) *[give decision]* déclarer *ou* statuer

ruling (adj) actuel (-elle) *ou* courant(e) *ou* en vigueur

ruling (n) décision (f) *ou* jugement (m)

run (n) *[regular route]* parcours (m)

run (n) *[work routine]* exécution (f); série (f) *ou* séquence (f)

run (v) *[be in force]* être valable *ou* durer

run (v) *[buses, trains]* fonctionner *ou* être en service

run (v) *[manage]* diriger *ou* gérer

run (v) *[work machine]* faire fonctionner

run a risk courir un risque

run into debt s'endetter

run out of manquer de

run to monter *ou* s'élever à

running (n) *[of machine]* marche (f) *ou* fonctionnement (m)

running costs *or* **running expenses** coûts opérationnels *ou* coûts d'exploitation

running total total (m) reporté

rush (n) ruée (f)

rush (v) accélérer *ou* activer

rush hour heures (fpl) de pointe

rush job travail (m) urgent *ou* travail d'urgence

rush order commande (f) urgente

Ss

sack someone renvoyer *ou* licencier quelqu'un

safe (adj) sûr(e); en sûreté

safe (n) coffre-fort (m)

safe deposit dépôt (m) en coffre-fort

safe investment placement (m) sûr

safeguard (v) sauvegarder *ou* protéger

safety (n) sécurité (f)

safety measures *or* safety precautions mesures (fpl) de sécurité

safety regulations consignes (fpl) de sécurité

salaried (adj) salarié(e)

salary (n) salaire (m)

salary cheque chèque (m) de salaire

salary review révision (f) de salaire

sale (n) *[at a low price]* solde (m)

sale (n) *[selling]* vente (f)

sale: on sale en vente

sale by auction vente (f) aux enchères

sale or return vente (f) à condition *ou* avec possibilité de reprise des invendus

saleability (n) qualité (f) marchande

saleable (adj) vendable

sales (n) *[clearance sale]* soldes (mpl & fpl)

sales (n) *[selling]* ventes (fpl)

sales analysis analyse (f) des ventes

sales book *[accounts]* journal (m) des ventes

sales budget budget (m) commercial

sales campaign campagne commerciale

sales chart diagramme (m) des ventes *ou* courbe (f) des ventes

sales clerk vendeur (m) *ou* vendeuse (f)

sales conference réunion (f) du service commercial

sales curve courbe (f) des ventes

sales department service (m) commercial

sales executive directeur (-trice) commercial(e)

sales figures chiffre (m) des ventes; chiffre d'affaires

sales force équipe (f) de vente *ou* force (f) de vente

sales forecast prévisions (fpl) des ventes

sales ledger grand livre (m) des ventes

sales ledger clerk employé(e) aux écritures (du grand livre des ventes)

sales literature brochures (fpl) *ou* prospectus (mpl)

sales manager directeur (-trice) commercial(e)

sales people commerciaux (mpl)

sales pitch baratin (m) (d'un vendeur)

sales promotion promotion (f) des ventes

sales receipt ticket (m) de caisse

sales representative représentant(e) *ou* délégué(e) commercial(e) *ou* VRP (mf)

sales revenue produit (m) des ventes; chiffre (m) d'affaires

sales target objectif (m) de vente

sales tax taxe (f) sur les ventes

sales team équipe (f) de vente; commerciaux (mpl)

sales volume volume (m) des ventes

salesman (n) *[in shop]* vendeur (m)

salesman *[representative]* représentant (m) *ou* délégué commercial

saleswoman (n) *[in shop]* vendeuse (f)

saleswoman *[representative]* représentante (f) *ou* déléguée commerciale

salvage (n) *[action]* sauvetage (m)

salvage (n) *[things saved]* matériel (m) sauvé *ou* récupéré

salvage (v) sauver *ou* effectuer un sauvetage

sample (n) *[group, part]* échantillon (m)

sample (v) *[ask questions]* faire un sondage (d'opinion)

sample (v) *[test]* essayer; *[tasting]* goûter

sampling *[statistics, testing]* échantillonnage (m)

satisfaction (n) satisfaction (f)

satisfy (v) *[customer]* satisfaire

satisfy a demand répondre à *ou* satisfaire à la demande

saturate (v) saturer

saturate the market saturer le marché

saturation (n) saturation (f)

save (v) *[money]* économiser *ou* faire des économies

save (v) *[not waste]* économiser

save (v) *[on computer]* sauvegarder

save on (v) économiser

save up (v) épargner *ou* économiser

savings (n) économies (fpl)

savings account compte (m) d'épargne

savings bank banque (f) d'épargne

scale (n) *[system]* échelle (f) *ou* barème (m)

scale down (v) réduire suivant un barème

scale (n) of charges tarif (m) *ou* barème (m) des prix

scale up (v) augmenter suivant un barème

scarcity value valeur (f) de rareté

scheduled flight vol (m) régulier

scheduling (n) établissement (m) d'un plan *ou* d'un programme

scheduling of worktime aménagement (n) du temps de travail

screen (v) (candidates) sélectionner (des candidats)

scrip (n) *[share, bond, etc.]* titre (m)

scrip issue émission (f) d'actions gratuites

seal (n) sceau (m)

seal (v) *[attach a seal]* sceller

seal (v) *[envelope]* fermer *ou* cacheter (une enveloppe)

sealed envelope enveloppe (f) fermée *ou* cachetée

sealed tenders soumissions (fpl) cachetées

season (n) *[time for something]* saison (f)

season *[time of year]* saison (f)

season ticket carte (f) d'abonnement

seasonal (adj) saisonnier (-ière)

seasonal adjustments corrections (fpl) des variations saisonnières

seasonal demand demande saisonnière

seasonal variations variations (fpl) saisonnières

seasonally adjusted figures chiffres (mpl) désaisonnalisés *ou* chiffres corrigés des variations saisonnières

second (adj) deuxième *ou* second(e)

second (v) *[member of staff]* détacher

second quarter deuxième trimestre (m)

second-class de deuxième classe; de seconde *[train]*

secondary industry industrie (f) de transformation *ou* secteur (m) secondaire

secondhand (adj) d'occasion

seconds (n) articles (mpl) déclassés *ou* de second choix

secret (adj) secret (-ète)

secret (n) secret (m)

secretarial college école (f) de secrétariat

secretary (n) secrétaire (mf)

secretary *[company official]* secrétaire général(e)

secretary *[government minister]* ministre (mf)

sector (n) secteur (m)

secure (v) funds se procurer des fonds

secure (adj) investment placement (m) sûr

secure (adj) job emploi (m) sûr

secured creditor créancier privilégié

secured debts dettes (fpl) garanties

secured loan emprunt (m) garanti

securities (n) titres (mpl) *ou* valeurs (fpl)

Securities and Investment Board (SIB) Commission (f) des opérations de Bourse (COB)

security (n) *[being safe]* sécurité (f)

security (n) *[guarantee]* garantie (f) *ou* caution (f)

security guard vigile (m) *ou* gardien (m) de la sécurité

security of employment sécurité (f) de l'emploi

security of tenure *[job]* stabilité (f) d'emploi

security of tenure *[rented home]* droit (m) d'occupation d'un logement

see-safe (n) vente (f) avec possibilité de retour des invendus

seize (v) saisir *ou* confisquer

seizure (n) saisie (f) *ou* confiscation (f)

selection (n) sélection (f) *ou* choix (m)

selection procedure procédure (f) de sélection

self-employed (adj) indépendant(e) *ou* qui travaille à son compte

self-financed (adj) autofinancé(e)

self-financing (adj) qui peut s'autofinancer

self-financing (n) autofinancement (m)

self-regulation (n) autorégulation (f)

self-regulatory (adj) autorégulateur (-trice)

sell (v) vendre

sell forward vendre à terme

sell off liquider *ou* écouler

sell out *[all stock]* vendre la totalité du stock

sell out *[sell one's business]* vendre son entreprise

sell-by date date (f) limite de vente

seller (n) vendeur (m)

seller's market marché (m) à la hausse

selling (n) vente (f)

selling price prix (m) de vente

semi-finished products produits (mpl) semi-finis

semi-skilled workers ouvriers (mpl) spécialisés

send (v) envoyer *ou* expédier

send a package by airmail expédier un paquet par avion

send a package by surface mail expédier un colis par courrier ordinaire

send a shipment by sea expédier des marchandises par mer *ou* par bateau

send an invoice by post envoyer une facture par la poste

sender (n) expéditeur (-trice)

senior (adj) plus âgé(e); plus important(e)

senior manager *or* **senior executive** cadre (m) supérieur

senior partner associé(e) principal(e)

separate (adj) séparé(e)

separate (v) diviser

separate: under separate cover sous pli séparé

sequester (v) *or* **sequestrate (v)** séquestrer *ou* mettre sous séquestre

sequestration (n) séquestration (f) *ou* mise (f) sous séquestre

sequestrator (n) administrateur (m) séquestre *ou* séquestre (m)

serial number numéro (m) de série

series (n) série (f)

serve (v) servir

serve a customer servir un client

service (n) *[company, bureau]* société (f) de services

service (n) *[dealing with customers]* service (m)

service (n) *[of machine]* entretien (m) *ou* maintenance (f)

service (n) *[train, bus]* service (m)

service (n) *[working for a company]* service (m)

service (v) *[a machine]* entretenir; réviser *[une machine]*

service a debt servir *ou* payer les intérêts d'une dette

service centre atelier (m) de réparations

service charge service (m)

service department service (m) d'entretien

service industry industrie (f) de services *[secteur tertiaire]*

service manual manuel (m) d'entretien

set (adj) fixé(e)

set (n) jeu (m) *ou* ensemble (m)

set (v) fixer

set against déduire

set (adj) price prix (m) imposé *ou* prix fixe

set (v) targets fixer des objectifs

set up (v) a company créer *ou* constituer *ou* fonder une société

set up in business monter *ou* démarrer une affaire; s'établir

setting up costs frais (mpl) de mise en route *ou* d'établissement

setback (n) revers (m) *ou* recul (m)

settle (v) *[an invoice]* payer *ou* régler (une facture)

settle *[arrange things]* (s')arranger

settle a claim payer des dommages-intérêts *ou* indemniser

settle an account régler un compte

settlement *[agreement]* accord (m)

settlement *[payment]* règlement (m) *ou* paiement (m)

setup (n) *[company]* boîte (f)

setup *[organization]* organisation (f)

share (n) part (f)

share (n) *[in a company]* action (f)

share (v) *[divide among]* partager

share (v) *[use with someone]* partager

share an office partager un bureau

share capital capital-actions (m)

share certificate certificat (m) d'action(s)

share issue émission (f) d'actions

shareholder (n) actionnaire (mf)

shareholding (n) actions (f); participation (f)

sharp practice combine (f) *ou* pratique (f) malhonnête

sheet (n) of paper feuille (f) de papier

shelf (n) étagère (f) *ou* rayon (m)

shelf filler employé(e) qui réassortit les stocks sur les rayons

shelf life of a product durée (f) de conservation d'un produit

shell (n) company société (f) prête-nom

shelter (n) abri (m)

shelve (v) repousser *ou* ajourner; abandonner *[un projet]*

shelving (n) *[postponing]* ajournement (m); abandon (n)

shelving *[shelves]* rayonnage (m)

shift (n) *[change]* mouvement (m) *ou* changement (m)

shift (n) *[team of workers]* équipe (f)

shift key *[on keyboard]* touche (f) de majuscules

shift work travail (m) posté *ou* travail par équipe

ship (n) navire (m)

ship (v) expédier *ou* envoyer

ship broker courtier (m) maritime

shipment (n) *[goods]* envoi (m) *ou* chargement (m)

shipment (n) *[sending]* envoi (m) *ou* expédition (f)

shipper (n) expéditeur (m)

shipping (n) *[sending]* envoi (m) *ou* expédition (f)

shipping agent *[maritime]* agent (m) maritime

shipping charges *or* **shipping costs** frais (mpl) de transport

shipping clerk expéditionnaire (m)

shipping company *or* **shipping line** compagnie (f) de navigation

shipping instructions instructions (fpl) pour l'expédition

shipping note note (f) de chargement *ou* billet (m) de bord

shop (n) magasin (m)

shop around comparer les prix *[dans différents magasins]*

shop assistant vendeur (-euse)

shop window vitrine (f) *[d'un magasin]*

shop-soiled (adj) défraîchi(e)

shopkeeper (n) commerçant(e)

shoplifter (n) voleur (-euse) à l'étalage

shoplifting (n) vol (m) à l'étalage *ou* vol dans les rayons

shopper (n) acheteur (-euse) *ou* client(e)

shopping (n) *[action]* courses (fpl)

shopping *[goods bought]* achats (mpl)

shopping arcade galerie (f) marchande

shopping centre centre (m) commercial

shopping mall galerie (f) marchande

shopping precinct zone (f) piétonnière

shopping: go shopping faire des courses

short (adj) court(e)

short credit *[short-term credit]* crédit (m) à court terme

short: be short of être à court de *ou* ne pas avoir assez de

short-dated bills effets (mpl) à courte échéance

short-term (adj) à court terme

short-term contract *[work]* contrat (m) à durée déterminée

short-term credit crédit (m) à court terme

short-term debts dettes (fpl) à court terme

short-term loan emprunt (m) à court terme; prêt (m) à court terme

shortage (n) manque (m) *ou* pénurie (f)

shortfall (n) déficit (m) *ou* manque (m)

shorthand (n) sténo(graphie) (f)

shorthand: take shorthand prendre en sténo

shortlist (n) liste (f) de sélection

shortlist (v) sélectionner (des candidats)

shorts (n) obligations (fpl) à court terme

show (n) *[exhibition]* salon (m) *ou* exposition (f)

show (v) révéler *ou* faire apparaître

show (v) a profit révéler un bénéfice

show (n) of hands *[vote]* vote (m) à main levée

showcase (n) vitrine (f) *[armoire vitrée]*

showroom (n) salle (f) d'exposition

shrink-wrapped (adj) sous emballage pelliculé *ou* sous film

shrink-wrapping (n) emballage (m) pelliculé *ou* emballage sous film

shrink-wrapping *[action]* pelliculage (m)

shrinkage (n) rétrécissement (m); diminution (f)

shrinkage (n) *[losses of stock]* coulage (m)

shut (adj) fermé(e)

shut (v) fermer

SIB (Securities and Investment Board) COB (= Commission (f) des opérations de Bourse)

side (n) côté (m)

sideline (n) activité (f) secondaire

sight (n) vue (f)

sight draft traite (f) à vue

sign (n) panneau (m) publicitaire *ou* enseigne (f)

sign (v) (a cheque, a contract) signer (un chèque, un contrat)

signatory (n) signataire (mf)

signature (n) signature (f)

simple interest intérêts (mpl) simples

single (adj) simple *ou* unique

Single European Market Marché (m) unique

sister company société-soeur (f)

sister ship sistership (m)

sit-down protest *or* **sit-down strike** grève (f) sur le tas

site (n) site (m) *ou* emplacement (m)

site engineer ingénieur (m) de chantier

sitting tenant locataire (mf) occupant les lieux

situated (adj) situé(e)

situation (n) *[place]* emplacement (m) *ou* situation (f)

situation (n) *[state of affairs]* situation (f) *ou* état (m)

situations vacant *[jobs]* offres (fpl) d'emploi; postes (mpl) à pourvoir

size (n) taille (f)

skeleton staff personnel (m) réduit *ou* personnel de base

skill (n) aptitude (f) *ou* talent (m); technique (f)

skilled (adj) qualifié(e)

skilled labour *or* **skilled workers** ouvriers (mpl) qualifiés

slack (adj) peu actif (-ive)

slash (v) prices casser les prix

slash (v) credit terms réduire le crédit

sleeping partner associé commanditaire (m); bailleur (m) de fonds

slip (n) *[mistake]* erreur (f)

slip (n) *[piece of paper]* fiche (f); bordereau (m)

slow (adj) lent(e)

slow down (v) ralentir

slow payer mauvais payeur

slowdown (n) ralentissement (m)

slump (n) *[depression]* crise (f) économique *ou* marasme (m)

slump (n) *[rapid fall]* chute (f) *ou* effondrement (m)

slump (v) s'effondrer

slump in sales effondrement (m) des ventes

small (adj) petit(e)

small ads petites annonces

small businesses petites entreprises; petites et moyennes entreprises (PME)

small businessman petit patron

small change petite monnaie

small-scale peu important(e) *ou* modeste

small-scale enterprise petite entreprise

soar (v) monter en flèche

social (adj) social(e)

social costs coûts (mpl) sociaux

social security sécurité (f) sociale

social security contributions contribution (f) sociale généralisée (CSG)

society (n) *[club]* club (m) *ou* société (f)

society *[general]* société (f)

socio-economic groups groupes (mpl) socio-économiques

soft currency devise (f) faible

soft loan prêt (m) bonifié *ou* de faveur

soft sell vente (f) non agressive

software (n) *[computer]* programme (m) *ou* logiciel (m)

sole (adj) seul(e) *ou* exclusif (-ive)

sole agency contrat (m) d'exclusivité

sole agent agent (m) exclusif *ou* concessionnaire exclusif

sole owner seul propriétaire (m)

sole trader commerçant (m) indépendant *ou* seul propriétaire

solicitor (n) *[GB]* notaire (mf); avocat(e)

solution (n) solution (f)

solve (v) a problem résoudre un problème

solvency (n) solvabilité (f)

solvent (adj) solvable

source (n) of income source (f) de revenus

spare part pièce (f) détachée *ou* pièce de rechange

spare time temps (m) libre

special (adj) spécial(e)

special drawing rights (SDRs) droits (mpl) de tirage spéciaux (DTS)

special offer offre (f) spéciale *ou* promotion (f)

specialist (n) spécialiste (mf)

specialization spécialisation (f)

specialize se spécialiser

specifications (n) specifications (fpl); cahier (m) des charges *[d'un contrat]*

specify (v) spécifier *ou* indiquer

speech (n) of thanks discours (m) de remerciement

spend (v) *[money]* dépenser

spend *[time]* consacrer du temps à *ou* passer du temps à

spending money argent (m) pour les dépenses courantes

spending power pouvoir (m) d'achat

spinoff (n) produit (m) dérivé

spoil (n) abîmer *ou* endommager; gâcher

sponsor (n) sponsor (m) *ou* commanditaire (m)

sponsor (v) sponsoriser *ou* commanditer *ou* parrainer

sponsorship sponsorisation (f) *ou* parrainage (m)

spot (n) *[place]* endroit (m)

spot cash argent (m) comptant

spot price prix (m) au comptant *ou* prix spot

spot purchase achat (m) immédiat

spread (v) a risk répartir un risque

spreadsheet (n) *[computer printout]* tableau (m)

spreadsheet (n) *[program]* tableur (m)

stability (n) stabilité (f)

stabilization (n) stabilisation (f)

stabilize (v) stabiliser *ou* se stabiliser

stable (adj) stable

stable currency monnaie (f) stable

stable economy économie (f) stable

stable exchange rate taux (m) de change stable

stable prices prix stables

staff (n) personnel (m)

staff (v) employer du personnel

staff (n) appointment nomination (f) au niveau du personnel

staff meeting réunion (f) du personnel

stage (n) phase (f) *ou* stade (m) *ou* étape (f)

stage (v) *[organize]* mettre sur pied

stage a recovery se remettre *ou* se redresser

staged (adj) payments paiements (mpl) échelonnés

stagger (v) étaler *ou* échelonner

stagnant (adj) stagnant(e)

stagnation (n) stagnation (f)

stamp (n) *[device]* tampon (m) *ou* timbre (m)

stamp (n) *[post]* timbre (m) *ou* timbre-poste (m)

stamp (v) *[letter]* affranchir *ou* timbrer *[coller un timbre]*

stamp (v) *[mark]* tamponner

stamp duty droit (m) de timbre

stand (n) *[at exhibition]* stand (m)

stand down (v) se désister *ou* se démettre

stand security for *[loan]* avaliser *ou* garantir *[un emprunt, un prêt]*

stand surety for (someone) se porter garant de *ou* se porter caution pour (quelqu'un)

standard (adj) ordinaire *ou* standard

standard (n) standard (m) *ou* norme (f)

standard letter lettre (f) standard *ou* lettre type

standard rate (of tax) taux (m) d'imposition moyen

standardization (n) standardisation (f) *ou* normalisation (f)

standardize (v) standardiser *ou* normaliser

standby arrangements *[IMF]* accord (m) (de crédit) de confirmation *ou* accord stand-by

standby credit crédit (m) d'appoint *ou* de soutien *ou* crédit stand-by

standby ticket billet (m) (d'avion) stand-by

standing (n) standing (m) *ou* réputation (f)

standing order (ordre de) prélèvement (m) automatique

staple (n) agrafe (f)

staple (v) agrafer

staple (adj) industry industrie (f) principale *ou* de base

staple (v) papers together attacher des feuilles avec une agrafe

staple (adj) product produit (m) principal

stapler (n) agrafeuse (f)

start (n) commencement (m) *ou* démarrage (m) *ou* début (m)

start (v) commencer *ou* démarrer *ou* débuter

start-up (n) démarrage (m) (d'une affaire, d'un produit)

start-up costs frais (mpl) de démarrage *ou* d'établissement

starting (adj) de départ

starting date date (f) d'ouverture; date d'entrée en vigueur

starting point point (m) de départ

starting salary salaire (m) de départ *ou* de débutant

state (n) *[condition]* état (m)

state (n) *[country]* état (m)

state (v) déclarer *ou* stipuler *ou* préciser

state-of-the-art (adj) de pointe

statement (n) déclaration (f)

statement of account relevé (m) de compte

statement of expenses état (m) des dépenses

station (n) *[train]* gare (f) (ferroviaire)

statistical (adj) statistique

statistical analysis analyse (f) statistique

statistician (n) statisticien (-ienne)

statistics (n) statistiques (fpl) *ou* chiffres (mpl)

status (n) statut (m) *ou* position (f)

status inquiry enquête (f) sur la solvabilité d'un client

status symbol marque (f) de prestige

statute (n) of limitations loi (f) de prescription

statutory (adj) statutaire *ou* réglementaire

statutory holiday congé (m) légal *ou* fête (f) légale

stay (n) *[time]* séjour (m)

stay (v) séjourner *ou* demeurer

stay (n) of execution ordonnance (f) à surseoir *ou* sursis (m)

steadiness (n) régularité (f); stabilité (f) *[du marché]*

sterling livre (f) sterling

stevedore (n) débardeur (m) *ou* docker (m)

stiff (adj) competition concurrence (f) farouche

stimulate (v) the economy encourager *ou* stimuler l'économie

stimulus (n) stimulant (m)

stipulate (v) stipuler

stipulation (n) stipulation (f)

stock (adj) *[normal]* courant(e) *ou* normal(e)

stock (n) *[goods]* stock (m)

stock (v) *[goods]* stocker *ou* entreposer

stock (n) code numéro (m) de stock

stock control contrôle (m) *ou* gestion (f) des stocks

stock controller contrôleur (m) *ou* gestionnaire (m) des stocks

Stock Exchange Bourse (f)

stock level niveau (m) de stocks

stock list inventaire (m)

stock market marché (m) *ou* Bourse (f) (des valeurs)

stock market valuation capitalisation (f) boursière *ou* valeur (f) boursière

stock movements mouvements (mpl) de stocks

stock size taille (f) courante

stock turn *or* **stock turnover** *or* **stock turnround** rotation (f) des stocks

stock up (v) faire des réserves *ou* des provisions

stock (n) valuation évaluation (f) des stocks

stockbroker (n) société (f) de Bourse *[agent de change]*

stockbroking (n) courtage (m)

stockist (n) stockiste (mf) *ou* dépositaire (mf)

stockpile (n) réserves (fpl)

stockpile (v) faire des réserves *ou* stocker

stockroom (n) réserve (f) *ou* entrepôt (m) *ou* magasin (m)

stocktaking (n) inventaire (m) (des stocks)

stocktaking sale solde (m) avant inventaire

stop (n) stop (m) *ou* arrêt (m) *ou* fin (f)

stop (v) *[doing something]* arrêter *ou* suspendre *ou* cesser

stop a cheque faire opposition à un chèque

stop an account bloquer un compte

stop payments suspendre les paiements

stoppage (n) *[act of stopping]* arrêt (m) *ou* suspension (f)

stoppage of payments arrêt (m) *ou* suspension (f) des paiements

storage (n) *[computer]* mémoire (f)

storage (n) *[cost]* frais (mpl) d'entrepôt

storage (n) *[in warehouse]* entreposage (m)

storage capacity capacité (f) d'entreposage

storage facilities entrepôt (m)

storage unit *[computer]* unité (f) de mémoire

store (n) *[items kept]* réserve (f)

store (n) *[large shop]* magasin (m); grand magasin

store (n) *[place where goods are kept]* magasin (m) *ou* dépôt (m) *ou* entrepôt (m)

store (v) *[keep for future]* mettre en réserve

store (v) *[keep in warehouse]* entreposer

storeroom (n) dépôt (m) *ou* entrepôt (m) *ou* magasin (m)

storm damage dégâts (mpl) *ou* dommages (mpl) causés par une tempête

straight line depreciation amortissement (m) linéaire

strategic (adj) stratégique

strategic planning stratégie (f)

strategy (n) stratégie (f)

street (n) rue (f)

street directory répertoire (m) des noms de rues *[sur un plan]*

strike (n) grève (f)

strike (v) faire (la) grève *ou* se mettre en grève

striker (n) gréviste (mf)

strong (adj) fort(e)

strong currency devise (f) forte

structural (adj) de structure *ou* structurel (-elle)

structural adjustment *or* **change** changement (m) structurel

structural unemployment chômage (m) structurel

structure (n) structure (f)

structure (v) *[arrange]* organiser

study (n) étude (f); examen (m)

study (v) étudier; examiner *ou* analyser

sub judice (affaire) qui passe devant les tribunaux

subcontract (n) contrat (m) de sous-traitance

subcontract (v) donner en sous-traitance *ou* sous-traiter

subcontractor (n) sous-traitant (m)

subject to sous réserve de

sublease (n) sous-location (f)

sublease (v) sous-louer

sublessee (n) sous-locataire (mf)

sublessor (n) locataire (mf) principal(e)

sublet (v) sous-louer

subsidiary (adj) secondaire

subsidiary (n) filiale (f)

subsidiary company filiale (f)

subsidize (v) subventionner

subsidy (n) subvention (f)

subtotal (n) sous-total (m)

subvention (n) subvention (f)

succeed (v) *[do as planned]* réussir

succeed (v) *[do well]* réussir

succeed (v) *[follow someone]* succéder à

success (n) succès (m)

successful (adj) qui réussit *ou* qui a du succès

successful *[candidate, bidder]* retenu(e)

sue (v) intenter un procès à *ou* contre quelqu'un; poursuivre quelqu'un (en justice)

suffer (v) damage subir des dégâts

sufficient (adj) suffisant(e)

sum (n) *[of money]* somme (f)

sum *[total]* total (m)

summons (n) convocation (f)

sundries (n) articles (mpl) divers

sundry items articles (mpl) divers

superior (adj) *[better quality]* supérieur(e) *ou* meilleur(e)

superior (n) *[person]* supérieur (m)

supermarket (n) supermarché (m)

superstore (n) hypermarché (m); grande surface (f)

supervise superviser *ou* surveiller

supervision (n) surveillance (f)

supervisor (n) surveillant(e)

supervisory (adj) de surveillance

supplement (n) supplément (m)

supplementary (adj) supplémentaire

supplier (n) fournisseur (m)

supply (n) *[action]* fourniture (f)

supply (n) *[stock of goods]* stock (m) *ou* provision (f)

supply (v) approvisionner *ou* fournir

supply and demand l'offre et la demande

supply price prix (m) livré

supply side economics économie (f) de l'offre

support price prix (m) de soutien

surcharge (n) supplément (m); surtaxe (f)

surety (n) *[person]* garant *ou* caution (f)

surety (n) *[security]* garantie (f) *ou* nantissement (m)

surface mail courrier (m) ordinaire

surface transport transport (m) par terre *ou* par mer

surplus (n) surplus (m) *ou* excédent (m)

surplus dividend superdividende (m) *ou* dividende (m) complémentaire

surrender (n) *[insurance policy]* résiliation (f) (d'un contrat) *ou* rachat (m) (d'une police)

surrender (v) *[insurance]* résilier (un contrat) *ou* racheter (une police)

surrender a policy racheter une police d'assurance

surrender value valeur (f) de rachat

survey (n) *[examination: building, damages]* expertise (f)

survey (n) *[general report]* enquête (f) *ou* sondage (m)

survey (v) *[inspect: building, damage]* expertiser

surveyor (n) expert (m) (en bâtiments)

suspend (v) suspendre

suspension (n) suspension (f) *ou* interruption (f) *ou* arrêt (m)

suspension of deliveries arrêt (m) des livraisons

suspension of payments suspension *ou* arrêt des paiements

swap (n) *or* **swop (n)** échange (m)

swap (v) *or* **swop (v)** échanger

swatch (n) (petit) échantillon (m)

switch (v) *[change]* changer *ou* remplacer

switch over to passer à

switchboard (n) standard (m) (téléphonique)

sympathy strike grève (f) de solidarité

syndicate (n) syndicat (m) (financier)

synergy (n) synergie (f)

system (n) système (m)

systems analysis analyse (f) de systèmes

systems analyst analyste (mf) de systèmes *ou* informaticien-analyste (m), informaticienne-analyste (f)

Tt

tabulate (v) disposer en tableau *ou* en colonnes

tabulation (n) disposition (f) en tableau! en colonnes

tabulator (n) tabulateur (m)

tachograph (n) tachygraphe (m)

tacit agreement *or* **tacit approval** accord (m) tacite

take (n) *[money received]* rentrée (f) *ou* recette (f)

take (v) *[need]* prendre; falloir *ou* nécessiter

take (v) *[receive money]* gagner

take a call *[phone]* répondre au téléphone *ou* prendre un appel

take a risk prendre un risque

take action agir *ou* intervenir *ou* prendre des mesures

take industrial action faire (la) grève

take legal action intenter un procès à

take legal advice consulter un avocat

take note prendre note (de)

take off (v) *[deduct]* enlever *ou* déduire *ou* rabattre

take off *[plane]* décoller

take off *[rise fast]* s'envoler

take on (v) freight charger des marchandises *ou* du fret

take on staff embaucher du personnel

take out (v) a policy souscrire *ou* contracter une assurance

take over (v) *[from someone else]* prendre la succession *ou* succéder

take place avoir lieu *ou* arriver

take someone to court poursuivre quelqu'un en justice

take stock faire l'inventaire

take the soft option choisir la solution de facilité

take time off work prendre un congé

take up an option lever une option

takeover (n) rachat (m); prise (f) de contrôle

takeover bid offre (f) publique d'achat (OPA)

takeover target société (f) opéable

takings (n) recettes (fpl)

tangible (adj) tangible

tangible assets biens (mpl) matériels *ou* actif (m) corporel

tanker (n) pétrolier (m) *ou* navire-citerne (m)

tare (n) tare (f)

target (n) objectif (m) *ou* but (m); cible (f)

target (v) avoir pour but; cibler

target market marché (m) ciblé

tariff (n) *[price]* tarif (m)

tariff barriers barrières (fpl) douanières

tax (n) impôt (m); taxe (f)

tax (v) imposer *ou* prélever un impôt; taxer

tax adjustment redressement (m) d'impôt

tax allowance abattement (m) à la base *ou* fiscal

tax assessment détermination (f) de l'assiette fiscale

tax avoidance évasion (f) fiscale

tax code catégorie (f) d'impôt

tax collection perception (f) des impôts

tax collector percepteur (m)

tax concession dégrèvement (m) fiscal *ou* d'impôt

tax consultant conseiller (m) fiscal

tax credit avoir (m) fiscal *ou* crédit (m) d'impôt

tax deducted at source impôt (m) retenu à la source

tax deductions *[taken from salary]* retenues (fpl) fiscales *ou* prélèvement (m) fiscal

tax evasion fraude (f) fiscale

tax exemption exonération (f) *ou* exemption (f) d'impôt

tax form formulaire (m) de déclaration de revenus

tax haven paradis (m) fiscal

tax inspector inspecteur (m) des impôts

tax loophole moyen (légal) d'échapper au fisc

tax offence infraction (f) fiscale

tax paid taxe (f) payée

tax rate taux (m) d'imposition

tax rebate remboursement (m) (d'un trop-perçu) d'impôt

tax relief dégrèvement (m) d'impôt *ou* allègement (m) fiscal

tax return *or* **tax declaration** déclaration (f) de revenus *ou* d'impôts

tax shelter abri (m) fiscal

tax system régime (m) fiscal

tax year année (f) fiscale

tax-deductible (adj) déductible (des impôts)

tax-exempt exonéré(e) *ou* exempt(e) d'impôt

tax-free hors taxe

taxable (adj) imposable *ou* taxable

taxable income revenu (m) imposable

taxation (n) imposition (f)

taxpayer (n) contribuable (mf)

telephone (n) téléphone (m)

telephone (v) téléphoner *ou* appeler (au téléphone)

telephone book annuaire (m) des téléphones

telephone call appel (m) (téléphonique)

telephone directory annuaire (m) des téléphones

telephone exchange central (m) téléphonique

telephone line ligne (f) téléphonique

telephone number numéro (m) de téléphone

telephone subscriber abonné(e) du téléphone

telephone switchboard standard (m) téléphonique

telephonist standardiste (mf) *ou* téléphoniste (mf)

telesales (n) *[telephone sales]* vente(s) (fpl) par téléphone

television (TV) (n) télévision (f)

telex (n) télex (m)

telex (v) télexer *ou* envoyer un télex

teller (n) *[bank]* préposé(e) à la caisse *ou* caissier (-ière)

temp (n) secrétaire (f) intérimaire

temp (v) faire de l'intérim

temp agency agence (f) d'intérim

temporary employment *or* **work** emploi (m) *ou* travail (m) temporaire

temporary staff personnel (m) temporaire

tenancy (n) *[agreement]* bail (m) de location

tenancy *[period]* durée (f) du bail

tenant (n) locataire (mf)

tender (n) *[offer to work]* soumission (f)

tender for a contract faire une soumission pour un travail *ou* soumissionner un travail

tenderer (n) soumissionnaire (mf)

tendering (n) soumission (f)

tenure (n) *[right]* jouissance (f) d'un droit (à une propriété *ou* à une fonction)

tenure *[time]* période (f) d'exercice d'une fonction

term (n) *[part of academic year]* trimestre (m) (juridique *ou* universitaire)

term *[time of validity]* terme (m) *ou* durée (f)

term insurance assurance (f) à terme

term loan prêt (m) à terme

terminal (adj) *[at the end]* terminal(e)

terminal (n) *[airport]* terminal (m)

terminal (n) *[computer]* terminal (m)

terminal (adj) bonus prime (f) de fin de contrat

terminate (v) terminer *ou* résilier; se terminer *ou* prendre fin

terminate a contract résilier un contrat

termination (n) terminaison (f) *ou* fin (f); résiliation (f) (d'un contrat)

termination clause clause (f) résolutoire

terms (n) conditions (fpl) *ou* termes (mpl)

terms of employment conditions (fpl) d'emploi

terms of payment modalités (fpl) de paiement

terms of reference *[of committee, etc.]* attributions (fpl) *ou* pouvoirs (mpl)

terms of sale conditions (fpl) de vente

territory (n) *[of salesman]* secteur (m)

tertiary industry *or* **tertiary sector** industrie (f) de services *ou* secteur (m) tertiaire

test (n) test (m) *ou* contrôle (m)

test (v) tester *ou* contrôler

theft (n) vol (m)

third party tiers (m); tierce personne (f)

third quarter troisième trimestre (m)

third-party insurance assurance (f) au tiers

threshold (n) seuil (m)

threshold agreement accord (m) d'indexation des salaires sur le coût de la vie

threshold price prix (m) de seuil

throughput (n) rendement (m)

ticket (n) billet (m) *ou* ticket (m)

tie-up (n) *[link]* association (f)

tight money argent (m) cher *ou* rare

tighten up (v) (on) resserrer (le contrôle)

till (n) tiroir-caisse (m)

time and motion study étude (f) des temps et des mouvements *ou* de l'organisation scientifique du travail

time deposit dépôt (m) à terme

time limit délai (m)

time limitation limitation (f) de temps

time rate tarif (m) horaire

time scale délai (m) *[d'exécution]*

time: on time à l'heure; à temps

timetable (n) *[appointments]* emploi (m) du temps *ou* calendrier (m)

timetable (n) *[trains, etc.]* horaire (m) *ou* indicateur (m)

timetable (v) établir un calendrier

timing (n) choix (m) d'une date *ou* d'une heure

tip (n) *[advice]* tuyau (m)

tip (n) *[money]* pourboire (m)

tip (v) *[give money]* donner un pourboire

tip (v) *[say what might happen]* pronostiquer

TIR (Transports Internationaux Routiers) Transports Internationaux Routiers

token (n) symbole (m)

token charge participation (f) symbolique

token payment paiement (m) symbolique

toll (n) péage (m)

toll free *[US]* gratuitement

toll free number *[US]* numéro (m) vert

ton (n) tonne (f)

tonnage (n) tonnage (m) *ou* jauge (f)

tonne (n) tonne (f) (métrique)

tool up (v) équiper *ou* outiller (une usine)

top (adj) supérieur(e) *ou* extra

top (n) *[highest point]* sommet (m)

top (n) *[upper surface]* dessus (m)

top (v) *[go higher than]* dépasser

top-flight *or* **top-ranking (adj)** de haut niveau *ou* très important(e)

top management direction (f) générale *ou* cadres (mpl) supérieurs

top quality qualité (f) supérieure

top-selling (adj) qui se vend le mieux

total (adj) total(e)

total (n) total (m)

total (v) s'élever à

total amount total (m) *ou* montant (m) total

total assets actif (m) total

total cost coût (m) total

total expenditure dépense (f) totale

total income revenu (m) total

total invoice value montant (m) total de la facture

total output production (f) totale

total revenue revenu (m) total

track record expérience (f) professionnelle; dossier (m)

trade (n) *[business]* commerce (m)

trade (v) faire des opérations commerciales

trade agreement accord (m) de commerce international

trade association association (f) professionnelle

trade cycle cycle (m) économique

trade deficit *or* **trade gap** déficit (m) commercial

trade description designation (f) de marchandises

trade directory répertoire (m) d'entreprises

trade discount remise (f) commerciale *ou* remise professionnelle

trade fair foire (f) commerciale

trade in (v) *[buy and sell]* faire le commerce (de) *ou* être négociant (en)

trade in *[give in old item for new]* donner en reprise

trade-in (n) *[old item in exchange]* reprise (f)

trade-in price valeur (f) de reprise

trade journal *or* **trade magazine** revue (m) professionnelle *ou* spécialisée

trademark (n) *or* **trade name** marque (f) de fabrique *ou* de commerce

trade mission mission (f) commerciale

trade price prix (m) de gros

trade terms remise (f) professionnelle

trade union syndicat (m) *ou* Trade-union (f)

trade unionist syndicaliste (mf) *ou* trade-unioniste (mf)

trader (n) commerçant(e) *ou* négociant(e) *ou* marchand(e)

trading (n) affaires (fpl)

trading company société (f) *ou* entreprise (f) commerciale

trading loss perte (f) d'exploitation

trading partner partenaire (m) commercial

trading profit bénéfice (m) d'exploitation

train (n) train (m)

train (v) *[learn]* suivre une formation

train (v) *[teach]* former quelqu'un

trainee (n) stagiaire (mf); apprenti(e)

traineeship (n) stage (m) de formation

training (n) formation (f)

training levy taxe (f) d'apprentissage

training officer responsable (mf) de la formation

transact (v) business traiter une affaire *ou* effectuer une transaction

transaction (n) transaction (f)

transfer (n) transfert (m)

transfer (v) *[move to new place]* transférer

transfer of funds virement (m) de crédit

transferable (adj) cessible *ou* transmissible

transit (n) transit (m)

transit lounge salle (f) de transit

transit visa visa (m) de transit

transit: in transit en transit

translate (v) traduire

translation (n) traduction (f)

translation bureau bureau (m) de traduction

translator (n) traducteur (-trice)

transport (n) transport (m)

transport (v) transporter

transport facilities moyens (mpl) de transport

travel agency agence (f) de voyages

travel agent agent (m) de voyages

travelling expenses frais (mpl) de déplacement

Treasury (n) Ministère (m) des Finances

treble (v) tripler

trend (n) tendance (f)

trial (n) *[court case]* procès (m)

trial (n) *[test of product]* essai (m)

trial and error (apprentissage par) essais (mpl) et erreurs

trial balance bilan (m) de vérification

trial period période (f) d'essai

trial sample échantillon (m) d'essai

triple (adj) triple

triple (v) tripler

triplicate: in triplicate en trois exemplaires

troubleshooter (n) expert (m) en problèmes de gestion d'entreprise

truck (n) *[lorry]* camion (m)

trucker (n) camionneur (m)

trucking (n) camionnage (m) *ou* transport (m) routier

true copy copie (f) conforme

trust company société (f) fiduciaire

tune (v) *[machine, etc.]* ajuster

turn down (v) refuser

turn over (v) *[make sales]* faire un chiffre d'affaires (de ...)

turnkey operation opération (f) clés en main

turnkey operator constructeur (m) clés en main

turnover (n) *[of staff]* rotation (f) (du personnel)

turnover (n) *[of stock]* rotation (f) (des stocks)

turnover (n) *[sales]* chiffre (m) d'affaires

turnover tax impôt (m) sur le chiffre d'affaires

turnround (n) *[goods sold]* rotation (f) (des stocks)

turnround *[making profitable]* redressement (m)

turnround *[of plane]* rotation (f); chargement, déchargement et entretien

Uu

unaccounted for (adj) inexpliqué(e)

unaudited (adj) non vérifié(e)

unaudited accounts comptes (mpl) non vérifiés

unauthorized expenditure dépenses (f) non autorisées

unavailability (n) indisponibilité (f)

unavailable (adj) non disponible

unchanged (adj) inchangé(e)

unchecked figures chiffres (mpl) non vérifiés

unclaimed baggage bagages (mpl) non réclamés

unconditional (adj) inconditionnel (-elle) *ou* sans réserve

unconfirmed (adj) non confirmé(e)

undated (adj) non daté(e) *ou* sans date

undelivered (adj) non livré(e)

under *[according to]* selon *ou* aux termes de

under *[less than]* moins de *ou* inférieur(e) à

under construction en construction

under contract lié(e) par contrat

under control sous contrôle *ou* en main(s)

under new management changement (m) de propriétaire *ou* de direction

undercharge (v) ne pas (faire) payer assez

undercut (v) a rival vendre moins cher qu'un concurrent

underdeveloped countries pays (mpl) en développement (PED)

underequipped (adj) sous-équipé(e)

underpaid (adj) sous-payé(e)

undersell (v) vendre moins cher que

undersigned (adj) soussigné(e)

underspend (v) dépenser moins (que prévu)

understand (v) comprendre

understanding (n) entente (f); arrangement (m)

undertake (v) *[something]* entreprendre *[quelque chose]*

undertake *[to do something]* s'engager à *[faire quelque chose]*

undertaking (n) *[company]* entreprise (f)

undertaking (n) *[promise]* engagement (m)

underwrite (v) *[guarantee]* garantir

underwrite (v) *[pay costs]* prendre les dépens en charge

underwriting syndicate syndicat (m) de garantie

undischarged bankrupt failli (m) non réhabilité

uneconomic rent loyer (m) non rentable

unemployed (adj) sans emploi; en *ou* au chômage

unemployment (n) chômage (m)

unemployment pay allocation (f) de chômage

unfair (adj) injuste

unfair competition concurrence (f) déloyale

unfair dismissal licenciement (m) abusif *ou* injuste

unfavourable (adj) défavorable

unfavourable exchange rate taux (m) de change défavorable

unfulfilled order commande (f) non exécutée

unilateral (adj) unilatéral(e)

union (n) syndicat (m) *[de travailleurs]*

union recognition reconnaissance (f) officielle d'un syndicat (dans une entreprise)

unique selling point *or* **proposition (USP)** avantage (m) spécifique d'un produit

unit (n) *[in unit trust]* action (f)

unit (n) *[item]* unité (f)

unit cost coût (m) unitaire

unit price prix (m) unitaire *ou* prix de l'unité

unit trust société (f) d'investissement à capital variable (SICAV)

unlimited liability responsabilité (f) illimitée

unload (v) *[goods]* décharger

unobtainable (adj) qu'on ne peut se procurer

unofficial (adj) officieux (-euse)

unpaid (adj) non payé(e) *ou* impayé(e)

unpaid invoices factures (fpl) impayées *ou* les impayés (mpl)

unsealed envelope enveloppe (f) non cachetée

unsecured creditor créancier (m) sans garantie

unskilled (adj) non qualifié(e)

unsold (adj) non vendu(e); invendu(e)

unsubsidized (adj) non subventionné(e)

unsuccessful (adj) qui ne réussit pas *ou* sans succès

up front à l'avance *ou* d'avance

up to jusqu'à *ou* jusqu'à concurrence de *ou* à hauteur de

up to date *[complete]* à jour

up to date *[modern]* moderne *ou* de pointe

up-market de luxe *ou* haut de gamme

update (n) mise (f) à jour

update (v) mettre à jour *ou* réviser

upset price *[reserve price]* prix (m) minimum fixé; mise (f) à prix

upturn (n) reprise (f)

upward trend tendance (f) à la hausse

urgent (adj) urgent(e)

use (n) emploi (m) *ou* utilisation (f)

use (v) utiliser *ou* se servir de

use up spare capacity utiliser la capacité disponible

useful (adj) utile

user (n) utilisateur (-trice)

user-friendly (adj) convivial(e)

USP (unique selling point *or* **proposition)** avantage (m) spécifique d'un produit

usual (adj) habituel (-elle) *ou* normal(e)

utilization (n) utilisation (f)

Vv

vacancy (n) *[for job]* poste (m) vacant *ou* poste à pourvoir

vacant (adj) vide *ou* libre *ou* inoccupé(e)

vacate (v) quitter *[les lieux]*

valid (adj) valide *ou* valable

validity (n) validité (f)

valuation (n) évaluation (f) *ou* expertise (f)

value (n) valeur (f)

value (v) évaluer *ou* estimer

value added tax (VAT) taxe (f) sur la valeur ajoutée (TVA)

valuer (n) expert (m) (en évaluation)

van (n) *[for delivery]* camionnette (f) (de livraison)

variable costs coûts (mpl) variables

variance (n) variation (f) *ou* écart (m)

variation (n) variation (f)

VAT (value added tax) TVA (taxe sur la valeur ajoutée)

VAT declaration déclaration (f) de TVA

VAT inspector inspecteur (m) de la TVA

VAT invoice facture (f) avec TVA

vehicle (n) véhicule (m)

vendor (n) vendeur (m), venderesse (f)

venture (n) *[business]* affaire (f) *ou* entreprise (f)

venture (v) *[risk]* risquer

venture capital capital-risque (m)

venue (n) lieu (m) (de réunion)

verbal (adj) verbal(e)

verbal agreement entente (f) verbale *ou* accord (m) verbal

verification (f) vérification (f)

verify (v) vérifier

vertical communication communication (f) verticale

vertical integration intégration (f) verticale

vested interest droits (mpl) acquis *ou* intérêts (mpl)

veto (n) *[right]* (droit de) veto (m)

veto (v) a decision s'opposer à une décision *ou* mettre son veto à une décision

via via *ou* par

viable (adj) viable

VIP lounge salon (m) réservé aux personnages de marque

visa (n) visa (m)

visible imports importations visibles

visible trade commerce (m) visible

void (adj) *[not valid]* nul (nulle)

void (v) annuler

volume (n) volume (m)

volume discount ristourne (f) *ou* remise (f) sur quantité

volume of sales volume (m) de ventes

volume of trade *or* **volume of business** volume (m) d'affaires

voluntary liquidation liquidation (f) volontaire

voluntary redundancy départ (m) volontaire

vote (n) vote (n)

vote (v) voter

vote (n) of thanks remerciements (mpl) *[votés par une assemblée]*

voucher (n) *[document from an auditor]* justificatif (m) comptable

voucher (n) *[paper given instead of money]* bon (m) (d'échange)

Ww

wage (n) paie (f) *ou* salaire (m)

wage claim revendication (f) salariale

wage freeze blocage (m) *ou* gel (m) de salaires

wage levels niveau (m) des salaires

wage negotiations négociations (f) salariales

wage scale échelle (f) des salaires *ou* grille (f) des salaires

waive (v) renoncer à

waive a payment refuser tout paiement

waiver (n) *[of right]* renoncement (m) *ou* abandon (m)

waiver clause clause (f) d'abandon

warehouse (n) entrepôt (m)

warehouse (v) entreposer

warehouseman (n) magasinier (m) *ou* responsable (m) d'un entrepôt

warehousing (n) entreposage (m)

warrant (n) *[document]* warrant (m)

warrant (v) *[guarantee]* garantir

warrant (v) *[justify]* justifier

warranty (n) garantie (f)

wastage (n) pertes (fpl) *ou* gaspillage (m)

waste (n) déchets (mpl); gaspillage (m)

waste (v) *[use too much]* gaspiller

waybill (n) lettre (f) de voiture

weak market marché (m) faible

wear and tear usure (f) normale

week (n) semaine (f)

weekly (adj & adv) hebdomadaire; par semaine

weigh (v) peser

weighbridge (n) pont (m) bascule

weight (n) poids (m)

weight limit poids (m) maximum

weighted average moyenne pondérée

weighted index indice pondéré

weighting (n) *[added to salary]* indemnité (f) de résidence

well-paid job travail (m) rémunérateur

wharf (n) quai (m)

white knight chevalier (m) blanc

whole-life insurance assurance vie entière

wholesale (adv) en gros

wholesale (selling) vente (f) en gros; commerce (m) de gros

wholesale dealer grossiste (mf)

wholesale discount remise (f) de gros

wholesale price index indice (m) des prix de gros

wholesaler (n) grossiste (mf)

wildcat strike grève (f) sauvage

win (v) **a contract** remporter un contrat

wind up (v) *[a company]* liquider une société

wind up *[a meeting]* lever la séance

winding up (n) liquidation (f) d'une société

window (n) *[of shop]* vitrine (f)

window display étalage (m)

withdraw (v) *[an offer]* retirer

withdraw *[money]* retirer (de l'argent)

withdraw a takeover bid retirer une OPA

withdrawal (n) *[of money]* retrait (m)

withholding tax retenue (f) à la source *[impôt]*

witness (n) témoin (m)

witness (v) *[a document]* signer en qualité de témoin

witness (v) **an agreement** être témoin à la signature d'un contrat; signer en qualité de témoin

word-processing (n) traitement (m) de texte

wording (n) formulation (f) *ou* termes (mpl)

work (n) travail (m)

work (v) travailler

work in progress travail en cours

work permit carte (f) *ou* permis (m) de travail

work-to-rule (n) grève (f) du zèle

worker (n) travailleur (-euse); employé(e)

worker director délégué(e) du personnel

workforce (n) main-d'oeuvre (f) *ou* personnel (m)

working (adj) qui travaille

working capital fonds (m) de roulement

working conditions conditions (fpl) de travail

working party groupe (m) de travail

workplace (n) lieu (m) de travail

workshop (n) atelier (m)

workstation (n) *[at computer]* poste (m) de travail

world (n) monde (m)

World Bank Banque (f) mondiale

world market marché (m) mondial

worldwide (adj) mondial(e)

worldwide (adv) partout dans le monde

worth (n) *[value]* valeur (f)

worth: be worth valoir

worthless (n) sans valeur

wrap up (v) *[discussion]* terminer *ou* mettre fin à

wrap up (v) *[goods]* emballer

wrapper (n) *or* **wrapping** (n) (papier d') emballage (m)

wrapping paper papier (m) d'emballage; papier cadeau

wreck (n) *[company]* entreprise qui a fait naufrage

wreck (n) *[ship]* épave (f)

wreck (v) *[ruin]* détruire; ruiner

writ (n) injonction (f)

write (v) écrire

write down (v) *[assets]* réduire la valeur; amortir

writedown (n) *[of asset]* amortissement (m)

write off (v) *[debt]* passer par profits et pertes

write-off (n) *[loss]* perte (f) sèche

write out (v) rédiger

write out a cheque libeller un chèque *ou* faire un chèque

writing (n) écrit (m); écriture (f)

written agreement convention écrite *ou* contrat écrit

wrong (adj) faux (fausse) *ou* inexact

wrongful dismissal renvoi (m) injustifié

Xx Yy Zz

year (n) année (f)

year end fin (f) d'exercice (financier)

yearly (adj) annuel (-elle)

yearly (adv) annuellement *ou* chaque année

yearly payment paiement annuel *ou* versement annuel

yellow pages pages (f) jaunes (de l'annuaire des téléphones)

yield (n) *[on investment]* rendement (m)

yield (v) *[interest]* rapporter

zero (n) zéro (m)

zero-rated (adj) assujetti(e) à un taux zéro (de TVA)

zip code *[US]* code (m) postal

zone (n) zone (f)

zoning regulations plan (m) d'occupation des sols

Français-Anglais
French-English

Aa

abandon (m) d'actions renunciation (n) of shares

abandon d'un projet shelving (n) of a plan

abandonner *[renoncer]* renounce (v) *[shares]*

abandonner un projet abandon (v) *or* shelve (v) a plan

abattement (m) à la base *[impôt]* personal allowance (n) *or* tax allowance

abattement (m) fiscal tax abatement (n)

abîmer *[endommager]* damage (v) *or* cause (v) damage; spoil (v)

abonné(e) *[téléphone, revue, etc.]* subscriber (n)

abonnement (m) subscription (n)

abonner: s'abonner (à) subscribe (v) (to)

abri (m) fiscal tax shelter (n)

absence (f) absence (n)

absent(e) (adj) absent (adj); off *or* away

absorber *[frais, entreprise]* absorb (v)

absorption (f) *[fusion]* absorption (n)

accaparer le marché corner (v) the market

accélérer speed up (v)

acceptable acceptable (adj)

acceptation (f) (d'une offre) acceptance (n) (of an offer)

acceptation irrévocable irrevocable acceptance

accepté(e) *[convenu]* agreed (adj)

accepter accept (v) *or* agree (v) (to)

accepter *[approuver]* approve (v)

accepter de faire quelque chose agree to do something

accepter la responsabilité (de) accept liability (for)

accepter les prix agree the prices

accepter une traite accept a bill

accessoire (m) *[équipement]* fitting (n)

accessoires (mpl) en option optional (adj) extras

accident (m) accident (n); crash (n) *[car, plane]*

accident du travail industrial accident *or* injuries (n)

accommodement (m) composition (n) *[with creditors]*

accompagnateur (-trice) (n) courier (n) *or* guide (n)

accompagner accompany (v)

accord (m) *[entre deux parties]* settlement (n)

accord (m) *[convention, contrat]* agreement (n) *or* contract (n)

accord (m) *[marché, entente]* deal (n) *or* arrangement (n)

accord à l'amiable out-of-court settlement

accord de commerce trade agreement

accord de commercialisation marketing agreement

Accord de libre-échange nord-américain (Aléna) North American Free Trade Agreement (NAFTA)

accord de longue date long-standing agreement

accord d'indexation des salaires threshold agreement

accord flexible *ou* **non limité** open-ended agreement

accord multilatéral multilateral agreement

accord réciproque reciprocal agreement

accord tacite tacit agreement

accord-type (m) model agreement

accord unilatéral one-sided agreement

accord verbal verbal agreement

accord: être d'accord agree (v) (with)

accord: se mettre d'accord sur to come to an agreement on

accorder give (v) *or* grant (v)

accroissement (m) gain (n)

accumulation (f) accumulation (n)

accumulation de provisions hoarding (n) of goods

accumuler : s'accumuler accumulate (v); accrue (v) *[interest]*

accusation (f) *[inculpation]* charge (n) *[in court]*

accusation (f) *[la partie plaignante]* (the) prosecution (n)

accusé (m) de réception acknowledgement (n)

accuser quelqu'un *[inculper]* charge (v) someone

accuser réception d'une lettre acknowledge receipt of a letter

achat (m) *[opération]* buying (n) *or* purchasing (n)

achat (m) *[article acheté]* purchase (n) *or* acquisition (n)

achat à tempérament hire purchase (HP)

achat à terme forward buying

achat (au) comptant cash purchase

achat en gros bulk buying

achat impulsif *ou* **d'impulsion** impulse purchase

achats (mpl) centralisés central purchasing

acheminement (m) *[expédition]* forwarding (n)

acheter (v) buy (v) *or* purchase (v)

acheter à terme buy forward

acheter au comptant buy for cash

acheter une société acquire (v) a company

acheteur (-euse) buyer (n) *or* purchaser (n)

acheteur impulsif impulse buyer

acheteur potentiel prospective buyer

acheteur sérieux genuine buyer

achèvement (m) (de travaux) completion (n)

acompte (m) down payment (n) *or* advance (n)

acompte (m) *[dividende intérimaire]* interim payment

acompte: en acompte on account

acquéreur (m) *[acheteur]* purchaser (n) *or* buyer (n)

acquérir *[acheter]* purchase (v) *or* buy (n)

acquérir *[obtenir]* gain (v) *or* get (v)

acquisition (f) acquisition (n)

acquisition (f) *[achat]* purchase (n) *or* acquisition (n)

acquisition d'immobilisations capital expenditure (n) *[accounts]*

acquisition: faire l'acquisition (de) acquire (v) (something)

acquit: pour acquit paid in full

acquitté(e) paid (adj)

acquittement (m) d'une dette paying (n) *or* clearing (n) of a debt

acquitter une dette *[régler]* pay (v) a debt *or* clear off (v) a debt

acquitter une traite *[honorer]* honour (v) a bill

acquitter: s'acquitter d'une dette pay (v) a debt *or* clear off (v) a debt

acte (m) *[document]* deed (n)

acte de cession deed of transfer

acte de cession *[de créance]* deed of assignment

acte de propriété title deeds

acte de vente bill of sale

Acte unique Single European Act

actif (m) *[avoir]* assets (n)

actif circulant current assets

actif corporel tangible assets

actif et passif assets and liabilities

actif immobilisé fixed assets *or* capital assets

actif net net assets *or* net worth

actif réalisable realizable assets

action (f) *[acte]* action (n)

action (f) *[juridique]* action (n)

action (f) *[valeur mobilière]* share (n) *or* stock (n)

action gratuite bonus share

actions (fpl) *[portefeuille]* shareholding (n)

actions cotées en Bourse listed shares

actions ordinaires ordinary shares; common stock *[US]*

actions privilégiées preference shares; preferred stock *[US]*

actionnaire (mf) shareholder (n) *or* stockholder (n)

actionnaire important major shareholder

actionnaire majoritaire majority shareholder

actionnaire minoritaire minority shareholder

actionnaire: petit actionnaire minor shareholder

activer *[accélérer]* speed up (v) *or* rush (v)

activer une commande chase (v) an order

activité (f) secondaire sideline (n)

actuaire (mf) actuary (n)

actuel (-elle) present (adj) *or* current (adj)

actuellement currently (adv)

ad valorem ad valorem

addition (f) *[facture au restaurant]* bill (n)

addition (f) *[somme]* addition (n) *[calculation]*

additionner *[ajouter]* add (v)

additionner (une colonne de chiffres) add up (v) (a column of figures)

adéquat *[suffisant]* adequate (adj)

adhésion (f) membership *[being a member]*

adjoint(e) (n & adj) assistant (n) *or* deputy (n)

adjuger un contrat à quelqu'un award (v) a contract to someone

admettre (quelqu'un) *[laisser entrer]* admit (v) *or* let in (v) (someone)

administrateur (-trice) administrator (n)

administrateur (-trice) (company) director (n)

administrateur dirigeant executive director

administrateur judiciaire official receiver (n)

administrateur non dirigeant non-executive director

administrateur séquestre sequestrator (n)

administratif (-ive) (adj) administrative (adj)

administratifs (mpl) admin people; admin (n)

administration (f) administration (n)

Administration des douanes Customs and Excise

admission (f) *[entrée]* admission (n) *or* entry (n)

adopter (une résolution) carry (v) *or* adopt (v) (a motion)

adoption (f) adoption (n) (of a proposal)

adresse (f) address (n)

adresse de l'expéditeur return address

adresse de réexpédition forwarding address

adresse du bureau *ou* **du lieu de travail** business address

adresse personnelle home address

adresse postale *[boîte à lettres]* accommodation address

adresser address (v)

adresser une lettre *ou* **un colis** address a letter *or* a parcel

adresser: s'adresser à quelqu'un speak (v) to someone

aérogare (f) air terminal (n)

aérogramme (m) air letter

aéroport (m) airport (n)

affacturage (m) *[factoring]* factoring (n)

affaire (f) *[entreprise]* business (n) *or* venture (n)

affaire (f) *[marché]* bargain (n) *or* deal (n)

affaire: faire affaire (avec) deal (v) *or* do business (with)

affaires (fpl) business (n)

affaires: pour affaires on business

affecter *[destiner]* allocate (v) *or* earmark (v) *[funds]*

affecter des fonds à un projet earmark funds for a project

affilié(e) affiliated (adj)

affirmatif (-ive) (adj) affirmative (adj)

afflux (m) (de capitaux) influx (n) (of capital)

affranchir *[avec machine]* frank (v) (a letter)

affranchir *[coller un timbre]* stamp (v) *or* put a stamp on (a letter)

affranchir: machine à affranchir franking machine

affrètement (m) *[nolisage]* charter (n) *or* chartering (n)

affréter *[noliser]* charter (v)

affréter un avion charter (v) an aircraft

affréteur (m) charterer (n)

âge (m) age (n)

âge de la retraite retirement age

âge limite age limit

agence (f) agency (n) *or* bureau (n)

agence (f) *[d'une banque]* branch (n) *[of a bank]*

agence de location letting agency

agence de notation financière credit agency; credit bureau *[US]*

agence de placement employment agency *or* bureau

agence de presse news agency

agence de publicité advertising agency

agence de recouvrement (de dettes) debt collection agency

agence de renseignements commerciaux trade bureau

agence de voyages travel agency

agence d'intérim temp agency

agence immobilière (real) estate agency

agenda (m) diary (n)

agenda de bureau desk diary

agenda de poche pocket diary

agent (m) *[intermédiaire]* agent (n); dealer (n); broker (n)

agent agréé authorized dealer

agent commercial *[représentant]* representative (n)

agent d'assurances insurance agent *or* broker

agent de change stockbroker (n) *or* broker (n)

agent de recouvrement (de dettes) debt collector (n)

agent de voyages travel agent

agent en brevets patent agent

agent en douane customs broker

agent exclusif sole agent

agent immobilier estate agent

agent maritime shipping agent

agios (mpl) *[frais bancaires]* bank charges (n)

agir *[prendre des mesures]* take action *or* act (v)

agrafe (f) staple (n)

agrafer staple (v)

agrafeuse (f) stapler (n)

agricole agricultural (adj)

agriculture (f) agriculture (n); farming (n)

agroalimentaire (m) food and agriculture industry

agro-industrie (f) agribusiness (n)

aide (f) *[assistance]* assistance (n)

aider assist (v) *or* help (v)

aire (f) de chargement loading bay (n)

ajournement (m) postponing (n) *or* deferment (n)

ajournement (m) d'une réunion postponing (n) *or* ajourning (n) of a meeting

ajourner (une réunion) postpone (v) *or* adjourn (v) (a meeting)

ajourner la réalisation d'un projet postpone (v) *or* shelve (v) a plan

ajouter add (on) (v)

ajouter 10% pour le service add on 10% for service

ajouter 10% pour le transport allow 10% for carriage

ajustement (m) *[de comptes]* reconciliation (n)

ajusteur (m) (d'assurances) average adjuster (n)

aléatoire random (adj)

Aléna (Accord de libre-échange nord-américain) (NAFTA) North-american Free Trade Agreement

allègement (m) fiscal tax relief (n)

aller go (v)

aller chercher collect (v) *or* fetch (v)

aller en augmentant be on the increase

aller de ... à ... *[s'étendre]* range (v) from ... to ...

allocation (f) *[somme allouée]* allowance (n)

allocation (f) *[prestation]* benefit (n)

allocation de chômage unemployment benefit *or* pay

allouer allocate (v)

alternative (f) alternative (n)

amélioration (f) improvement (n)

améliorer *ou* **s'améliorer** improve (v)

aménagement (m) *[emploi du temps]* scheduling (n)

aménagement (m) *[magasin]* fitting out (n)

aménagement (m) *[région]* (planning and) development (n)

aménagement du territoire national planning and development

aménagement urbain town planning (n)

aménager *[emploi du temps]* schedule (v)

aménager *[magasin, etc.]* fit out (v)

aménager *[région]* develop (v)

amende (f) fine (n) *or* penalty (n)

amendement (m) amendment (n)

amener *[apporter]* bring (v)

Américain (-aine) American (n)

américain (-aine) (adj) American (adj)

amortir depreciate (v) *or* write down (v)

amortir *[rembourser]* amortize (v) *or* redeem (v)

amortissement (m) *[dépréciation]* depreciation (n) *or* writedown (n)

amortissement (m) *[remboursement]* amortization (n) *or* redemption (n)

amortissement linéaire straight line depreciation

amortissement accéléré accelerated depreciation

analyse (f) analysis (n)

analyse de projet project analysis

analyse de systèmes systems analysis

analyse des coûts cost analysis

analyse des tâches job analysis

analyse des ventes sales analysis

analyse du marché market analysis

analyser analyse (v) *or* analyze (v); study (v)

analyste (mf) analyst (n)

analyste de systèmes *[informatique]* systems analyst

anglais (-aise) *[britannique]* british (adj)

année (f) year

année budgétaire financial year

année civile calendar year

année de référence base year

année fiscale tax year *or* fiscal year

année: l'année dernière last year

année: par année per year *or* per annum *or* yearly

années d'ancienneté years of service

annexe (f) *[document]* attached document

annexe: en annexe attached

annonce (f) *[déclaration]* announcement (n); news (n)

annonce (f) *[publicité]* advertisement (n) *or* ad (n)

annonce: mettre une annonce advertise (v); put (v) an ad

annoncer announce (v) *or* report (v)

annoncer *[faire de la publicité]* advertise (v)

annoncer un déficit report a loss

annoncer un poste (dans un journal) advertise (v) a vacancy

annonces classées classified ads (n)

annonceur (m) advertiser (n)

annuaire (m) des téléphones telephone directory *or* book

annuel (-elle) annual (adj)

annuellement *[chaque année]* annually (adv)

annulation (f) d'un contrat annulment (n) of a contract

annulation d'un rendez-vous cancellation (n) of an appointment

annulé(e) cancelled (adj) *or* off (adv)

annuler annul (v); cancel (v)

annuler un chèque cancel a cheque

annuler une commande cancel an order

annuler un contrat annul (v) *or* rescind (v) a contract

annuler une facture void (v) an invoice

annuler un rendez-vous cancel an appointment

antérieur(e) *[préalable]* prior (adj)

antérieur(e) *[précédent]* previous (adj)

anticipé(e) advance (adj) (payment, etc.)

antidater antedate (v) *or* backdate (v)

anti-inflationniste anti-inflationary (adj)

appareil (m) machine (n); device (n)

appareil de démonstration demonstration model

appartement (m) flat (n) *or* apartment (n)

appartenir à belong to (v)

appel (m) *[d'un jugement]* appeal (n) *[against a decision]*

appel (m) *[téléphonique]* (telephone *or* phone) call (n)

appel de personne *[bip]* (radio-)paging (n)

appel d'offres *[pour un contrat]* invitation (n) to tender

appel en PCV reverse charge call; collect call *[US]*

appel international international call

appel venant de l'extérieur incoming call

appeler *[téléphoner]* phone (v) *or* call (v)

appeler d'un jugement appeal (v) against a decision

appeler en direct dial (v) direct

appeler en PCV reverse (v) the charges *or* call (v) collect

application (f) *[mise en pratique]* implementation (n)

appliquer *[mettre en pratique]* implement (v)

appréciation (f) *[augmentation en valeur]* appreciation (n) *[in value]*

apprécier: s'apprécier *[augmenter de valeur]* appreciate (v) *or* increase (v) in value

approbation (f) approval (n)

approbation: donner son approbation give (v) one's approval

approprié(e) relevant (adj)

approuver *[accepter]* approve (v) *or* agree (v)

approuver *[sanctionner]* approve *or* pass (v) *or* sanction (v)

approuver les comptes agree the accounts

approuver les termes d'un contrat approve the terms of a contract

approvisionnement (m) supply (n)

approvisionner *[fournir]* supply (v)

approvisionner: s'approvisionner shop at (v); obtain (v) supplies from

approximatif (-ive) approximate (adj) *or* rough (adj)

approximativement *[environ]* approximately (adv)

appui (m) (financier) backing (n)

appuyer (financièrement) back up (v)

apurer les comptes audit (v) the accounts

arbitrage (m) *[médiation]* arbitration (n)

arbitre (m) *[juge]* arbitrator (n) *or* adjudicator (n)

arbitrer un conflit arbitrate (v) in a dispute

archives (fpl) records (n) *or* archives (n)

argent (m) money (n)

argent (m) *[fonds]* funds (n)

argent (m) *[métal]* silver (n)

argent au jour le jour money at call *or* call money

argent bon marché cheap money

argent cher dear money

argent comptant *[espèces]* cash (n)

argent frais new money *or* fresh money

argent pour les dépenses courantes spending money

arranger *[organiser]* arrange (v) (a meeting, etc.)

arranger: s'arranger à l'amiable settle (v) out of court

arranger: s'arranger avec ses créanciers compound (v) with creditors

arrérages (mpl) arrears (n) (of payment)

arrêt (m) stop (n)

arrêt (m) *[action]* stoppage (n) *or* suspension (n)

arrêt (m) *[panne]* failure (n)

arrêt (m) *[pause]* break (n)

arrêt des livraisons stoppage *or* suspension of deliveries

arrêt des paiements stoppage of payments

arrêt: sans arrêt non-stop

arrêter stop (v) *[doing something]*

arrêter les comptes close (v) *or* balance (v) the accounts

arrêter les négociations break off (v) negotiations

arrêter le travail *[débrayer]* stop work *or* knock off

arrêter un plan d'action *[décider]* decide (v) on a course of action

arrhes (fpl) *[acompte]* deposit (n) *[paid in advance]*

arrhes non remboursables non-refundable deposit

arriéré (m) arrears (n) *or* back payment (n)

arriéré de loyer back rent (n)

arrivage (m) consignment (n)

arriver *[avoir lieu]* take (v) place

arriver à *[atteindre]* reach (v) *or* come to (v)

arriver à *[réussir à]* manage to (v)

arriver à échéance mature (v)

arriver à un accord reach an agreement

arriver à une impasse deadlock (v)

arrondir au chiffre inférieur round down (v)

arrondir au chiffre supérieur round up (v)

article (m) article (n) *or* item (n)

article (m) *[d'un contrat]* clause (n)

article unique *ou* **non suivi** one-off item

article imparfait reject (n)

article-réclame (m) *[produit d'appel]* loss-leader (n)

articles (mpl) de luxe luxury goods

articles déclassés *ou* **de second choix** seconds (n)

articles divers sundry items *or* sundries (n)

articles manufacturés manufactured goods

articles qui se vendent rapidement fast-selling items

ascenseur (m) lift (n); elevator (n) *[US]*

assemblage (m) *[montage]* assembly (n)

assemblée (f) assembly (n) *or* meeting (n)

assemblée d'actionnaires shareholders' meeting

assemblée générale general meeting

assemblée générale annuelle annual general meeting (AGM)

assistance (f) judiciaire legal aid (n)

assistance sociale welfare (n)

assistant(e) assistant (n)

assistante de direction *[secrétaire]* personal assistant (PA)

assister à (une réunion) attend (v) (a meeting)

association (f) *[groupement]* association (n) *or* council (n)

association (f) *[société]* partnership (n)

association de consommateurs consumer council

Association européenne de libre-échange (AELE) European Free Trade Association (EFTA)

association professionnelle trade association

associé(e) (n) partner (n)

associé(e) *[collègue]* associate (n)

associé(e) principal(e) senior partner

associer: s'associer go into partnership with someone

assujetti(e) liable to (adj) *or* subject to (adj)

assujetti à un taux zéro (de TVA) zero-rated (adj)

assurable insurable (adj)

assurance (f) insurance (n)

assurance au tiers third-party insurance

assurance-automobile motor insurance

assurance-habitation house insurance

assurance-incendie *ou* **contre l'incendie** fire insurance

assurance maladie medical insurance

assurance multirisque general insurance

assurance tous risques comprehensive insurance

assurance-vie life assurance *or* life insurance

assurance vie entière whole-life insurance

assurer insure (v)

assurer quelqu'un sur la vie assure (v) someone's life

assurer une permanence *[à un stand, etc.]* man (v) (a stand, etc.) 24 hours a day

assurer: s'assurer take out (v) an insurance

assureur (m) *[compagnie d'assurances]* insurer (n)

assureur maritime marine underwriter

atelier (m) workshop (n)

atelier de réparations repair shop

attaché(e) commercial(e) commercial attaché (n)

atteindre reach (v) *or* arrive (v)

atteindre un objectif meet a target

atteindre une moyenne average (v)

atteindre: ne pas atteindre son objectif miss (v) one's target

attendu(e) due (adj); expected (adj)

attente: en attente pending (adj)

attention (f) attention (n)

attention: à l'attention de for the attention of (FAO)

atterrir *[avion]* land (v)

attestation (f) provisoire d'assurance cover note

attirer attract (v)

attractif (-ive) attractive (adj)

attribution (f) d'actions share allocation (n) *or* allotment (n)

aubaine (f) good value (for money)

audit (m) *[commissaire aux comptes]* auditor (n)

audit (m) *[vérification comptable]* audit (n)

audit externe external audit

audit interne internal audit

auditeur (m) *[commissaire aux comptes]* auditor (n)

auditeur *ou* **audit externe** external auditor

auditeur *ou* **audit interne** internal auditor

augmentation (f) rise (n) *or* increase (n); raise (n) *[US]*

augmentation (f) *[valeur]* appreciation (n) *or* increase in value

augmentation de salaire salary increase *or* pay rise

augmentation indexée sur le coût de la vie cost-of-living increase

augmentation annuelle moyenne mean annual increase

augmentation: en augmentation increasing (adj)

augmenter increase (v) *or* rise (v)

augmenter *[majorer]* mark up (v) (an item)

augmenter de prix increase (v) in price

augmenter en valeur *[s'apprécier]* appreciate (v) *or* increase (v) in value

augmenter le prix d'un article increase (v) the price of an item

augmenter suivant un barème scale up

austérité (f) austerity (n)

authentifier authenticate (v)

authentique *[véritable]* genuine (adj)

autocopiant(e) *[sans carbone]* carbonless (adj

autofinancé(e) self-financed (adj)

autofinancement (m) self-financing (n)

autogéré(e) self-managed (adj)

autogestion (f) self-management (n)

autorisation (f) authorization (n)

autorisation (f) *[permis]* licence (n) *or* permit (n)

autorisation d'absence leave (n) of absence

autorisation de découvert overdraft facility

autorisé authorized (adj); entitled (adj)

autoriser authorize (v); entitle (v)

autoriser le paiement authorize payment

autorité (f) authority (n)

autorités (fpl) portuaires port authority

avaliser back (v) *or* guarantee (v)

avaliseur (m) *ou* **avaliste (mf)** *[garant]* guarantor (n)

avance (f) *[acompte]* advance (n) on account

avance (f) *[paiement d'avance]* money up front

avance (f) *[prêt]* advance (n) *or* loan (n)

avance bancaire bank advance

avance de caisse cash advance

avance sur salaire advance against salary

avance: à l'avance *ou* **d'avance** in advance

avancement (m) *[progrès]* progress (n)

avancement (m) *[promotion]* promotion (n)

avancement: avoir de l'avancement earn (v) promotion

avancer (de l'argent) advance (v) *or* lend (v) (money)

avancer *[progresser]* progress (v)

avant-projet (m) draft project (n)

avantage (m) advantage (n)

avantage (m) spécifique d'un produit unique selling point (USP)

avantages sociaux fringe benefits *or* perks (n)

avantageux (-euse) favourable (adj); economical (adj)

avarie (f) *[assurance]* average (n)

avarie commune general average

avenant (m) *[à un contrat]* rider (n)

avenant (m) *[à une police d'assurance]* endorsement (n) *[on insurance]*

avenir (m) future (n)

avenir: à l'avenir in future

avertissement (m) notice (n) *or* warning (n)

avion (m) aircraft (n) *or* plane (n)

avion-cargo (m) freight plane *or* freighter (n)

avion charter *ou* **avion nolisé** charter plane

avis (m) note (n) *or* notification (n)

avis d'exécution contract note

avis d'expédition advice note

avis de renouvellement renewal notice

aviser *[informer]* notify (v)

avocat(e) lawyer (n); barrister (n) *[GB]*

avocat-conseil (m) counsel (n)

avocat de la défense defence counsel

avocat représentant la partie plaignante prosecution counsel

avoir (m) *[actif]* assets (n)

avoir (m) fiscal *[crédit d'impôt]* tax credit (n)

avoir (v) de l'importance *[importer]* matter (v)

avoir (v) en stock carry (v) *or* have (v) in stock

avoir (v) lieu *[se tenir]* take (v) place *or* be held

ayant droit (m) beneficiary (n) *or* rightful claimant (n)

Bb

bagages (mpl) luggage (n) *or* baggage (n)

bagages à main hand luggage

bagages non réclamés unclaimed baggage

bail (m) *[loyer]* lease (n)

bail à céder lease for sale

bail de courte durée short lease

bail de longue durée long lease

bailleur (m), bailleresse (f) *[qui donne à bail]* lessor (n)

bailleur (m) de fonds *[commanditaire]* backer (n)

baisse (f) *[chute]* drop (n) *or* fall (n)

baisse (f) *[diminution]* decrease (n)

baisse (f) *[ralentissement]* decline (n)

baisse (f) *[recul, repli]* downturn (n)

baisse des prix drop in prices *or* price cut

baisse: en baisse *[marché, franc]* falling (adj)

baisser *[chuter]* drop (v) *or* fall (v) *or* go down (v)

baisser *[réduire]* lower (v) *or* cut (v) *or* reduce (v)

baisser les prix lower prices

baisser un prix reduce a price

baisser: faire baisser les prix bring down (v) *or* force down (v) prices

baisser: faire baisser les stocks run down (v) stocks

baissier (m) *[spéculateur à la baisse]* bear (n) *[Stock Exchange]*

balance (f) *[appareil]* weighing machine (n); (pair of) scales (n)

balance (f) *[bilan]* balance (n)

balance commerciale balance of trade

balance commerciale bénéficiaire favourable balance of trade

balance commerciale en déficit unfavourable balance of trade

balance commerciale en dollars dollar balance

balance des comptes trial balance

balance des paiements balance of payments

balancer balance (v)

bancable *[effet]* bankable (paper)

bande (f) magnétique magnetic tape *or* mag tape (n)

banque (f) bank (n)

banque (f) *[activité bancaire]* banking (n)

banque centrale central bank

banque d'affaires merchant bank

banque de compensation clearing bank

banque de crédit credit bank

banque de données *[informatique]* data bank

banque d'épargne savings bank

banque d'escompte discount house *or* bank

banque émettrice *ou* **banque d'émission** issuing bank

Banque Européenne d'Investissement (BEI) European Investment Bank (EIB)

Banque mondiale World Bank

banqueroute (f) *[faillite]* bankruptcy (n) *or* commercial failure (n)

banqueroute : faire banqueroute go (v) bankrupt

banquier (m) banker (n)

baratin (m) (d'un vendeur) sales pitch (n)

barème (m) scale (n)

barème des prix scale of charges

barème fixe fixed scale (of charges)

barème d'imposition tax schedules

barrer *[rayer ou radier]* cross out (v)

barrer un chèque cross (v) a cheque

barrière (f) *[obstacle]* barrier (n)

barrières (fpl) douanières customs barriers *or* tariff barriers

bas (m) bottom (n)

bas (basse) (adj) low (adj)

bas de gamme down-market (adj)

bas: au bas de (la facture, etc.) at the bottom of (the invoice, etc.)

base (f) *[fondement]* basis (n) *or* base (n)

base de données *[informatique]* database

baser: se baser (sur) base (v) (on)

bassin (m) dock (n)

bâtiment (m) building (n)

bâtiment principal main building

battre un record break (v) a record

bénéfice (m) profit (n); earnings (n)

bénéfice avant impôts pretax profit *or* profit before tax

bénéfice brut gross profit

bénéfice commercial operating profit

bénéfice d'exploitation trading profit

bénéfice imposable taxable profit

bénéfice net clear profit *or* net profit

bénéfice net *[après impôts]* after-tax profit *or* profit after tax

bénéfice net (d'un bilan) bottom line (n)

bénéfice théorique paper profit

bénéfice: faire un bénéfice make (v) a profit

bénéfices (mpl) d'une société corporate profits

bénéfices (mpl) exceptionnels excess profits

bénéfices (mpl) non distribués retained earnings

bénéficiaire (mf) beneficiary (n); payee (n) *or* recipient (n)

bénéficiaire (adj) profitable (adj) *or* profit-making (adj)

bénéficier de benefit from (v)

besoins (mpl) requirements (n) *or* needs (n)

besoins en main-d'oeuvre manpower requirements

bien (n) property (n); goods (n); asset (n)

bien masqué hidden asset

biens (mpl) de consommation consumer goods *or* consumable goods

biens de consommation durables consumer durables *or* durable goods

biens d'équipement capital goods *or* capital equipment

biens immobiliers real estate

biens incorporels intangible assets

biens matériels *[actif corporel]* tangible assets

biens meubles moveable property

biens personnels personal property

biens sociaux company assets *or* company property

bilan (m) balance sheet (n)

bilan de fin d'exercice closing balance (n)

bilan de vérification trial balance

bilan initial opening balance

bilatéral(e) bilateral (adj)

billet (m) *[voyage, théâtre, etc.]* ticket (n)

billet à ordre *[banque]* promissory note *or* note of hand

billet de banque (bank) note (n); (bank) bill *[US]*

billet gratuit *ou* **billet de faveur** complimentary ticket

billet open *[voyage]* open ticket

billet stand-by standby ticket

billet vert *[dollar américain]* greenback (n) *or* (american) dollar (n)

billetterie (f) cash dispenser (n) *or* cashpoint (n)

bimensuel (-elle) *[deux fois par mois]* twice a month *or* fortnightly (adv)

blanc (m) *[case]* blank (n)

blanchiment (m) (de capitaux) laundering (n) (of money)

blanchir (des capitaux) launder (v) (money)

blister (m) blister pack *or* bubble pack (n)

bloc (m) (d'actions) block (n) *[of shares]*

bloc d'immeubles block (n) *[building]*

blocage (m) *[gel]* freeze (n)

bloquer block (v) *or* freeze (v)

bloquer des capitaux *[immobiliser]* lock up (v) capital

bloquer les prix *[à un niveau déterminé]* peg (v) prices

bloquer les salaires et les prix freeze (v) wages and prices

bloquer un compte stop (v) an account

boîte (f) box (n)

boîte (f) *[petite compagnie]* setup (n) *or* small company (n)

boîte à *ou* **aux lettres** letter box

boîte en carton *[carton]* cardboard box (n) *or* carton (n)

boîte postale PO Box

bon (m) coupon (n)

bon (m) *[d'échange]* voucher (n)

bon (bonne) (adj) good (adj)

bon-cadeau (m) gift voucher (n)

bon d'achat gift coupon

bon de caisse *[certificat de dépôt]* certificate (n) of deposit

bon du Trésor *[obligation]* (government) bond (n)

bon marché (adj & adv) cheap (adj & adv)

bonne affaire good buy

bonne gestion good management

bonne qualité good quality

bonus (m) bonus (n)

bonus (m) *[assurance]* no-claims bonus

boom (m) *[expansion]* boom (n)

bord: à bord *[navire, etc.]* on board

bordereau (m) note (n) *or* slip (n) *[piece of paper]*

bordereau d'expédition dispatch note *or* consignment note

bordereau de versement *[banque]* deposit slip *or* paying-in slip

Bourse (f) Stock Exchange (n)

Bourse (f) *[marché]* stock market (n)

bourse de commerce *[matières premières]* commodity exchange (n)

Bourse de Paris Paris Stock Exchange

bouteille (f) bottle (n)

bouteilles (fpl) consignées returned empties

boutique (f) shop (n) *or* boutique (n)

boutique hors taxe duty-free shop

boycottage (m) boycott (n)

boycotter boycott (v)

bras droit (m) *[personne]* right-hand man

brevet (m) d'invention patent (n) *or* letters patent

breveté(e) patented (adj)

breveter: faire breveter (une invention) patent (v) *or* take out (v) a patent

britannique *[anglais, -aise]* British (adj)

brochure (f) brochure (n)

brouillon (m) rough draft (n)

brouillon: faire un brouillon de lettre draft (v) a letter

brut(e) gross (adj)

budget (m) *[gouvernement, société]* budget (n)

budget de publicité publicity budget *or* advertising budget

budget des frais généraux overhead budget

budget des ventes sales budget

budget opérationnel operational budget *or* operating budget

budget promotionnel promotion *or* promotional budget

budget provisoire provisional budget

budgétaire budget *or* budgetary (adj)

budgéter *ou* **budgétiser** budget (v)

budgétisation (f) budgeting (n)

bulletin (m) *[formulaire]* form (n)

bulletin (m) *[revue, journal, etc.]* newsletter (n); journal (n)

bulletin de commande order form (n)

bulletin de livraison delivery note (n)

bulletin de paie pay slip (n)

bulletin de vote ballot paper (n)

bureau (m) *[meuble]* desk (n)

bureau (m) *[pièce]* office (n)

bureau (m) *[service]* department (n) *or* office (n)

bureau à modules *ou* **bureau paysager** open-plan office

bureau central *ou* **principal** *[siège]* head office *or* main office

Bureau d'assurance crédit à l'exportation Export Credit Guarantee Department (ECGD)

bureau de change bureau de change

bureau de la réception *ou* **d'accueil** reception desk

bureau de l'état civil registry office

bureau de location *[places de théâtre]* booking office *or* ticket office

bureau de placement employment agency *or* bureau

bureau de poste post office

bureau de renseignements inquiry office; information bureau

bureau de tourisme tourist information office

bureau de traduction translation bureau

bureau d'études design department *or* design studio

bus (m) *[autobus]* bus (n)

but (m) *[objectif]* aim (n); target (n)

Cc

cabinet-conseil (m) consultancy firm (n)

cachet (m) de la poste date stamp (n)

cacheter *[une enveloppe]* seal (v)

cadastre (m) land register (n)

caddie (m) *[de supermarché]* trolley (n); cart (n) *[US]*

cadeau (m) gift (n) *or* present (n)

cadeau d'affaires business gift

cadre (m) débutant *ou* **jeune cadre** junior manager (n) *or* junior executive

cadre supérieur senior manager (n) *or* senior executive

cadre moyen middle manager

cadres (mpl) *[direction]* management (n) *or* managerial staff (n)

cadres supérieurs top management

CAF (coût, assurance, fret) c.i.f. (cost, insurance and freight)

cahier (m) des charges (contract) specification (n)

caisse (f) *[argent]* (cash) float (n) *or* petty cash

caisse (f) *[boîte d'emballage]* packing case (n) *or* crate (n)

caisse (f) *[dans un magasin]* cash desk (n) *or* pay desk

caisse (f) *[dans un supermarché]* checkout (n)

caisse (f) *[pour monnaie]* (petty) cash box (n)

caisse de retraite pension fund (n)

caisse enregistreuse cash register (n) *or* till (n)

caisse noire *[réserves occultes]* hidden reserves (n)

caissier (-ière) cashier (n) *or* pay desk attendant (n)

calcul (m) calculation (n)

calcul approximatif rough calculation

calcul du prix de revient costing (n) (of a product)

calculatrice (f) calculator (n)

calculatrice de poche *ou* **calculette (n)** pocket calculator

calculer calculate (v) *or* work out (v) (figures)

calendrier (m) calendar (n); diary (n)

calendrier (m) *[emploi du temps]* timetable (n) *or* schedule (n)

cambiste (mf) foreign exchange dealer *or* broker (n)

camion (m) lorry (n) *or* truck (n)

camion (n) *[contenu]* lorry-load (n) *or* truck-load (n)

camionnage (m) *[transport]* road haulage (n) *or* trucking (n)

camionnette (f) de livraison delivery van

camionneur (m) lorry driver (n) *or* trucker (n)

campagne (f) *[promotion]* compaign (n) *or* drive (n)

campagne (f) *[province]* country (n) *[not town]*

campagne commerciale sales campaign

campagne publicitaire publicity *or* advertising campaign

canal (m) (de distribution) (distribution) channel (n)

candidat(e) candidate (n) *or* applicant (n)

candidature (f) (à un emploi) application (n) (for a job)

capacité (f) *[rendement, volume]* capacity (n)

capacité d'emprunt borrowing power

capacité d'entreposage storage capacity

capacité de production manufacturing capacity

capacité industrielle industrial capacity

capital (m) principal (n) *[money]*

capital (m) *ou* **capitaux (mpl)** capital (n)

capital actions share capital

capital à risque *ou* **capital-risque** risk capital *or* venture capital

capital disponible available capital

capital initial *ou* **d'investissement** initial capital

capital nominal nominal capital

capital obligations debenture capital *or* debenture stock

capital roulant *ou* **capital circulant** circulating capital

capital social equity capital

capitalisation (f) capitalization (n)

capitalisation boursière market valuation *or* capitalization

capitaliser capitalize (v)

capitaliser les intérêts add (v) interest to the capital

capitaux (mpl) capital (n)

capitaux propres equity (n) *or* shareholders' equity

carat (m) carat (n)

carbone (m) carbon paper (n)

carbone: sans carbone *[autocopiant]* carbonless

cargaison (f) cargo (n)

cargo (m) cargo ship *or* cargo boat

carnet (m) (de banque, de chèques, de quittances) (bank, cheque, receipt) book (n)

carnet de commandes order book

carte accréditive *[d'un magasin]* charge card (n)

carte à puce *ou* **à mémoire** smart card

carte bancaire cheque (guarantee) card

carte d'abonnement *[concert, etc.]* season ticket (n)

carte de crédit credit card

carte de débarquement landing card

carte d'embarquement boarding card *or* boarding pass

carte de membre (membership) card

carte de retrait cash card

carte de séjour residence permit

carte de travail work permit

carte professionnelle (business) card

cartel (m) cartel (n)

carton (m) *[matériau]* carton (n) *or* cardboard (n) *[material]*

carton (m) *[boîte en carton]* cardboard box (n) *or* carton (n) *[box]*

cash (m) *[argent comptant]* cash (n) *or* ready cash

cash (adv) cash (adv)

cash-flow (m) cash flow (n)

cash-flow (m) négatif negative cash flow

cash-flow positif positive cash flow

cash-flow actualisé discounted cash flow (DCF)

casse (f) breakages (n)

casser les prix slash (v) prices

catalogue (m) catalogue (n); list (n)

catalogue de vente par correspondance mail-order catalogue

catastrophe (f) naturelle act (n) of God

catégorie (f) category (n) *or* class (n)

catégorie: de première catégorie high-quality (adj)

caution (f) *[garantie]* guarantee (n)

caution (f) *[personne]* surety (n) *or* guarantee (n)

caution: se porter caution (pour quelqu'un) stand (v) security *or* go guarantee (for)

cautionner quelqu'un bail (v) someone out

central (m) téléphonique telephone exchange (n)

central(e) central (adj)

centralisation (f) centralization (n)

centraliser centralize (v)

centre (m) centre (n) *[important town]*

centre commercial shopping centre *or* shopping precinct

centre de coût *[comptabilité]* cost centre

centre de production *[unité]* production unit (n)

centre de profit *[comptabilité]* profit centre

centre des affaires business centre

centre industriel industrial centre

centre(-)ville (m) downtown (n)

certificat (m) certificate (n)

certificat d'action(s) share certificate

certificat de douanes customs clearance certificate

certificat de garantie certificate of guarantee

certificat d'homologation certificate of approval

certificat d'immatriculation *[société]* certificate of incorporation

certificat d'origine certificate of origin

certificat médical doctor's certificate

certifier certify (v)

cesser stop (v); discontinue (v) *[doing something]*

cessible *[transmissible]* transferable (adj)

cession (f) *[transfert]* cession (n) *or* assignment (n) *or* assignation (n)

cession-bail (m) lease-back (n) (arrangement)

cessionnaire (mf) assignee (n)

chaîne (f) de magasins chain (n) *[of stores]*

chaîne (f) de montage assembly line (n)

chaîne (f) de production production line

chambre (f) d'hôtel hotel room (n) *or* hotel accommodation (n)

Chambre de commerce et d'industrie Chamber (n) of Commerce

chambre (f) froide cold store (n)

change (m) (foreign) exchange (n) *[currency]*

changement (m) *[modification]* change (n) *or* alteration (n)

changement de propriétaire *ou* **de direction** under new management *[shop]*

changer *[modifier]* change (v) *or* alter (v)

changer de l'argent change (v) some money

changer de propriétaire change hands (n) *[shop]*

chapardage (m) pilferage (n) *or* pilfering (n)

charge (f) *[chargement]* load (n)

charge (complète) d'un camion lorry-load (n) *or* truck-load (n)

charge en lourd deadweight (n)

charge utile payload (n) *or* commercial load

charge: (frais) à la charge de (costs) payable by

chargé(e) (n) (de) manager (n) *or* officer (n)

chargé(e) des relations publiques public relations officer

chargement (m) load (n); loading (n) *[action]*

charger des marchandises *ou* **du fret** take on (v) freight *or* cargo

charger un camion *ou* **un navire** load (v) a lorry *or* a ship

charger un programme *[informatique]* load (v) a (computer) program

charges (fpl) costs (n) *or* charges (n)

charges constatées d'avance *[comptabilité]* accruals (n)

charges d'exploitation running costs

charges sociales social benefit contributions (n)

chariot (m) élévateur fork-lift truck

chef (m) *[directeur]* chief (n) *or* head (n) *or* manager (n)

chef comptable chief accountant; controller *[US]*

chef de bureau chief clerk *or* head clerk

chef de la fabrication production manager

chef d'entreprise company head

chef de projet project manager

chef de rayon *[d'un magasin]* department manager

chef de service head of department *or* manager

chef du personnel personnel manager

chef du service des réclamations claims manager

chef du service export export manager

chemin (m) de fer rail (n) *or* railway (n); railroad *[US]*

chèque (m) cheque (n); check *[US]*

chèque au porteur cheque to bearer

chèque barré crossed cheque

chèque-cadeau (m) gift voucher (n)

chèque certifié certified cheque

chèque de caisse cheque to self

chèque de dividende dividend warrant (n)

chèque de salaire salary cheque *or* pay cheque

chèque en blanc blank cheque

chèque-livre (m) book token (n)

chèque non barré *ou* **chèque négociable** open cheque *or* uncrossed cheque

chèque postal Post Office cheque

chèques personnalisés personalized cheques

chèque-repas (m) luncheon voucher (n)

chèque sans provision *ou* **chèque en bois** dud cheque; rubber check *[US]*

chéquier (m) *[carnet de chèques]* cheque book (n)

cher (chère) (adj) *[coûteux]* dear (adj) *or* expensive (adj)

cher (chère) (adj) *[début de lettre]* dear *[Sir, Madam, etc.]*

cher: coûter *ou* **être plus cher** be more expensive *or* cost (v) more

chercheur (-euse) researcher (n) *or* research worker (n)

chevalier (m) blanc white knight (n)

chez *[aux bons soins de]* care of (c/o) *[on letter]*

chiffre (m) figure (n) *or* digit (n)

chiffre d'affaires turnover (n)

chiffre de vente(s) sales figures

chiffres (mpl) figures (n)

chiffres d'origine historical figures

chiffres réels actuals (n)

choisir choose (v)

choisir *[élire]* elect (v)

choisir la solution de facilité take (v) the soft option

choix (m) choice (n)

choix (m) *[sélection]* choice *or* selection (n)

choix: de choix choice (adj)

chômage (m) unemployment (n)

chômage: au *ou* **en chômage** out of work (adj) *or* unemployed (adj)

chômeur (-euse) unemployed person

chômeur (-euse): les chômeurs the unemployed (n)

chute (f) *[baisse]* drop (n) *or* fall (n) *or* slump (n)

chuter *[baisser]* drop (v) *or* fall (v) *or* slump (v)

chuter *[baisser rapidement]* plummet (v)

cible (f) target (n)

cibler *[avoir pour but]* target (v)

circulaire (f) circular (n) *or* circular letter (n)

circulation (f) *[distribution, argent, voitures]* circulation (n)

citer *[un prix]* quote (v) (a price)

clair(e) clear (adj) *or* easy to understand

classe (f) *[catégorie]* class (n)

classe affaires *[voyage]* business class

classe touriste *[voyage]* economy class *or* tourist class

classement (m) *[de documents]* filing (n) *[action]*

classer classify (v) *or* order (v)

classer (des documents, dans un classeur) file (v) (documents)

classeur (m) filing cabinet (n)

classification (f) classification (n)

clause (f) clause (n) *or* provision (n)

clause d'exclusion exclusion clause

clause d'indexation *ou* **de révision des coûts** escalator clause

clause échappatoire escape clause

clause pénale penalty clause

clause résolutoire termination clause

clause supplémentaire *[avenant]* rider (n)

clavier (m) keyboard (n)

clavier numérique *[pavé]* numeric keypad (n)

claviste (m) keyboarder (n)

clé (f) *ou* **clef (f)** key *[to door; important]*

client fidèle regular customer

client(e) customer (n) *or* client (n)

client(e) *[acheteur]* shopper (n)

client potentiel prospect (n) *or* potential customer

clientèle (f) custom (n) *or* clientele (n)

clôture (f) close (n) *or* end (n) *or* finish (n)

clôture: après clôture *[Bourse]* after hours

clôturer un compte *[fermer]* close (v) an account

club (m) *[société]* club (n) *or* society (n)

coassocié(e) (n) copartner (n)

coassurance (f) co-insurance (n)

COB (Commission des opérations de Bourse) SIB (Securities and Investments Board)

cocréancier (-ière) (n) co-creditor (n)

code (m) code (n)

code (à) barres bar code

code civil *[droit civil]* (French) code of civil law

code postal postcode (n); zip code *[US]*

codirecteur (-trice) co-director (n)

codirection (f) *ou* **cogestion (f)** joint management (n)

coefficient (m) de remplissage *[avion]* load factor (n) *[of plane]*

coefficient de rentabilité profitability (n)

coentreprise (f) joint venture (n)

coffre-fort (m) safe (n)

coffret (m) *[jeu d'outils, etc.]* boxed set (n)

colis (m) parcel (n)

collaborateur (-trice) contributor (n)

collaborateur (-trice) indépendant(e) freelancer (n) *or* freelance (worker)

collaboration (f) collaboration (n)

collaborer collaborate (v) *or* co-operate (v)

collectif (-ive) collective (adj) *or* joint (adj)

collectivités (fpl) locales local authorities (n)

collègue (mf) *[associé]* associate (n)

colonne (f) column (n)

colonne des crédits credit column *or* credit side

colonne des débits debit column *or* debit side

combine (n) *[pratique malhonnête]* fiddle (n); sharp practice (n)

comité (m) committee (n) *or* board (n) *or* council (n)

comité de consommateurs consumer council

comité consultatif advisory board

comité d'entreprise *[travailleurs]* works committee *or* works council

commande (f) order (n) *[for goods]*

commande de réapprovisionnement repeat order *or* reorder (n)

commande par téléphone telephone order

commande urgente rush order

commandes en attente outstanding orders *or* back orders

commandes en attente *[anticipées]* dues (n) *[items not yet on the market]*

commandé(e) (adj) on order

commander order (v) (goods)

commanditaire (m) sleeping partner (n)

commencement (m) start (n)

commencer start (v) *or* begin (v); initiate (v)

commerçant(e) shopkeeper (n) *or* trader (n)

commerçant indépendant independant trader

commerce (m) commerce (n) *or* trade (n)

commerce *[entreprise]* business (n)

commerce bilatéral reciprocal trade

commerce d'exportation export trade

commerce extérieur overseas trade *or* foreign trade

commerce intérieur domestic trade

commerce international international trade

commerce invisible invisible trade

commerce multilatéral multilateral trade

commerce unilatéral one-way trade

commerce visible visible trade

commercial(e) commercial (adj)

commercialisation (f) commercialization (n); marketing (n)

commercialiser *[rendre commercial]* commercialize (v)

commercialiser *[vendre]* market (v) *or* put (v) on the market

commerciaux (mpl) sales people *or* sales team

commissaire (m) aux comptes *[audit]* auditor (n)

commission (f) *[comité]* commission (n) *or* committee (n)

commission (f) *[d'agent]* commission (n) *[money]*

commission (f) *[d'agent de change* ou **courtage]** brokerage (n) *or* broker's commission

commission d'enquête commission of inquiry

Commission des opérations de Bourse (COB) Securities and Investments Board (SIB)

commission du logement rent tribunal

commission: faire partie d'une commission sit (v) on a committee

commun(e) *[conjoint]* common *or* joint (adj)

commun(e) *[courant]* common (adj) *or* frequent (adj)

communauté (f) community (n)

communication (f) communication (n)

communication (f) *[message]* communication *or* message (n)

communication (f) (téléphonique) (phone *or* telephone) call (n)

communication avec pré-avis *[téléphone]* person-to-person call

communication interurbaine *[téléphone]* trunk call *or* long distance call

communication urbaine *[téléphone]* local call

communications (fpl) communications (n)

communiqué (m) de presse press release (n)

communiquer communicate (v)

compagnie (f) *[société]* company (n) *or* firm (n) *or* house (n)

compagnie aérienne airline (n); air carrier (n)

compagnie d'assurances insurance company

compagnie d'assurance-vie assurance company

compagnie de navigation shipping company *or* shipping line

comparabilité (f) comparability (n)

comparable comparable (adj)

comparaison (f) comparison (n)

comparaître (en justice) appear (v) before a court

comparer compare (v)

comparer les prix *[de différents magasins]* shop around (v)

compensation (f) *[dédommagement]* compensation (n)

compensation (f) *[d'un chèque]* clearance (n) of a cheque

compenser *[dédommager]* make up (v) (a loss)

compenser un chèque clear (v) a cheque

compétence (f) *[autorité]* jurisdiction (n) *or* authority (n)

compétence (f) *[habileté, savoir-faire]* expertise (n) *or* know-how (n)

compétent(e) (adj) *[habile]* competent (adj); skilled (adj)

compétent(e) *[expérimenté]* experienced (adj)

compétitif (-ive) competitive (adj)

compétition (f) *[concurrence]* competition (n)

compétitivité (f) competitiveness (n)

complémentaire complementary (adj)

complet *[annonce devant un hôtel, etc]* no vacancy

complet (-ète) *[achevé]* complete (adj)

complet (-ète) *[entier]* clear (adj) *[day]*

complet (-ète) *[hôtel, vol]* fully booked *or* booked up (adj)

complexe (m) industriel industrial complex (n)

composer un numéro *[téléphone]* dial (v) a number

comprendre understand (v)

comprendre *[consister en]* consist of (v)

comprendre *[inclure]* include (v)

comprendre *[se rendre compte]* realize (v) *or* understand (v)

compression (f) *[des dépenses, etc.]* retrenchment (n)

compris(e) *[inclus]* inclusive of (adj)

compris(e): non compris exclusive of (adj)

compromis (m) compromise (n); arrangement (n)

comptabiliser enter (v) in an account

comptabilité (f) *[comptes]* accounts (n)

comptabilité (f) *[système]* accounting (n)

comptabilité (f) *[tenue de livres]* bookkeeping (n)

comptabilité analytique cost accounting

comptabilité de gestion management bookkeeping

comptabilité en partie double double-entry bookkeeping

comptabilité en partie simple single-entry bookkeeping

comptabilité générale *ou* **financière** financial accounting

comptabilité: tenir la comptabilité keep (v) the accounts

comptable (mf) accountant (n)

comptant *ou* **au comptant** cash (adv)

compte (m) account (n)

compte à découvert overdrawn account

compte bancaire bank account

compte bloqué account on stop

compte-chèque postal (CCP) Post Office account

compte clients *[créances]* accounts receivable *or* receivables (n)

compte courant current account *or* drawing account

compte crédit *[à la banque]* budget account

compte créditeur account in credit

compte d'achat *ou* **compte permanent** credit account *or* charge account

compte d'affectation appropriation account

compte de caisse cash account

compte de capital capital account

compte de chèques cheque account

compte de contrepartie contra account

compte de dépôt *ou* **compte sur livret** deposit account

compte d'épargne savings account

compte d'épargne en actions (CEA) Personal Equity Plan (PEP)

compte de non-résident external account

compte de régularisation *[société]* accruals

compte de résultat *ou* **de pertes et profits** profit and loss account

compte détaillé detailed account *or* itemized account

compte d'exploitation trading account

compte fournisseurs *[dettes]* accounts payable *or* payables (n)

compte joint joint account

compte numéroté numbered account

compte oisif *ou* **compte qui dort** dormant account *or* dead account

compte ouvert open account

compte: avoir un compte have (v) an account

compte: suivant compte remis for account rendered

comptes (mpl) (de la société) company's accounts

comptes consolidés consolidated accounts

comptes de fin de mois month-end accounts

comptes de gestion management accounts

comptes de l'exercice annual accounts

comptes de quinzaine mid-month accounts

comptes semestriels half-yearly accounts

compter count (v) *or* add (v)

compter sur (quelqu'un, quelque chose) count on (v) *or* depend on (v) *or* rely on (v)

comptoir (m) counter

conception (f) (de produit) *[design]* (product) design (n)

concerner concern (v); affect (v)

concession (f) *[droit exclusif de vente]* concession (n) *or* distributorship (n)

concessionnaire (mf) concessionaire (n) *or* distributor (n)

concevoir *[dessiner]* design (v)

conciliation (f) conciliation (n)

conclure un accord conclude (v) an agreement

conclure une affaire, un marché clinch (v) a deal *or* make (v) a deal

concorder (avec) *[correspondre]* agree with (v) *or* be the same as

concorder: faire concorder *[comptes, états]* reconcile (v)

concurrence (f) competition (n)

concurrence déloyale unfair competition

concurrence farouche stiff *or* cut-throat *or* keen competition

concurrence: faire concurrence à quelqu'un compete (v) with someone

concurrencer compete (v)

concurrent(e) (n) competitor (n) or rival (n)

concurrent(e) (adj) competing (adj) or rival (adj)

concurrentiel (-elle) *[en concurrence]* competing (adj) or competitive (adj)

condamner (quelqu'un) à une amende fine (v) (someone)

condition (f) condition (n)

condition (f) *[état]* condition or state (n)

condition: (acheter) à condition (buy) on approval or on appro

condition: à (la) condition que on condition that or provided that

condition: (vente) sous condition conditional (adj) (sale)

conditions (fpl) *[modalités, état]* terms (n) or conditions (n)

conditions avantageuses favourable terms

conditions d'emploi terms of employment or of service

conditions de travail working conditions

conditions de vente conditions or terms of sale

conditionnel (-elle) conditional (adj)

conditionnement (m) *[emballage]* packaging *[action, material]*

conditionnement (m) *[présentation]* display pack or display box (n)

conditionner *[emballer]* package (v)

conducteur (-trice) *[voiture]* driver (n)

conduire (une voiture) drive (v) (a car)

confection (f) ready-to-wear (adj) (clothing)

conférence (f) conference (n)

conférence de presse press conference

conférence: en conférence in a meeting

confiance (f) confidence (n)

confidentialité (f) confidentiality (n)

confidentiel (-elle) confidential (adj)

confidentiellement confidentially (adv) or in confidence

confier entrust (v)

confirmation (f) confirmation (n)

confirmer confirm (v)

confirmer une embauche confirm someone in a job

confirmer une réservation confirm a booking

confiscation (f) seizure (n) or forfeiture (n)

confisquer seize (v) or declare (v) forfeit

conflit (n) conflict (n); dispute (n)

conflit d'intérêts conflict of interest

conflits du travail industrial disputes or labour disputes

conformément à (l'échantillon, la facture) as per (sample, invoice, etc.)

conformément à un contrat contractually (adv)

conformer: se conformer à comply with (v)

congé (m) *[autorisation d'absence]* leave (n) or leave of absence

congé (m) *[vacances]* holiday (n)

congé de maladie ou **congé-maladie (m)** sick leave

congé de maternité maternity leave

congé légal *[fête légale]* statutory holiday

congé payé paid leave or paid holiday

congé sans solde unpaid leave

congé: partir en congé go on holiday

congé: prendre un congé take time off ; take a short holiday

congédier dismiss (v) or pay off (v) or sack (v)

conglomérat (m) conglomerate

congrès (m) conference (n)

conjointement jointly (adv)

conjoncture (f) économique economic trends (n) or situation (n)

connaissement (m) bill of lading (n)

conseil (m) *[comité]* board (n) or council (n)

conseil (m) *[personne]* consultant (n)

conseil (m) *[recommandation]* (piece of) advice (n)

conseil d'administration board of directors

conseil d'arbitrage adjudication tribunal

conseil de prud'hommes industrial (arbitration) tribunal

conseil juridique *[recommandation]* legal advice

conseil municipal town council

conseillé(e) recommended (adj)

conseiller (v) advise (v); recommend (v)

conseiller (-ère) (n) adviser (n) *or* advisor (n); consultant (n)

conseiller en gestion d'entreprise management consultant (n)

conseiller fiscal tax consultant *or* tax adviser

conseiller juridique legal adviser

conserver *[maintenir]* maintain (v) *or* keep (v) at same level

considération: sans considération de regardless of

consignataire (mf) *[destinataire]* consignee (n)

consigne (f) left luggage office

consigné(e) returnable (adj)

consigné(e): non consigné(e) non-returnable (adj) (packing, etc.)

consigner *[donner en dépôt]* consign (v)

consigner *[enregistrer]* record (v); minute (v) *[at a meeting]*

consignes (fpl) de sécurité safety regulations (n)

consignes (fpl) en cas d'l'incendie fire regulations

consister en consist of (v)

consolidation (f) (d'une dette) funding (n) (of debt)

consolidé(e) *[compte]* consolidated (adj)

consolidé(e) *[dette]* funded (adj)

consolider consolidate (v)

consommateur (-trice) consumer (n)

consommateur (m) final end user (n)

consommation (f) consumption (n)

consommation des ménages household consumption

consommation domestique *ou* **nationale** domestic *or* home consumption

consortium (m) consortium (n)

constant(e) constant (adj)

constituer *[créer]* form (v) *or* set up (v) (a company)

constitution (f) *[statuts d'une société]* constitution (n)

constructeur (m) constructor (n) *or* builder (n)

constructeur (m) *[fabricant]* manufacturer (n) *or* maker (n)

constructeur clés en main turnkey operator

construction (f) construction (n) *or* building (n)

construction: en construction under construction

consultant (m) consultant (n)

consulter consult (v)

consulter un avocat take legal advice

contact (m) contact (n) *[general]*

contact (m) *[relation]* contact (n) *[person]*

contacter *[joindre]* contact (v)

contenant (m) *[récipient]* container (n)

conteneur (m) container (n)

conteneurisation (m) *ou* **mise (f) en conteneur(s)** containerization (n)

conteneuriser *ou* **mettre en conteneurs** containerize (v) *or* put into containers

contenir contain (v) *or* hold (v)

contentieux (m) legal department (n) *[of company]*

contenu (m) *[physique]* contents (n)

contenu (m) *[teneur]* content (n)

contingent (m) *ou* **contingentement (m)** quota (n)

contingentement d'importation import quota

contingenté(e) (adj) *[produit]* subject to a quota

continu(e) continuous (adj)

continuel (-elle) continual (adj)

continuellement *[sans cesse]* continually (adv)

continuer continue (v) *or* carry on (v) *or* go on (v)

contourner (une difficulté) get round (v) (a problem)

contracter contract (v)

contracter des dettes incur (v) debts

contracter une assurance take out (v) an insurance policy

contractuel (-elle) contractual (adj)

contraire contrary (adj)

contraste (m) contrast (n)

contrat (m) contract (n) *or* agreement (n)

contrat d'association *ou* **de société** deed of partnership

contrat d'assurance insurance contract

contrat d'exclusivité exclusive agreement

contrat de productivité productivity agreement

contrat de service service contract

contrat de sous-traitance subcontract (n)

contrat de travail contract of employment

contrat de travail à durée déterminée (CDD) fixed-term contract

contrat de vente *[acte de vente]* bill (n) of sale

contrat forfaitaire *ou* **contrat à prix ferme** fixed-price agreement

contrat global blanket agreement; package deal

contrat sous seing privé private contract

contrefaçon (f) *[copie]* imitation (n) *or* copy (n) *or* forgery (n)

contrefaçon (f) *[délit]* infringement (n) (of patent, etc.)

contrefaire counterfeit (v); pirate (v)

contrefaire un produit protégé par un brevet infringe (v) a patent

contre-OPA (f) reverse takeover (n)

contrepassation (f) rectifying (n) (an entry)

contrepasser une écriture rectify (v) an entry

contre-proposition (f) counter-offer (n)

contresigner countersign (v)

contribuable (mf) taxpayer (n)

contribuer (une somme) contribute (v)

contribution (f) contribution (n)

contributions directes direct taxes *or* direct taxation

contributions indirectes indirect taxes *or* indirect taxation

contrôle (m) *[administration]* control (n)

contrôle (m) *[essai]* control *or* test (n)

contrôle (m) *[maîtrise]* control (n)

contrôle (m) *[restriction]* control *or* limitation (n) *or* restriction (n)

contrôle (m) *[vérification]* control *or* check (n) *or* examination (n)

contrôle budgétaire budgetary control

contrôle de qualité quality control

contrôle des changes exchange control

contrôle des loyers rent control

contrôle des prix price control

contrôle des stocks stock control; inventory control *[US]*

contrôle douanier customs examination; baggage check

contrôlé(e) par l'Etat government-controlled (adj)

contrôler control (v)

contrôler *[faire l'essai]* test (v) *or* control (v)

contrôler *[vérifier]* inspect (v) *or* monitor (v) *or* control (v)

contrôleur (m) controller (n)

contrôleur des stocks stock controller

convenir *[être d'accord]* agree with (v) *[of same opinion]*

convenir *[faire l'affaire]* fit (v) *or* be suitable

convention (f) agreement (n)

convention collective sur les salaires collective wage agreement

convention écrite *ou* **contrat écrit** written agreement

convenu(e) *[accepté]* agreed (adj)

conversion (f) conversion (n)

convertibilité (f) convertibility (n)

convertible convertible (adj)

convivial(e) user-friendly (adj)

convocation (f) summons (n)

convoquer (une assemblée) call (v) *or* convene (v) (a meeting)

coopératif (-ive) (adj) co-operative (adj)

coopération (f) co-operation (n)

coopérative (f) *[société]* co-operative (n) *or* co-operative society

coopérer co-operate (v)

coopter quelqu'un co-opt (v) someone

coordonnées (fpl) *[détails]* particulars (n)

coordonnées bancaires bank details (n)

coparticipation (f) copartnership (n)

copie (f) *[d'un document]* copy (n) *or* duplicate (n)

copie carbone carbon copy

copie certifiée conforme certified copy

copie conforme true copy

copie (sur) papier) *[d'imprimante]* hard copy

copropriétaire (mf) joint owner (n) *or* part owner

copropriété (f) joint ownership (n) or part-ownership (n)

copyright (m) copyright (n)

corbeille *[Bourse]* trading floor (n)

corporation (f) *[guilde]* guild (n)

correction (f) correction (n)

correspondance (f) *[courrier]* correspondence (n)

correspondance (f) *[transport]* connecting flight, etc.

correspondance commerciale business correspondance

correspondant(e) *[courrier, journaliste]* correspondent (n)

correspondre (à quelque chose) correspond (v) (with something)

correspondre avec quelqu'un correspond with someone

corrigé(e) des variations saisonnières seasonally adjusted (figures)

corriger correct (v); adjust (v)

corrompre (quelqu'un) bribe (v) (someone)

cosignataire (mf) joint signatory (n)

cote (f) *[Bourse]* quotation (n)

cote (de crédit) (financial) rating (n)

coté(e) (adj) en Bourse quoted (adj) or listed (adj) on the Stock Exchange

côté (m) side (n)

coter (en Bourse) quote (v) (on the Stock Exchange)

cotisation (f) *[à un club, à une revue, etc.]* subscription (n)

cotisation (f) *[contribution]* contribution (n)

cotiser *[à un club, à une revue, etc.]* subscribe (v)

cotiser *[contribuer]* contribute (v)

coulage (m) *[perte]* leakage (n)

coulage (m) *[vol]* shrinkage (n)

coupon (m) coupon (n)

coupon attaché cum coupon

coupon détaché ex coupon

coupon-prime (m) gift voucher (n)

coupon-réponse (m) reply coupon

coupure (f) *[billets de banque]* denomination (n)

cour (f) *[tribunal]* court (n)

cour de justice law courts

courant *[de ce mois]* instant (adj) or inst.

courant(e) current (adj)

courant(e) *[actuel]* current (adj) or going (adj) *[price]*

courant(e) *[commun]* common (adj) or frequent (adj)

courant(e) *[de base]* stock (adj) *[normal]*

courant(e) *[quotidien]* day-to-day *[expenses]*

courbe (f) curve (n)

courbe des ventes sales curve

courir *[s'accumuler]* accrue (v)

courir un risque run (v) a risk

couronne (f) *[unité monétaire: Danemark, Norvège]* krone (n)

couronne (f) *[unité monétaire: Suède, Islande]* krona (n)

courrier (m) post (n) or mail (n)

courrier à l'arrivée incoming mail

courrier au départ outgoing mail

courrier électronique electronic mail or email (n)

courrier ordinaire surface mail

cours (m) *[études]* course (n)

cours (m) *[taux]* rate (n); price (n)

cours à terme forward rate

cours de clôture *[Bourse]* closing price

cours de commerce commercial course

cours de gestion d'entreprise *[management]* management course

cours demandé asking price

cours de recyclage refresher course

cours d'ouverture *[Bourse]* opening price

cours du change rate of exchange

cours du jour today's rate

cours du marché market rate

cours par correspondance correspondence course

cours: au cours de during (adv) or in the course of

cours: en cours in progress

cours: (monnaie) qui a cours legal tender

courses (fpl) shopping (n) *[action]*

courses: faire des *ou* **ses courses** go shopping or do some shopping

coursier (m) *[commissionnaire]* (office) messenger (n)

coursier (m) *[en vélo, moto, voiture]* courier (n)

court(e) short (adj)

court(e): à court de short of

court(e): à court terme short-term (adj)

courtage (m) [profession] stockbroking (n)

courtage (m) [commission d'agent] brokerage (n) or broker's commission (n)

courtier (m) broker (n)

courtier d'assurances insurance broker

courtier en devises foreign exchange broker or dealer (n)

courtier en valeurs mobilières stockbroker (n) or broker (n)

courtier maritime ship broker

couru(e) (adj) [intérêt] accrued (adj)

coût (m) cost (n)

coût, assurance, fret (CAF) cost, insurance and freight (c.i.f.)

coût courant current cost

coût d'acquisition d'immobilisations capital expenditure

coût de fabrication ou de production production cost; manufacturing cost

coût de la main-d'oeuvre labour cost(s)

coût de lancement launching cost

coût de la vie cost of living

coût de revient (de marchandise vendue) cost of sales

coût d'exploitation ou coût opérationnel operating cost or running cost

coût fixe fixed cost

coût historique ou coût d'acquisition historical cost

coût majoré cost plus

coût marginal marginal cost

coût unitaire unit cost

coût proportionnel ou coût variable variable cost

coûter cost (v)

coûteux (-euse) [cher] dear (adj) or expensive (adj) or costly (adj)

couvert (m) [au restaurant] cover charge (n)

couverture (f) [garantie] cover (n)

couverture contre l'inflation hedge (n) against inflation

couverture d'assurance insurance cover

couverture des dividendes dividend cover

couverture (f) médiatique media coverage

couvrir [dépenses] cover (v) [expenses, a position]

couvrir les coûts de production cover costs

créance (f) debt (n)

créance douteuse bad debt

créance exigible debt due

créances (fpl) outstanding debts or monies owing

créances (fpl) [comptes clients] accounts receivable or receivables (n)

créancier (m) creditor (n)

créancier chirographaire unsecured creditor

créancier prioritaire preferential or preferred creditor

créancier privilégié secured creditor

créancier sans garantie unsecured creditor

crédit (m) credit (n)

crédit à court terme short credit or short-term credit

crédit à découvert [découvert autorisé] open credit

crédit à long terme long credit or extended credit

crédit-bail (m) [leasing] leasing (n) (with option to purchase)

crédit bancaire bank credit

crédit d'appoint ou crédit stand-by standby credit

crédit d'impôt [avoir fiscal] tax credit

crédit gratuit interest-free credit

crédit immédiat instant credit

crédit permanent ou renouvelable revolving credit

crédit-relais (m) bridging loan (n)

crédit: à crédit on credit

crédit: faire crédit give credit

créditer un compte (d'une somme) credit (a sum) to an account

créditeur (-trice) (adj) in credit

créditrentier (-ière) annuitant (n)

crédits (mpl) à la consommation consumer credit

crédits gelés frozen credits

créer (une société) set up (v) (a company)

créneau (m) sur le marché gap (n) *or* niche (n) in the market

crise (f) crisis (n)

crise du dollar dollar crisis

crise économique slump (n) *or* recession (n)

crise financière crash (n) *or* financial crisis

croissance (f) growth (n) *or* expansion (n)

croissance économique economic growth

croissance externe external growth

culminer *[atteindre un niveau élevé]* peak (v)

cumulatif (-ive) cumulative (adj)

cumulé(e) accrued (adj)

curriculum (m) vitae (CV) curriculum vitae (CV)

cycle (m) cycle (n)

cycle économique economic cycle *or* trade cycle

cyclique cyclical (adj)

Dd

date (f) date (n)

date d'achèvement (de travaux) completion date

date d'échéance maturity date

date de livraison delivery date

date d'entrée en vigueur effective date; starting date

date d'ouverture opening date

date de réception date of receipt

date d'expiration expiry date

date limite closing date *or* deadline (n)

date limite de vente sell-by date

date: de longue date long-standing (adj)

date: en date de dated (adj)

date: sans date undated

daté(e) dated (adj)

daté(e): non daté(e) undated

dater date (v)

débardeur (m) *[docker]* stevedore (n)

débarquer land (v) *[passengers, cargo]*

débarquer des marchandises land goods (at a port)

débarrasser: se débarrasser de get rid of (something)

débit (m) debit (n)

débit et crédit *[passif et actif]* debits and credits

débiter un compte debit (v) an account

débiteur (m) debtor (n)

débiteur (-trice) (adj) *[compte]* showing a debit; in the red

débours (mpl) out-of-pocket expenses (n)

débourser disburse (v)

débrayer *[arrêter le travail]* knock off (v) *or* stop (v) work

débrouiller: se débrouiller cope (v) *or* get along (v)

début (n) beginning (n)

débutant(e) (n) beginner (n)

débuter begin (v) *or* start (v)

décentralisation (f) decentralization (n)

décentraliser decentralize (v)

déchargement (m) unloading (n)

décharger *[marchandises]* unload (v) (goods)

déchets (mpl) (industriels) (industrial) waste (n)

déchiqueteur (m) *ou* **déchiqueteuse (f)** shredder (n)

décider *ou* **prendre une décision** decide (v) *or* come (v) to a decision *or* reach a decision

décider : se décider make up (v) one's mind

décideur (m) decision maker (n)

décimale (f) decimal (n)

décisif (-ive) deciding (adj)

décision (f) decision (n)

déclaration (f) declaration (n) *or* statement (n)

déclaration (f) *[annonce]* announcement (n)

déclaration de revenus declaration of income

déclaration de sinistre insurance claim

déclaration de TVA VAT declaration

déclaration d'impôts tax return *or* tax declaration

déclaration en douane customs declaration

déclaration sous serment affidavit

déclarer declare (v) *or* state (v)

déclarer *[statuer]* rule (v)

déclarer des marchandises à la douane declare goods to customs

déclarer quelqu'un en faillite declare someone bankrupt

déclarer un dividende declare a dividend

déclarer: rien à déclarer nothing to declare

décoller *[avion]* take off (v)

décommander *[un rendez-vous]* cancel (v)

découler de result from (v)

découvert (m) *[à la banque]* overdraft (n)

découvert autorisé *[crédit]* open credit

découvert: (compte) à découvert overdrawn (adj) (account)

décroissant(e) decreasing (adj) *or* diminishing (adj)

dédommagement (m) compensation (n) (for damage) *or* indemnification (n)

dédommager *[indemniser]* compensate (v) *or* indemnify (v)

dédommager: se dédommager recoup (v) (one's losses)

dédouanage (m) *ou* **dédouanement (m)** customs clearance

dédouané(e) *[marchandise]* duty-paid *[goods]*

dédouaner des marchandises clear (v) goods through customs

déductible deductible (adj)

déductible des impôts tax-deductible (adj)

déduction (f) deduction (n)

déduire *[retrancher]* deduct (v) *or* take off (v)

déduire des impôts set (v) against tax

défaillance (f) *[d'un appareil]* breakdown (n)

défaillance (f) *[d'une société]* bankruptcy (n)

défaillant(e) *[témoin]* defaulter (n)

défaut (m) defect (n) *or* fault (n)

défaut (m) de paiement non-payment (n)

défavorable adverse (adj) *or* unfavourable (adj)

défectueux (-euse) defective (adj) *or* faulty (adj)

défectuosité (f) *[imperfection]* imperfection (n) *or* defect (n)

défendeur (m), défenderesse (f) defendant (n)

défendre *[en justice]* defend (v)

défendre *[interdire]* forbid (v)

défendre: se défendre en justice defend (v) a lawsuit

défense (f) *[interdiction]* interdiction (n)

défense (f) *[juridique, protection]* defence (n)

déficit (m) deficit (n) *or* loss (n)

déficit (m) *[manque]* shortfall (n)

déficit commercial trade deficit *or* trade gap

déficitaire showing a deficit *or* unfavourable (adj)

défiscaliser exempt (v) from tax

déflation (f) deflation (n)

déflationniste deflationary (adj)

défraîchi(e) (en magasin) shop-soiled (item)

défrayer defray (v) (costs)

dégâts (mpl) *[dommage]* damage (n)

dégâts causés par le feu fire damage

dégâts causés par la tempête storm damage

dégrèvement (m) fiscal *ou* **d'impôt** tax concession (n) *or* tax relief (n)

déjeuner (m) d'affaires business lunch

délai (m) time limit (n) *or* deadline (n)

délai de livraison delivery time

délai d'exécution *ou* **de production** lead time

délai de préavis *ou* **délai-congé (m)** period of notice

délai de réflexion cooling off period *[after purchase]*

délai de remboursement *ou* **d'amortissement** payback period

délai: à bref délai at short notice

délai: dans les délais within the time limits

délai: dernier délai final date

délégation (f) delegation (n)

délégué(e) (n) delegate (n)

délégué(e) commercial(e) (sales) representative (n) *or* rep (n)

délégué(e) du personnel worker director (n)

délégué(e) syndical(e) *[à un congrès]* trade union delegate

délégué(e) syndical(e) *[dans l'usine]* shop steward (n)

déléguer delegate (v)

délit (m) d'initié(s) insider dealing (n)

délit (m) par abstention nonfeasance (n)

demande (f) *[des consommateurs]* demand (n)

demande (f) *[réclamation]* demand (n) *or* claim (n)

demande (f) *[requête]* request (n) *or* requisition (n)

demande (f) *[de remboursement]* call (n) *[for money]*

demande de brevet déposée patent (n) applied for *or* patent pending

demande d'emploi job application *or* application for a job

demande de reseignement(s) inquiry (n) *or* enquiry (n)

demande reconventionnelle counter-claim (n)

demande saisonnière seasonal demand

demande: faire une demande par écrit apply (v) in writing

demande: sur demande on demand *or* on request

demander *[exiger]* demand (v)

demander *[faire payer]* charge (v)

demander *[réclamer]* ask for (v) *or* request (v) *[something]*

demander de faire quelque chose ask (v) (someone) to do something

demander des renseignements ask for details *or* for particulars

demander un remboursement ask for a refund

démarchage (m) *[porte-à-porte]* door-to-door selling (n) *or* canvassing (n)

démarcheur (m) door-to-door salesman (n) *or* canvasser (n)

démarquer *[réduire le prix]* mark down (v) (an article)

démarrage (m) start (n)

démarrage à *ou* **de zéro** cold start

démarrage (d'une affaire *ou* **d'un produit)** start-up (n)

démarrer start (v) *or* begin (v); open (v)

démarrer une affaire *[s'établir]* set up in business

démettre: se démettre (de ses fonctions) stand down (v)

demeurer *[habiter]* live (v)

demeurer *[séjourner]* stay (v)

demi(e) (adj) half (adj)

demi-douzaine (f) half a dozen *or* a half-dozen (n)

demie (f) half (n)

démission (f) resignation (n)

démissionner resign (v) *or* leave (v)

démodé(e) old-fashioned (adj) *or* out of date (adj)

démonstrateur (-trice) (n) demonstrator (n)

démonstration (f) demonstration (n)

déni (m) de responsabilité disclaimer (n)

denrée (f) commodity (n)

denrées alimentaires foodstuffs (n)

denrées périssables perishable goods *or* perishables (n)

dépareillé(e) odd (adj) *[not a pair]*

départ (m) departure (n)

départs naturels *[employés]* natural wastage (n)

départs volontaires *[employés]* voluntary redundancy (n)

départemental(e) departmental (adj)

dépassé(e) *[démodé(e)]* old-fashioned (adj) *or* out of date (adj)

dépasser go (v) higher than

dépasser *[excéder]* exceed (v)

dépasser son budget overspend one's budget

dépeçage (m) *[d'une société]* asset-stripping (n)

dépendre de *ou* **compter sur** depend on (v)

dépense (f) expense (n) *or* expenditure (n)

dépense exceptionnelle *[hors bilan]* below-the-line expenditure

dépenses (fpl) outgoings (n) *[money paid out]*

dépenses de consommation consumer spending

dépenser spend (v) *[money]*

dépenser trop overspend (v)

dépenser trop peu underspend (v)

déport (m) backwardation (n)

déposant(e) (n) depositor (n)

déposer une demande de brevet file (v) an application for a patent

déposer une marque de commerce register (v) a trademark

déposer une motion propose (v) a motion

déposer une requête file (v) a request

dépositaire (mf) *[stockiste]* stockist (n)

dépôt (m) *[d'argent]* deposit (n) *[in bank]*

dépôt (m) *[entrepôt]* depot (n)

dépôt (m) *[magasin]* store (n) *or* storeroom (n)

dépôt à terme time deposit

dépôt à terme fixe fixed deposit

dépôt à vue demand deposit

dépôt bancaire bank deposit

dépôt de nuit *[coffre]* night safe (n)

dépôt en coffre-fort safe deposit

dépôt en espèces cash deposit

dépôt rémunéré interest-bearing deposit

dépréciation (f) depreciation (n)

déprécier depreciate (v)

déprécier: se déprécier depreciate (v)

dépression (f) (economic) depression (n)

déréglementation (f) deregulation (n)

dernier (-ière) last one (n)

dernier (-ière) *[final]* last (adj) *or* closing (adj) *or* final (adj)

dernier (-ière) *[plus récent]* latest (adj)

dernier entré, premier sorti (DEPS) last in first out (LIFO)

dernier rappel final demand (n)

dernier trimestre last quarter (n)

dernière enchère closing bid (n)

dérouler: se dérouler *[opération]* progress (v)

description (f) description (n)

description de la fonction job description

description mensongère false description

déséconomies (fpl) d'échelle diseconomies of scale

désencadrer le crédit lift (v) credit restrictions

désendettement (n) *[d'une société]* degearing (n)

design (m) design (n)

désinflation (f) disinflation (n)

désinvestir disinvest (v)

désister: se désister stand down (v)

dessin (m) industriel industrial design (n)

dessiner *[concevoir]* design (v)

destinataire (mf) addressee (n)

destinataire (mf) *[consignataire]* consignee (n)

destination (f) destination (n)

détacher second (v) *[member of staff]*

détail (m) *[précision]* detail (n)

détail (m) *[ventilation]* breakdown (n)

détail *ou* **vente au détail** retail (n); retailing (n)

détaillant(e) retailer (n) *or* retail dealer (n)

détaillé(e) *[compte]* detailed *or* itemized (account)

détailler detail (v) *or* itemize (v)

détailler: se détailler retail (v) (at)

détails (mpl) *[coordonnées]* particulars (n) *or* details (n)

détenir *[garder]* hold (v) *or* keep (v)

détenir *[posséder]* hold (v) *or* own (v)

détenteur (-trice) holder (n) *[person]*

détermination (f) *[fixation]* fixing (n)

détermination de l'assiette fiscale tax assessment (n)

déterminer *[fixer]* determine (v)

déterminer un prix fixe (v) a price

détournement (m) de fonds misappropriation (n) *or* embezzlement (n)

détourner des fonds misappropriate (v) *or* embezzle (v) funds

dette (f) *[argent]* debt (n) *or* liability (n)

dette irrécouvrable irrecoverable debt

dettes (fpl) à court terme short-term liabilities

dettes à long terme long-term liabilities

dettes garanties secured debts

dettes privilégiées senior debts

Deutschemark (m) *[unité monétaire en Allemagne]* Deutschmark (n)

deuxième *[second]* second (adj)

deuxième trimestre second quarter (n)

dévalorisation (f) fall (n) in value

dévaloriser: se dévaloriser fall (v) in value

dévaluation (f) devaluation (n) *or* depreciation (n)

dévaluer devalue (v)

développement (m) development (n)

développement (m) *[croissance]* expansion (n)

développement économique economic development

développement industriel industrial expansion

développer develop (v)

développer: se développer *[grandir]* expand (v) *or* grow (v)

devenir become (v)

devenir prospère boom (v)

devis (m) estimate (n) *or* quote (n) *or* quotation (n)

devise (f) (étrangère) (foreign) currency (n); foreign exchange (n)

devise convertible convertible currency

devise faible soft currency

devise forte hard currency

devise non convertible blocked currency

devoir (de l'argent) owe (v) (money)

diagramme (m) diagram (n) *or* chart (n)

diagramme circulaire *ou* **en camembert** pie chart

diagramme des ventes sales chart

diagramme en bâtons bar chart

Dictaphone (m) dictating machine (n)

dictée (f) dictation (n)

dictée: prendre en dicté take (v) dictation

dicter dictate (v)

différé(e) deferred (adj)

différence (f) difference (n)

différence de prix price difference *or* difference in price

différent(e) different (adj)

différentiel (-elle) differential (adj)

différer *[être différent]* differ (v)

différer *[remettre à plus tard]* defer (v)

différer un paiement defer payment

diffuser *[distribuer]* distribute (v)

diffusion (f) *[distribution]* distribution (n)

dilution (f) du capital dilution (n) of equity

dimensions (fpl) measurements (n)

diminuer *[chuter]* diminish (v) *or* fall (v) *or* decrease (v)

diminuer *[supprimer]* cut (v) *or* reduce (v) *or* lower (v)

diminuer de valeur *[se déprécier]* depreciate (v) *or* lose (v) value

diminution (f) *[chute]* fall (n) *or* decrease (n) *or* reduction (n)

direct(e) direct (adj)

directement direct (adv)

directeur (-trice) (n) (company) director (n) *or* manager (n)

directeur (-trice) *[chef de service]* (department) head (n) *or* manager (n)

directeur (-trice) adjoint(e) assistant manager *or* deputy manager

directeur (-trice) commercial(e) sales manager *or* sales executive

directeur (-trice) d'agence branch manager

directeur (-trice) d'agence *[banque]* bank manager

directeur (-trice) de la production production manager

directeur (-trice) de la publicité publicity manager

directeur (-trice) du marketing marketing manager

directeur (-trice) général(e) (DG) general manager *or* managing director (MD)

directeur (-trice) général(e) adjoint(e) deputy managing director

directeur (-trice) intérimaire acting manager

direction (f) direction (n)

direction (f) *[poste de directeur]* directorship (n) *or* managership (n)

direction (f) *[l'administration, les cadres]* management (n) *or* managerial staff

direction générale *[cadres supérieurs]* top management

directive (f) directive (n) *or* guideline (n)

dirigeant (m) executive (n)

diriger *[gérer]* manage (v) *or* run (v)

diriger *[mener]* lead (v) *or* conduct (v) *or* direct (v)

discours (m) speech (n)

discrimination (f) sexiste sexual discrimination (n)

discussion (f) discussion (n)

discuter discuss (v)

disponibilité (f) availability (n)

disponibilités (fpl) *[liquidités]* liquid assets (n); cash reserves (n)

disponible available (adj); obtainable (adj)

disponible: non disponible unavailable (adj); unobtainable (adj)

disposer en tableau *ou* **en colonnes** tabulate (v)

dispositif (m) device

disposition (f) en tableau *ou* **en colonnes** tabulation (n)

disque (m) disk (n)

disque CD *ou* **disque compact** compact disc *or* CD

disque (m) dur hard disk

disquette (f) diskette (n) *or* floppy (disk)

disquette de sauvegarde backup copy (n)

dissimulation (f) d'actif concealment of assets

dissoudre (une association) dissolve (v) (a partnership)

distancer: se laisser distancer fall behind (v)

distribuer *[actions, marchandises)* distribute *[shares, goods]*

distribuer *[partager]* distribute (v); allocate (v)

distributeur (m) distributor (n)

distributeur automatique de billets (DAB) cash dispenser (n); cashpoint (n)

distribution (f) *[diffusion]* distribution (n)

divers (mpl) sundries (n)

divers(e) (adj) miscellaneous (adj)

diversification (f) diversification (n)

diversifier diversify (v)

dividende (m) dividend (n)

dividende à recevoir *ou* **dividende cumulé** accrued dividend

dividende complémentaire surplus dividend

dividende intérimaire interim dividend

dividende: avec dividende cum dividend

dividende: sans dividende ex dividend

division (f) *[secteur d'une société]* division (n)

docker (m) stevedore (n)

document (m) document (n) *or* paper (n)

document justificatif documentary evidence

documentaire (adj) documentary (adj)

documentation (f) documentation (n); literature (n)

dollar (m) (américain) (US) dollar (n) *or* greenback (n)

domicile (m) domicile (n)

domicilier domicile (v)

dommage (m) *[dégâts]* damage (n)

dommages-intérêts *ou* **dommages et intérêts** damages (n) *[insurance]*

dommages matériels damage to property

données (fpl) *[informatique]* data (n)

données de sortie output (n) *[computer]*

donner give (v)

donner de l'avancement *[promouvoir]* promote (v)

donner des explications inform (v); brief (v)

donner en reprise trade in *[give in old item in part exchange]*

donner en sous-traitance *[sous-traiter]* subcontract (v)

donner un pourboire tip (v) *or* give (v) a tip

dos (m) back (n)

dossier (m) *[ensemble des documents]*
file (n) *or* record (n)

dossier *[pochette avec documents]* file
(n)

doter en capital *[capitaliser]*
capitalize (v)

douane (f) customs (n)

douanier (m) customs official (n) *or*
customs officer (n)

double double (adj)

double (m) *[copie]* copy (n) *or*
duplicate (n); carbon copy

double imposition double taxation

doubler double (v)

douzaine (f) dozen (n)

douze douzaines *[grosse]* gross (n) (=
144)

drachme (f) *[unité monétaire en Grèce]*
drachma (n)

droit (m) *[à quelque chose]* right (n) *or*
entitlement (n)

droit (m) *[science]* law (n) *[study]*

droit (m) *[taxe]* duty (n) *or* tax (n) *or*
charge (n)

droit(e) (adj) *[côté]* right (adj)

droit (d'entrée) *[redevance]*
(admission) charge (n) *or* fee (n)

droit civil, droit commercial civil
law, commercial law

droit d'auteur copyright (n)

droit d'enregistrement *ou* **d'inscription**
registration fee

droit de douane customs duty

droit de participation equity (n)

droit de timbre stamp duty

droit de veto right of veto

droit des contrats et des obligations
contract law

droit des sociétés company law

droit international international law

droit maritime maritime law

droits acquis *[intérêts]* vested interest
(n)

droits (mpl) de bassin port charges *or*
port dues

droits de régie excise duty

droits de tirage spéciaux (DTS)
special drawing rights (SDRs)

dû (due) due (adj) *or* owing (adj)

ducroire del credere

dûment duly

dumping (m) dumping (n)

duplicata (m) *[copie]* duplicate (n) *or*
copy (n)

durée (f) *[période]* period (n) *or* term
(n)

durée de conservation d'un produit
shelf life of a product

durée d'un bail tenancy (n)

durer last (v)

Ee

écart (m) discrepancy (n) *or*
differential (n)

écart de prix price differential

écarts de salaires wage differentials

échange (m) exchange (n) *or* swap (n)

échange (m) *[troc]* bartering (n)

échange: en échange in exchange

échanges commerciaux trade (n)

échangeable exchangeable (adj)

échanger exchange (v) *or* swap (v)

échanger *[un article acheté]* exchange
(v)

échantillon (m) sample (n)

échantillon aléatoire random sample

échantillon d'essai trial sample

échantillon gratuit free sample

échantillon-témoin (m) check sample

échantillonnage (m) sampling (n)

échec (m) failure (n); flop (n)
[familiar]

échelle (f) *[barème]* scale (n)

échelle de prix fixe fixed scale of
charges

échelle des salaires wage scale

échelle des tarifs scale of charges

échelle mobile des salaires incremental scale

échelonner *[étaler]* stagger (v)

échouer fail (v) *or* not to succeed (v) *or* flop (v)

échouer *[négociations]* break down (v)

échouer *[projet]* fall through (v)

école (f) school (n); college (n)

école (f) de secrétariat secretarial college

école supérieure de commerce commercial college

économie (f) *[épargne]* economy (n)

économie (f) *[système]* economy (n)

économie (f) de l'offre supply side economics

économie de marché *ou* **économie libérale** free market economy

économie dirigée controlled economy

économie mixte mixed economy

économie parallèle *ou* **non officielle** black economy

économie politique economics (n)

économies (fpl) savings

économies d'échelle economies of scale

économies: faire des économies economize (v) *or* save (up) (v)

économique economic (adj)

économique *[moins cher]* economical

économiquement economically (adv)

économiser economize (v) *or* save (up) (v)

économiser l'énergie save energy

économiser: qui économise l'énergie energy-saving (adj)

économiste (mf) economist (n)

économiste financier market economist

écouler *[liquider]* sell off (v)

écouler le surplus de stock dispose (v) of excess stock

écouler: s'écouler flow (v)

écran (m) (d'ordinateur) monitor (n) *or* screen (n)

écrire write (v)

écrit (m) written document (n)

écrit(e) written (adj)

écrit(e) à la main *[manuscrit]* handwritten (adj)

écriture (f) handwriting (n)

écriture (f) *[comptabilité]* entry (n)

écriture au crédit credit entry

écriture au débit debit entry

écriture de contrepartie contra entry (n)

écrouler: s'écrouler *[s'effondrer]* collapse (v) *or* slump (v)

ECU (m) *ou* **écu (m)** ecu *or* ECU (European currency unit)

éditeur (-trice) *[qui corrige]* editor (n)

éditeur (-trice) *[qui publie]* publisher (n)

éditeur de texte *[programme]* (text) editor

édition (f) *[d'un livre]* edition (n)

effectif (m) labour force (n) *or* workforce (n)

effectuer carry out (v)

effet (m) *[document]* bill (n)

effet (m) *[réaction]* effect (n) *or* result (n)

effet à courte échéance short-dated bill

effet à longue échéance long-dated bill

effet bancaire bank bill (n)

effet de commerce negotiable instrument (n)

effet de levier *[de la dette]* gearing (n) *or* leverage (n)

effet escomptable *ou* **bancable** bankable paper (n)

effet négociable negotiable instrument

effet non négociable non-negotiable instrument

effets à payer bills payable *or* payables (n)

effets à recevoir bills receivable *or* receivables (n)

efficace efficient (adj *or* effective (adj)

efficacité (f) efficiency (n) *[ability to work well]*

efficacité (f) effectiveness (n) *[producing results]*

effondrement (m) collapse (n) *or* slump (n) *or* crash (n)

effondrement des ventes slump in sales

effondrer: s'effondrer slump (v) *or* collapse (v)

effondrer: s'effondrer *[faire faillite]* collapse (v) *or* go bankrupt *or* crash (v)

égal(e) equal (adj)

égaler equal (v)

égalisation (f) equalization (n)

égalité (f) equality (n)

élasticité (f) elasticity (n)

élection (f) election (n)

élever: s'élever *[se monter à]* amount to (v) *or* run to (v) *or* total (v)

élire elect (v)

emballage (m) *[action]* packing (n) *or* packaging (n)

emballage (m) *[matériau]* packing material *or* packaging material

emballage consigné returnable packing

emballage de présentation display pack

emballage factice dummy pack

emballage non consigné *ou* **perdu** non-returnable packing

emballage pelliculé shrink-wrapping (n)

emballer pack (v) *or* package (v) *or* parcel up (v)

emballer *[envelopper]* wrap up (v)

emballer *[dans des cartons]* pack (v) goods *[into cartons]*

emballeur (-euse) packer (n)

embargo (m) embargo (n)

embargo: lever l'embargo lift (an embargo

embargo: mettre l'embargo (sur) embargo (v) *or* put an embargo (on)

embarquement (m) embarkation (n)

embarquer *[des marchandises]* load (v)

embarquer *[monter à bord]* embark (v)

embaucher du personnel hire (v) *or* take on (v) staff

émettre (des actions, une lettre de crédit) issue (v) (shares, a letter of credit)

émission (f) d'actions share issue (n)

émission d'actions gratuites scrip issue *or* bonus issue

émission d'obligations debenture issue

émission prioritaire rights issue

empaqueter pack (v); parcel up (v)

emplacement (m) location (n) *or* site (n) *or* situation (n)

emploi (m) *[travail]* job (n) *or* employment (n) *or* post (n)

emploi (m) *[utilisation]* use (n)

emploi du temps schedule (n) *or* timetable (n)

emploi temporaire temporary employment

emploi: sans emploi *[au chômage]* unemployed (adj)

employé(e) (n) *[salarié]* employee (n)

employé(e) (adj) *[utilisé]* used (adj) *or* employed (adj)

employé(e) à temps partiel *ou* **à mi-temps** part-timer (n)

employé(e) aux écritures bookkeeper

employé(e) aux écritures (du grand livre des achats) bought ledger clerk

employé(e) aux écritures (du grand livre des ventes) sales ledger clerk

employé(e) de bureau office clerk (n) *or* office worker (n)

employé(e) qui réassortit les stocks sur les rayons shelf filler (n)

employé(e) subalterne junior clerk

employer use (v) *or* employ (v)

employer *[du personnel]* employ (v) *[staff]*

employeur (-euse) employer (n)

emprunt (m) *[somme reçue]* borrowing (n)

emprunt (m) *[somme prêtée]* loan (n)

emprunt à court terme short-term loan

emprunt à long terme long-term loan

emprunt bancaire bank borrowing

emprunt garanti secured loan

emprunt obligataire loan stock

emprunter borrow (v)

emprunteur (-euse) borrower (n)

emprunteur sur hypothèque mortgager *or* mortgagor (n)

en dehors des heures de bureau outside office hours

en dehors des heures de pointe off-peak

en plus *ou* **en sus** extra

encadrement (m) du crédit credit control (n) *or* credit squeeze (n)

encadrer *[limiter]* limit (v) *or* freeze (v) *or* squeeze (v)

encaissable cashable

encaisse (f) float (n)

encaissement (m) cashing (n)

encaisser un chèque cash (v) a cheque

encart (m) publicitaire magazine insert (n)

enchère (f) *[offre]* bid (n) *or* bidding (n)

enchère (f) *ou* **vente aux enchères** auction (n)

enchérir sur quelqu'un put (v) a higher bid than someone

enchérisseur (m) bidder (n)

encombrer (le marché) glut (v) (the market)

endetté(e) (adj) in debt; debtor (nation)

endettement (m) indebtedness (n); debt (n)

endettement: société à fort coefficient d'endettement highly-geared company

endetter get (v) (someone) into debt

endetter: s'endetter get (v) into debt *or* run (v) into debt

endommagé(e) damaged (adj)

endommager *[abîmer]* damage (v)

endossataire (mf) endorsee (n)

endossement (m) endorsement (n)

endosser un chèque endorse (v) a cheque

endosseur (m) endorser (n)

endroit (m) place (n)

énergie (f) *[électricité]* energy (n) *or* electricity (n)

enfreindre la loi break (v) the law

engagement (m) commitment (n) *or* engagement (n)

engager *[entamer]* enter (v) into (negotiations)

engager (des dépenses) incur (v) (costs)

engager: s'engager à agree (v) to (do something)

enlèvement (m) collection (n) *[of goods]*

enlever *[déduire ou rabattre]* take off (v) *or* deduct (v)

enlever *[supprimer]* remove (v)

énoncé (m) *[formulation]* form (n) of words

enquête (f) investigation (n) *or* survey (n)

enquêter investigate (v)

enregistré(e) registered (adj)

enregistrement (m) *[à l'aéroport]* check-in (n) *[at airport]*

enregistrement (m) *[immatriculation]* registration (n)

enregistrer *[immatriculer ou inscrire]* register (v)

enregistrer *[noter]* enter (v) *or* write in (v)

enregistrer: se faire enregistrer *[s'inscrire]* register (v) *[at hotel, etc.]*

enseigne (f) sign (n)

entamer *[démarrer]* open (v) *or* begin (v) *or* enter into (v)

entamer des négociations open negotiations

entente (f) *[arrangement]* understanding (n) *or* agreement (n)

entier (-ière) complete (adj)

entrée (f) admittance (n) *or* admission (n)

entrée (f) *[prix]* admission charge (n) *or* entry (n)

entreposage (m) storage (n) *or* warehousing (n)

entreposer store (v) *or* keep (v) in warehouse

entrepôt (m) *[bâtiment]* warehouse (n) *or* depot (n)

entrepôt (m) *[magasin]* storeroom (n)

entrepôt (m) *[port]* entrepot port

entrepôt de douanes bonded warehouse

entrepôt frigorifique cold store

entreprendre undertake (v) *or* embark on (v)

entrepreneur (m) *[homme d'affaires]* entrepreneur (n)

entrepreneur (m) *[en construction, etc.]* contractor (n)

entrepreneur de transports routiers haulage contractor

entreprise (f) *[opération]* undertaking (n) *or* venture (n)

entreprise (f) *[organisation]* enterprise (n) *or* business (n)

entreprise du secteur public state enterprise

entreprise privée private enterprise

entreprise: dans l'entreprise in-house

entrer enter (v) *or* go in (v)

entretenir *[faire durer]* maintain (v)

entretien (m) *[d'une machine]* service (n) *or* maintenance (n)

entretien (m) *[pour un poste]* interview (n) *[for a job]*

enveloppe (f) envelope (n)

enveloppe à fenêtre window envelope

enveloppe (f) budgétaire *[montant]* budget (n)

enveloppe longue foolscap envelope

environ *[approximativement]* approximately (adv) *or* about (adv)

envoi (m) *[expédition]* dispatch (n) *or* shipment (n); delivery (n)

envoi (m) *[marchandises]* consignment (n) *or* shipment (n)

envoi groupé consolidated shipment

envoi par la poste *[publipostage]* mailing (n)

envoler: s'envoler *[monter rapidement]* rise (v) fast

envoyer *[expédier]* send (v) *or* ship (v)

envoyer par avion send by air; airmail (v) *[post]*

envoyer par fax *ou* **par télécopie** fax (v)

envoyer par la poste send (v) by post *or* mail (v) *or* post (v)

envoyeur (-euse) sender (n)

épargne (f) *[économie]* saving (n)

épargne (f) *[sommes]* savings (n)

épargner save (v) (money) *or* put (v) (money) aside

épuisé(e) (adj) *[article]* out of stock

équilibrer balance (v)

équilibrer un budget balance (v) a budget

équipe (f) shift (n) *or* team (n)

équipe de jour day shift (n)

équipe de nuit night shift

équipe de vente *[les commerciaux]* sales team *or* sales force

équipe dirigeante management team

équipement (m) equipment (n)

équiper equip (v)

équiper *[outiller]* tool up (v) *[a factory]*

équitable *[raisonnable]* fair (adj)

erreur (f) error (n) *or* mistake (n)

erreur (f) *[écart]* discrepancy (n)

erreur aléatoire random error

erreur de calcul miscalculation (n)

erreur d'ordinateur computer error

erreur: faire une erreur make (v) a mistake

erreur: faire une erreur de calcul miscalculate (v)

escomptable discountable (adj)

escompte (m) discount (n)

escompte de caisse cash discount

escudo (m) *[unité monétaire au Portugal]* escudo (n)

espace (m) publicitaire advertising space (n)

espèces (fpl): en espèces (in) cash

espérance (f) de vie life expectancy (n)

espionnage (m) industriel industrial espionage (n)

esquisse (f) (d'un plan) draft (n)

esquisser *[ébaucher]* draft (v)

essai (m) trial (n) *or* test (n)

essai (m) *[machine, voiture]* test run (n)

essai: (acheter) à l'essai (buy) on approval *or* on appro

essai: (prendre quelqu'un) à l'essai (take someone) on probation

essayer try (v) *or* test (v)

essayer *[une voiture]* test drive (a car)

essence (f) petrol (n)

essentiel (-elle) essential (adj) *or* basic (adj)

esthétique (f) industrielle industrial design (n)

estimatif (-ive) estimated (adj)

estimation (f) estimate (n)

estimation approximative rough estimate *or* (rough) guess (n)

estimation des ventes estimated sales

estimation prudente conservative estimate

estimé(e) (adj) estimated (adj)

estimer *[calculer]* estimate (v) *or* calculate (v)

estimer *[évaluer]* estimate (v) *or* assess (v) *or* value (v)

estimer *[juger]* estimate (v) *or* judge (v)

établi(e) established (adj) *or* fixed (adj)

établi(e) depuis longtemps *[société]* old-established (adj) (company)

établir *[fonder]* establish (v)

établir les comptes make up (v) the accounts

établir un chèque, une facture write out a cheque, an invoice

établir un devis (pour un travail) estimate (v) for a job

établir un nouveau record set (v) a new record

établissement (m) setting up (n)

établissement (m) *[bâtiment]* building (n) *or* premises (n)

établissement d'un plan *ou* **d'un programme** scheduling (n)

étage (m) floor (n)

étagère (f) shelf (n)

étalage (m) *[en vitrine]* window display (n)

étalage (m) *[présentation]* display (n)

étalage (m) *[présentoir]* display stand (n)

étaler *[échelonner]* stagger (v)

état (m) *[condition]* state (n) *or* condition (n)

état (m) *[division d'un pays]* state (n)

état (m) *[document]* statement (n)

Etat (m) *[gouvernement]* government (n) *or* State (n)

état (m) *[situation]* situation (n) *or* state of affairs

état civil (civil) status (n)

état: en parfait état de marche in full working order

étendre: s'étendre de ... à ... range (v) from ... to ...

étiquetage (m) labelling (n)

étiqueter label (v)

étiquette (f) label (n) *or* tag (n)

étiquette-adresse (f) address label

étiquette de prix price tag *or* price label

étranger (-ère) (n) foreigner (n)

étranger (-ère) (adj) foreign (adj)

étranger: à l'étranger overseas

être be (v)

étude (f) *[conception]* design (n)

étude (f) *[recherche]* study (n) *or* research (n); analysis (n)

étude de marché market research

étude des temps et des mouvements time and motion study

étude du rapport coût-bénéfice cost-benefit analysis

études (fpl) *[universitaires, etc.]* studies (n)

étudier study (v) *or* research (v); analyze (v)

étudier le potentiel du marché analyse the market potential

eurochèque (m) Eurocheque (n)

eurodevise (f) Eurocurrency (n)

eurodollar (m) Eurodollar (n)

Euromarché (m) Euromarket (n)

européen (-éenne) European (adj)

évaluation (f) evaluation (n) *or* estimate (n)

évaluation (f) *[expertise]* valuation (n)

évaluation des dommages assessment (n) of damages

évaluation du rendement performance rating (n)

évaluer *[biens, coût]* evaluate (v) *or* estimate (v)

évaluer *[expertiser]* value (v)

évaluer les dommages assess (v) damages

évasion (f) fiscale tax avoidance

éventail (m) range (n)

éventualité (f) contingency (n)

éviter avoid (v)

ex-dividende ex dividend

exact(e) correct (adj)

exact(e) *[précis]* exact (adj) *or* accurate (adj)

examen (m) examination (n) *or* test (n)

examen (m) *[contrôle]* examination (n) *or* inspection (n)

examiner examine (v); consider (v)

excédent (m) excess (n) *or* surplus (n)

excédent de bagages excess baggage

excédentaire *[balance commerciale]* favourable (adj) (balance of trade)

excédents (mpl) de stock overstocks (n)

excédents (mpl) de personnel overmanning (n)

excéder exceed (v)

excellent(e) excellent (adj) *or* A1

excepté except (for)

exception: à l'exception de excluding

exceptionnel (-elle) *[inattendu]* exceptional (adj)

exceptionnel (-elle) *[très grand]* exceptional (adj) *or* outstanding (adj)

exclure exclude (v)

exclusif (-ive) exclusive (adj) *or* sole (adj)

exclusion (f) exclusion (n)

exclusivité (f) exclusivity (n)

excuse (f) apology (n)

excuser: s'excuser apologize (v)

exécuter implement (v) *or* fulfil(l) (v)

exécuter une commande fulfil an order

exécutif (-ive) executive (adj)

exécution (f) implementation (n) *or* fulfilment (n)

exécution de commandes order fulfilment

exemplaire (m) copy (n)

exemplaire: en deux exemplaires in duplicate

exemplaire: en trois exemplaires in triplicate

exempt(e) exempt (from)

exempt(e) de droit *ou* de taxe duty-free (adj)

exempt(e) d'impôt tax-exempt (adj) *or* tax-free (adj)

exempter exempt (v)

exemption (f) exemption (n)

exemption (f) d'impôt tax exemption

exercer exercise (v)

exercice (m) exercise (n)

exercice (m) social *[financier]* accounting year *or* financial year

exonération (f) d'impôt tax exemption *or* exemption from tax

exonéré(e) d'impôt exempt (adj) from tax *or* tax-exempt (adj)

exonérer *[exempter]* exempt (v) (from)

exorbitant(e) *[inabordable]* prohibitive (adj)

expédier *[des marchandises]* dispatch (v) *or* send (v) *or* ship (v)

expédier par avion airfreight (v) *[goods]*

expédier (un colis) par avion *[poste]* send (a package) by airmail

expédier par conteneurs containerize (v) *or* ship (v) in containers

expédier par courrier ordinaire send (v) by surface mail

expédier par exprès express (v)

expédier par la poste mail (v) *or* post (v) *or* send (v) by post

expédier par mer *ou* par bateau send (v) by sea

expéditeur (-trice) *[de lettre, colis]* sender (n)

expéditeur *[de marchandises]* shipper (n) *or* consignor (n)

expédition (f) *[acheminement]* shipping (n) *or* forwarding (n)

expédition (f) *[envoi]* consignment (n) *or* shipment (n)

expédition en vrac bulk shipment

expéditionnaire (m) shipping clerk (n)

expérience (f) experience (n)

expérimenté(e) experienced (adj)

expert (m) *[consultant]* expert (n); consultant (n)

expert (m) *[en bâtiments]* surveyor (n)

expert (m) *[en évaluation]* valuer (n)

expert-comptable (m) chartered accountant

expert en problèmes de gestion troubleshooter (n)

expertise (f) *[de bijoux, etc.]* valuation (n)

expertise (f) *[de dégâts, de bâtiment]* survey (n)

expertiser *[des bijoux, etc.]* value (v)

expertiser *[des dégâts, un bâtiment]* survey (v)

expiration (f) expiration (n); expiry (n) (date)

expirer *[n'être plus valable]* lapse (v)

expirer *[venir à expiration]* expire (v)

explication (f) explanation (n)

expliquer explain (v)

exploitation (f) *[entreprise]* enterprise (n)

exploitation agricole farm (n)

exploiter *[mettre en valeur]* exploit (v)

exploiter *[profiter de]* capitalize on (v)

export (m) *[exportation]* export (n)

exportateur (-trice) *[qui exporte]* exporting (adj)

exportateur (-trice) exporter (n)

exportation (f) export (n)

exportations (fpl) *[marchandises exportées]* exports (n)

exporter export (v)

exposant(e) exhibitor (n)

exposer *[à un salon]* exhibit (v)

exposer *[des faits]* set out (v) *or* describe (v)

exposition (f) *[salon]* exhibition (n)

exprès (-esse) *[explicite]* express (adj)

exprès: (envoyer) par exprès (send) by express delivery

express (adj) *[rapide]* express (adj) (letter, delivery)

exprimer express (v) *[state]*

expropriation (f) compulsory purchase (n)

extérieur(e) external (adj)

extérieur(e) à l'entreprise out-house (adj)

externe external (adj)

extra (adj) *[qualité]* high (adj) *or* top (adj) *or* premium (adj)

extraordinaire extraordinary (adj)

Ff

---

fabricant (m) *[constructeur]* manufacturer (n) *or* maker (n)

fabrication (f) production (n) *or* manufacture (n)

fabrication en série mass production

fabrique (f) *[usine]* factory (n)

fabriquer produce (v) *or* manufacture (v)

fabriquer en série mass-produce (v)

facile easy (adj)

facilité (f) facility (n)

facilités (fpl) de crédit credit facilities

facilités (fpl) de paiement easy terms

facteur (m) factor (n)

facteur de coût cost factor

facteur décisif deciding factor

facteur négatif minus factor *or* downside factor

facteurs cycliques cyclical factors

facteurs de production factors of production

factor (m) *[société, personne]* factor (n)

factoring (m) *[affacturage]* factoring (n)

facturation (f) invoicing (n) *or* billing (n)

facture (f) invoice (n) *or* bill (n)

facture avec TVA VAT invoice

facture d'avoir credit note

facture détaillée itemized invoice *or* detailed invoice

facture pro forma pro forma (invoice)

facturer invoice (v) *or* bill (v) *or* charge (v)

facultatif (-ive) optional (adj)

failli(e) (n) bankrupt (n)

failli(e) (adj) bankrupt (adj)

failli concordataire certificated bankrupt

failli non réhabilité undischarged bankrupt (n)

faillite (f) bankruptcy (n) *or* failure (n)

faillite: causer une faillite bankrupt (v)

faillite: faire faillite fail (v) *or* go bust (v) *or* crash (v)

faire exécuter *ou* **faire observer** enforce

faire face aux dépenses meet (expenses)

faisabilité (f) feasibility

fait(e) sur mesure *ou* **sur commande** custom-built *or* custom-made (adj)

falloir *[nécessiter]* need (v) *or* take (v)

falsification (f) fake (n) *or* forgery (n) *or* falsification (n)

falsifier fake (v) *or* forge (v) *or* falsify (v)

falsifier les comptes falsify the accounts

faute (f) *[blâme]* fault (n)

faute (f) *[erreur]* fault *or* mistake (n) *or* error (n)

faute de *[manque de]* for lack of

faute de frappe typing error

faute de quoi failing which

faux (fausse) false (adj) *or* wrong (adj) *or* inaccurate (adj)

faux (fausse) *[falsifié]* counterfeit (adj) *or* faked (adj)

faux (m) fake (n) *or* forgery (n)

faux frais (mpl) incidental expenses (n)

faux poids (m) false weight (n)

faveur: de faveur complimentary (adj) *[ticket, etc.]*

fax (m) *[télécopie]* fax (n)

femme d'affaires businesswoman (n)

ferme *[définitif, soutenu]* firm (adj)

fermé(e) closed (adj) *or* shut (adj)

fermer close (v) *or* shut (v)

fermer *[cacheter]* seal (v) (an envelope)

fermer à clé lock (up) (v)

fermer un compte close an account

fermer un compte en banque close a bank account

fermer un magasin, un bureau *[le soir]* lock up a shop, an office

fermer un magasin, une usine *[pour toujours]* close down a shop, a factory

fermeture (f) closure (n); closing (n) (down)

ferry (m) ferry (n)

fête (f) légale statutory holiday (n)

feu (m) *[incendie]* fire (n)

feuille (f) sheet (n) (of paper)

feuille de paie pay slip (n)

feuillet (m) *[publicitaire]* leaflet (n)

fiabilité (f) reliability (n)

fiable reliable (adj)

fiche (f) *[bordereau]* slip (n)

fiche (f) *[carte de fichier]* index card (n) *or* filing card

fiche (f) *[de contenu]* docket (n)

fiche (f) *[électricité]* plug (n)

fichier (m) card index (n)

fichier d'adresses address list (n) *or* mailing list

fichier (m) (informatique) (computer) file (n)

fidélité (f) à la marque brand loyalty (n)

fidélité de la clientèle customer loyalty

fiducie (f) trust (n)

filiale (f) affiliated company *or* associate company

fin (f) end (n)

fin (f) *[clôture]* close (n) *or* end (n)

fin d'exercice year end

fin de mois month end

final(e) final (adj) *or* last (adj)

finance (f) finance (n)

financement (m) financing (n) *or* funding (n)

financement du déficit budgétaire deficit financing

financer finance (v) *or* fund (v)

financer une opération finance an operation

finances (fpl) finances (n)

financier (-ière) financial (adj)

financièrement financially (adv)

fini(e) ended (adj) *or* finished (adj)

finir end (v) *or* finish (v)

firme (f) *[entreprise]* company (n) *or* firm (n) *or* house (n)

fisc (m) Inland Revenue (n)

fiscal(e) fiscal (adj)

fiscalisé(e) liable to tax *or* taxed (adj)

fiscaliser put (v) a tax on (something)

fixation (f) fixation (n) *or* fixing (n)

fixe *[prix]* fixed (adj) *or* set (adj)

fixé(e) fixed (adj) *or* set (adj)

fixer fix (v) *or* set (v) *or* determine (v)

fixer des objectifs set targets

fixer le prix du lingot fix (v) the bullion price (for gold)

fixer une date fix a date

fixer une réunion à 15h fix a meeting for 3 p.m.

fixing (m) (du cours de l'or) gold fixing (n)

flamber *[augmenter]* rocket (v) *or* go up (v) rapidly

flexibilité (f) flexibility (n)

florin (m) *[unité monétaire en Hollande]* guilder (n)

florissant(e) flourishing (adj) *or* booming (adj)

flottant(e) *[devise]* floating (adj)

flotter *[devise]* float (v)

fluctuation (f) fluctuation (n)

fluctuation (f) *[mouvement]* movement (n)

fluctuer fluctuate (v)

flux (m) flow (n); outflow (n)

flux de trésorerie cash flow

flux: (production, etc.) à flux tendus just-in-time (adj) (production, etc.)

FMI (Fonds Monétaire International) IMF (International Monetary Fund)

foi: de bonne foi in good faith; bona fide

foire (f) commerciale trade fair (n)

fonction (f) function (n)

fonctionnaire (m) civil servant (n)

fonctionnement (m) *[marche]* working (n)

fonctionnement: en fonctionnement in operation *or* operative (adj)

fonctionner *[appareil]* work (v)

fonctionner *[être en service]* run (v) *[buses, trains]*

fonctionner: faire fonctionner operate (v)

fond (m) bottom (n)

fondé (m) de pouvoir person with power of attorney; proxy (n)

fonds (m) fund (n)

fonds (mpl) funds (n) *or* money (n)

fonds de commerce business (n); goodwill (n)

fonds de prévoyance contingency fund (n)

Fonds Monétaire International (FMI) International Monetary Fund (IMF)

fonds bloqués *[actif gelé]* frozen assets

fonds de roulement working capital (n)

fonds de secours emergency reserves

fonds publics public funds

force (f) de vente sales force (n)

force (f) majeure force majeure (n)

forcé(e) forced (adj)

forfait (m) flat rate (n) *or* fixed rate (n)

formalité (f) formality (n)

formalités douanières customs formalities

formation (f) training (n)

formation dans l'entreprise in-house training

formation dans un centre spécialisé off-the-job training

formation en gestion d'entreprise management training

formation sur le tas *ou* **sur le terrain** on-the-job training

former *[une société]* form (v) *or* set up (v)

former (quelqu'un) train (v) (someone)

formulaire (m) form (n)

formulaire de candidature (à un poste) application form

formulaire de déclaration de sinistre insurance claim form

formulaire de déclaration en douane customs declaration form

formulaire d'inscription registration form

formulation (f) wording (n)

fort(e) strong (adj)

fortune (f) fortune (n) *or* wealth (n)

fortune: faire fortune make a fortune *or* make a lot of money

foule (f) mass (n)

fourchette (f) de prix price range (n)

fournir *[approvisionner]* supply (v) *or* provide (v)

fournir: se fournir (chez) buy at (v) (someone's shop)

fournisseur (m) supplier (n)

fournisseur du gouvernement government contractor (n)

fournitures (fpl) de bureau office stationery (n) *[paper]*

fragile fragile (adj)

frais (mpl) *[prix ou coût]* cost(s) (n) *or* charge(s) (n)

frais (mpl) *[dépense]* expenses (n)

frais administratifs *ou* **frais de gestion** administrative costs *or* charges

frais bancaires *[agios]* bank charges

frais de débarquement landing charges

frais de démarrage *ou* **d'établissement** start-up costs

frais de déplacement travel expenses

frais de distribution *ou* **de diffusion** distribution costs

frais de fabrication manufacturing overheads (n) *or* costs

frais de manutention handling charge

frais d'emballage packing charges

frais d'enlèvement collection charges *or* collection rates

frais d'entrepôt storage (n) (cost)

frais de port et d'emballage postage and packing (p & p)

frais de représentation *ou* **frais professionnels** expenses (n)

frais de transport shipping costs; carriage (n); freight (n)

frais de transport aérien air freight (charges)

frais de transports routiers haulage (n) (costs *or* charges)

frais financiers *[intérêts à payer]* interest charges

frais généraux *ou* **frais d'administration générale** overheads (n) *or* overhead costs *or* oncosts (n)

frais juridiques legal costs *or* legal charges

frais supplémentaires additional charges

franc (m) *[unité monétaire: France, Belgique, Suisse]* franc (n)

franc de port carriage free; post free

franchisage (m) franchising

franchise (f) franchise (n)

franchisé(e) (n) franchisee (n)

franchiser franchise (v)

franchiseur (m) franchiser (n)

franco franco *or* free

franco à bord (FAB) free on board (FOB *or* f.o.b)

franco à quai price ex quay

franco de port *ou* **franc de port** carriage free; post free

franco wagon free on rail

fraude (f) fraud (n)

fraude fiscale tax evasion (n)

frauder le fisc evade (v) tax

frauduleusement fraudulently (adv)

frauduleux (-euse) fraudulent (adj)

free-lance (adj) freelance (adj)

free-lance (mf) freelance (n) *or* freelancer (n)

fréquent(e) frequent (adj)

fret (m) freight (n)

fret aérien air freight

frontière (f) border (n)

fuite (f) de capitaux flight (n) of capital

fusion (f) merger (n)

fusionner merge (v)

futur(e) future (adj)

Gg

gâcher spoil (v) *or* damage (v)

gagner earn (v)

gagner net net (v)

gain (m) gain (n) *or* profit (n)

gain net net profit

gain théorique paper profit

gain: faire un gain make (v) a profit *or* make money

galerie (f) marchande shopping arcade (n) *or* shopping mall (n)

gamme (f) *[variété]* range (n)

gamme de produits product line *or* product range

garant (m) *[avaliste]* guarantor (n) *or* guarantee (n)

garant: se porter garant de quelqu'un go (v) guarantee for someone

garant: se porter garant d'une dette guarantee (v) a debt

garantie (f) guarantee (n) *or* warranty (n)

garantie (f) *[nantissement]* collateral (n) *or* security (n) *or* cover (n)

garantir guarantee (v)

garantir *[une émission d'actions]* underwrite (v)

garde-meuble (m) furniture storage (n)

garder *[détenir]* hold (v) *or* keep (v)

gardien (m) de la sécurité security guard (n)

gare (f) (ferroviaire) (railway) station (n)

gaspillage (m) wastage (n)

gaspiller waste (v)

gauche *[côté]* left (adj)

gel (m) (des prix et des salaires) (price and wage) freeze (n)

gelé(e) frozen (adj)

geler *[bloquer]* freeze (v)

geler les crédits freeze credits

général(e) general (adj)

général(e) *ou* **généralisé(e)** across-the-board

général(e) *[global]* overall (adj) *or* comprehensive (adj)

gentleman's agreement (m)
gentleman's agreement (n)

gérant(e) manager (n), manageress (f)

gérer manage (v) *or* run (v)

gérer une propriété manage a property

gérer: mal gérer mismanage (v)

gestion (f) *[administration]*
administration (n) *or* management (n)

gestion d'entreprise business
management

gestion de portefeuilles portfolio
management

gestion des stocks stock control

gestion du personnel personnel
management

gestion: mauvaise gestion
mismanagement (n)

gestionnaire (mf) administrator (n) *or*
controller (n)

gestionnaire (m) des stocks stock
controller

global(e) global *or* comprehensive (adj)

gold-point (m) gold point (n)

goodwill (m) goodwill (n)

gonflé(e) *[prix]* inflated (adj) (prices)

goulet (m) *ou* **goulot (m)**
d'étranglement bottleneck (n)

gouvernement (m) government (n)

gouvernemental *[du gouvernement]*
government (adj)

gramme (m) (g) gram *or* gramme (n)

grand(-)livre (m) ledger (n)

grand(-)livre des achats bought ledger
or purchase ledger

grand(-)livre des ventes sales ledger

grand(-)livre général general ledger *or*
nominal ledger

grand magasin department store

grande surface (f) hypermarket (n) *or*
superstore (n)

grande taille (f) *[vêtements]* outsize (n
& adj) (OS)

grandissant(e) mounting (adj) *or*
increasing (adj)

graphique (m) diagram (n) *or* graph (n)
or chart (n)

graphique d'évolution flow chart *or*
flow diagram

graphique des ventes sales chart

gratis *[gratuitement]* gratis (adv) *or*
free (adv) (of charge)

gratuit(e) free (adj)

gratuitement free (adv) (of charge) *or*
gratis (adv)

greffier (m) registrar (n)

grève (f) strike (n)

grève de protestation protest strike

grève de solidarité sympathy strike

grève du zèle *ou* **grève perlée** go-slow
(n) *or* work-to-rule (n)

grève générale total strike *or* all-out
strike

grève sauvage wildcat strike

grève sur le tas sit-down strike (n) *or*
sit-down protest (n)

grève: se mettre en grève *ou* **faire (la)**
grève strike (v) *or* go on strike

gréviste (mf) striker (n)

grille (f) grid (n)

grille (f) des salaires wage scale (n) *or*
structure (n)

grimper climb (v)

gros (m) *ou* **en gros** wholesale (m)

grosse (f) *[douze douzaines]* gross (n)
(= 144 items)

grossiste (mf) wholesale dealer (n) *or*
wholesaler (n)

groupage (m) d'envois consolidation
(n)

groupe (m) group (n)

groupe de travail working party (n)

groupe industriel industrial group

groupes socio-économiques
socio-economic groups

grouper batch (v)

grouper *[envoi]* consolidate (v)
[shipments]

grouper *[sur une liste]* bracket (v)
together

guerre (f) des prix price war *or*
price-cutting war (n)

guilde (f) guild (n)

Hh

hall (m) (d'exposition) (exhibition) hall (n)

harmonisation (f) harmonization (f)

harmoniser harmonize (v)

hausse (f) *[augmentation]* increase (n)

haussier (m) *[spéculateur à la hausse]* bull (n)

haut(e) high (adj)

haut de gamme up-market (adj)

hautement qualifié highly qualified

hauteur (f) height (n)

hauteur: à hauteur de up to

hebdomadaire (adj) weekly (adj)

hectare (m) hectare (n)

heure (f) hour (n); time (n)

heure de fermeture closing time

heure d'enregistrement *[à l'aéroport]* check-in time (n)

heure d'ouverture opening time

heure/homme (f) *ou* **heure travaillée** man-hour (n)

heure: (de) l'heure per hour

heure: de bonne heure early (adv)

heures (fpl) de bureau office hours *or* business hours

heures de pointe peak period (n) *or* rush hour

heures d'ouverture business hours *or* opening hours

heures d'ouverture des banques banking hours

heures supplémentaires *[de travail]* overtime (n)

holding (m) holding company

homme (m) *[ouvrier]* man (n)

homme d'affaires businessman (n)

homologuer *[authentifier]* authenticate (v)

honnête *[correct]* fair (adj)

honnête *[fiable ou sûr]* reliable (adj)

honoraire (adj) honorary (adj)

honoraires (mpl) *[pour services]* fee (n); honorarium (n)

honorer sa signature honour (v) one's signature

honorer une traite honour (v) a bill

horaire (m) *[indicateur]* timetable (n) *[train, etc.]*

horaire (adj) hourly (adv) *or* by the hour; per hour

hors taxe *[taxe non comprise]* exclusive of tax

hors taxe *[exempt de taxe]* duty-free (adj); tax-free (adj)

hôtel (m) hotel (n)

hôtel classé graded hotel

hôtel des ventes (aux enchères) saleroom (n) *or* auction room

hôtelier (-ière) hotelier (n)

hôtellerie (f) hotel trade (n)

hyperinflation (f) hyperinflation (n)

hypermarché (m) hypermarket (n) *or* superstore (n)

hypothèque (f) *ou* **prêt (m) hypothécaire** mortgage (n)

hypothéquer mortgage (v)

Ii

illégal(e) illegal (adj) *or* unlawful (adj); against the law

illégalement illegally (adv)

illégalité (f) illegality (n)

illicite illicit (adj)

image (f) (d'une société) (corporate) image (n)

image de marque *[réputation]* public image

imitation (f) imitation (n)

immatriculer une société register (v) a company

immédiat(e) immediate (adj)

immédiatement immediately (adv)

immobilier (-ière) immovable (adj)

immobilisations (fpl) *[actif immobilisé]* fixed assets (n)

immobilisations corporelles fixed tangible assets

immobilisations incorporelles fixed intangible assets

immobiliser des capitaux lock up (v) capitals

impair(e) odd (adj) *[not even]*

impasse (f) deadlock (n)

impayé(e) outstanding (adj) *or* unpaid (adj)

imparfait(e) imperfect (adj)

imperfection (f) imperfection (n)

implanter *[une industrie]* establish (v) *or* set up (v)

implanter: s'implanter sur un marché penetrate (v) a market

importance (f) importance (n)

important(e) important (adj) *or* major (adj)

important(e) *[massif ou lourd]* important *or* heavy (adj)

importateur (-trice) (n) importer (n)

importateur (-trice) (adj) importing (adj)

importation (f) *[action]* importation (n) *or* importing (n)

importation: (article) d'importation imported (adj) (article)

importations (fpl) imports (n) *or* imported goods

importations visibles visible imports

importer import (v)

importer *[avoir de l'importance]* matter (v) *or* be important

import-export (mf) import-export (n & adj)

imposable *[taxable]* taxable (adj)

imposé(e) taxed (adj)

imposer *[prescrire]* impose (v)

imposer *[taxer]* tax (v)

imposition (f) taxation (n)

imposition directe direct taxation

imposition indirecte indirect taxation

impôt (m) tax (n); taxation (n)

impôt direct direct tax

impôt indirect indirect tax

impôt progressif graded tax *or* graduated income tax

impôt retenu à la source tax deducted at source

impôt sur le chiffre d'affaires turnover tax

impôt sur le revenu income tax

impôt sur les bénéfices des sociétés corporation tax

impôt sur les gains exceptionnels excess profits tax

impôt sur les grosses fortunes wealth tax

impôt sur les plus-values capital gains tax

imprévu (m) *[éventualité]* contingency (n)

imprimante (f) (d'ordinateur) (computer) printer (n)

imprimante à marguerite daisy-wheel printer

imprimante laser laser printer

imprimante ligne à ligne line printer

imprimante matricielle dot-matrix printer

imprimé (m) printed matter (n)

imprimé (m) *[copie sur papier]* hard copy (n)

imprimé(e) (adj) printed (adj)

imprimer print (out) (v)

imprimeur (m) printer (n)

imputable chargeable (adj)

imputation (f) charging (n) *or* charge (n)

imputer charge (v) *[to an account]*

inabordable *[exorbitant]* prohibitive (adj) *or* exorbitant (adj) (price)

incendie (m) fire (n)

inchangé(e) unchanged (adj)

incidence (f) repercussion (n) *or* effect (n)

incitation (f) incentive (n)

inclure include (v) *or* count (v)

inclus(e) *[compris]* inclusive (adj)

inclusivement inclusive (adv)

incompétent(e) incompetent (adj)

inconditionnel (-elle) *[sans réserve]* unconditional (adj)

incorporé(e) *[intégré]* built-in (adj)

incorporel (-elle) intangible (adj)

incorporer *[intégrer]* incorporate (v) *or* build in (v)

incorrect(e) incorrect (adj)

incorrectement incorrectly (adv)

inculpation (f) *[accusation]* charge (n)

inculper *[accuser]* charge (v)

indemnisation (f) *[dédommagement]* compensation (n) *or* indemnity (n)

indemniser *[dédommager]* indemnify (v) *or* compensate (v)

indemniser quelqu'un d'une perte indemnify someone for a loss

indemnité (f) *[allocation]* benefit (n)

indemnité (f) *[dédommagement]* indemnity (n) *or* compensation (n)

indemnité (de déplacement, de vie chère) (travel, cost-of-living) allowance (n)

indépendant(e) independent (adj)

indépendant(e) *[qui travaille à son compte]* self-employed (adj); independent (adj)

index (m) index (n)

indexation (f) indexation (n)

indexé(e) (sur l'indice du coût de la vie) index-linked (adj)

indexer index (v)

indicateur (m) *[horaire]* timetable (n) *[trains, etc.]*

indicateurs (mpl) économiques economic indicators (n)

indicatif (m) (téléphonique) (dialling) code (n)

indicatif de zone *[telephone]* area code

indicatif du pays *[telephone]* country code

indicatif international *[telephone]* international access code

indice (m) *[des prix, etc.]* index (n)

indice de croissance growth index

indice de la production industrielle manufacturing output index

indice des prix à la consommation retail price index (RPI)

indice des prix à la production producer price index (PPI)

indice du coût de la vie cost-of-living index

indice pondéré weighted index

indiquer *[spécifier]* specify (v)

indirect(e) indirect (adj)

indispensable necessary (adj) *or* essential (adj)

indisponibilité (f) unavailability (n)

industrialisation (f) industrialization (n)

industrialiser industrialize (v)

industrie (f) industry (n)

industrie à fort coefficient de capital capital-intensive industry

industrie clé key industry

industrie de base basic *or* primary industry

industrie de croissance growth industry

industrie de services service industry *or* tertiary industry

industrie de transformation manufacturing industry *or* secondary industry

industrie légère light industry

industrie lourde heavy industry

industrie nationalisée nationalized industry

industriel (-elle) (adj) industrial (adj)

industriel (m) industrialist (n)

inefficacité (f) inefficiency (n)

inexact(e) inaccurate (adj) *or* wrong (adj)

inférieur(e) à under; less than

inflation (f) inflation (n)

inflation par la demande demand-led inflation

inflation par les coûts cost-push inflation

inflationniste inflationary (adj)

influence (f) influence (n)

influencer influence (v)

informaticien (-ienne) *[programmeur]* computer programmer (n)

informaticien (-ienne)-analyste systems analyst (n)

information (f) information (n)

information en retour feedback (n)

informatique (f) information technology (n)

informatique (f) *[traitement de données]* data processing (n)

informatisé(e) computerized (adj)

informatiser computerize (v)

informer *[aviser, renseigner]* inform (v)

informer *[donner des explications]* brief (v)

infrastructure (f) infrastructure (n)

ingénieur (m) engineer (n)

ingénieur conseil consulting engineer

ingénieur de chantier site engineer

ingénieur de production *ou* **ingénieur-produit** product engineer

ingénieur de projet project engineer

initial(e) (adj) initial (adj) *or* opening (adj)

initiale (f) *[lettre]* initial (n)

initialer *[signer de ses initiales]* initial (v)

initiation (f) induction (n)

initiative (f) initiative (n)

injonction (f) writ (n)

injuste unfair (adj)

innovateur (-trice) (adj) innovative (adj)

innovateur (m) innovator (n)

innovation (f) innovation (n)

innover innovate (v)

inonder (le marché) flood (v) (the market)

inscrire *[noter]* enter (v)

inscrire *[immatriculer ou enregistrer]* register (v) *[in official list]*

inscrire à l'ordre du jour put (v) on the agenda

inscrire une propriété au cadastre register a property

inscrire: s'inscrire register (v)

inscrire: s'inscrire à l'arrivée (à l'hôtel) check in (v) (at the hotel)

insérer une annonce put (v) an ad (in the paper)

insolvabilité (f) insolvency (n)

insolvable insolvent (adj)

inspecter inspect (v)

inspecteur (-trice) inspector (n)

inspecteur de la TVA VAT inspector

inspecteur des impôts tax inspector

inspecteur du travail factory inspector

inspection (f) inspection (n)

Inspection du travail factory inspectorate (n)

installations (fpl) *[bâtiments, etc.]* facilities (n)

installations portuaires harbour facilities

instantané(e) instant (adj) *or* immediate (adj)]

instituer *[commencer]* institute (v)

institut (m) institute (n)

institution (f) institution (n)

institution (f) financière financial institution

institutionnel (-elle) institutional (adj)

instruction (f) instruction (n)

instructions pour la livraison delivery instructions

instructions relatives à l'expédition shipping *or* forwarding instructions

instrument (m) *[document]* instrument (n) *or* document (n)

instrument (m) *[outil]* implement (n) *or* device (n)

intégration (f) horizontale horizontal integration (n)

intégration (f) verticale vertical integration

intégré(e) *[incorporé]* built-in (adj)

intégrer *[incorporer]* incorporate (v) *or* build in (v)

intenter un procès à *ou* **contre** take (v) legal action against *or* sue (v) (someone)

interdiction (f) ban (n)

interdiction d'importer import ban

interdire ban (v) *or* forbid (v)

intéressant(e) interesting (adj)

intéressement (m) *[aux bénéfices]* profit-sharing (scheme)

intéresser (quelqu'un) interest (v)

intérêt (m) *[considération]* interest (n)

intérêt (m) *[droit acquis]* vested interest

intérêt (m) *[d'un capital, d'une dette]* interest (n)

intérêt(s) composé(s) compound interest

intérêt couru *[d'un placement]* accrued interest

intérêt élevé high interest

intérêt fixe fixed interest

intérêt(s) simple(s) simple interest

interface (f) interface (n)

intérieur(e) inland

intérieur(e) *[national]* internal (adj) *or* domestic (adj)

intérim (m) *[travail temporaire]* temporary work (n)

intérim: assurer l'intérim de quelqu'un deputize (v) for someone

intérim: faire de l'intérim temp (v)

intérim: (président) par intérim acting (adj) (president)

intérimaire *[dividende, etc.]* interim (adj) (dividend, etc.)

intérimaire *[remplaçant]* acting (adj) (manager, etc)

intérimaire *[temporaire]* temporary (adj)

intermédiaire (mf) middleman (n) *or* intermediary (n)

international(e) international (adj)

interne internal (adj)

interprète (mf) interpreter (n)

interpréter *ou* **servir d'interprète** interpret (v)

interrompre *[suspendre]* suspend (v)

interruption (f) *[arrêt]* stop (n) *or* suspension (n)

intervenir intervene (v)

intervenir comme médiateur mediate (v)

intervention (f) intervention (n)

interviewé(e) interviewee (n)

interviewer (m) interviewer (n)

interviewer interview (v)

introduction (f) introduction (n)

invalidation (f) invalidation (n)

invalider invalidate (v)

invalidité (f) invalidity (n)

invendable unsellable (adj)

invendus (mpl) unsold items

inventaire (m) inventory (n) *or* stocklist (n)

inventaire (m) (des stocks) *[action]* stocktaking (n)

inventaire de position picking list (n)

inventaire: faire l'inventaire *[stocks]* take (v) stock

inventaire: faire l'inventaire *[maison]* inventory (v) the contents of a house

inventaire: nous faisons l'inventaire we are stocktaking

inventorier *[faire l'inventaire]* inventory (v)

inverse reverse (adj)

inverser reverse (v)

investi(e) invested (adj)

investir invest (v)

investissement (m) *[placement]* investment (n)

investissement à intérêt fixe fixed-interest investment

investissement à l'étranger foreign investment

investissement: faire un investissement invest (v)

investisseur (m) investor (n)

investisseurs institutionnels institutional investors

invitation (f) invitation (n)

inviter (quelqu'un à) invite (v) (someone to)

irrégularité (f) irregularity (n)

irrégulier (-ière) irregular (adj)

irrévocable irrevocable (adj)

isolé(e) *[unique]* one-off (adj)

itinéraire (m) itinerary (n)

Jj

jargon (m) administratif officialese (n)

jauge (f) *[d'un navire]* tonnage (n)

jauge brute gross tonnage

jeter throw away (v) *or* discard (v)

jeter: à jeter après usage disposable (adj)

jeu (m) *[ensemble]* set (n)

joindre *[relier]* attach (v) *or* join (v)

joindre *[contacter]* contact (v) *or* join (v)

joint-venture (f) joint venture (n)

jouissance (f) à vie *[usufruit]* life interest (n)

jour (m) day (n) *[24 hours]*

jour (m) *[journée de travail]* day *or* working day

jour de congé day off

jour de règlement trimestriel quarter day

jour férié bank holiday (n) *or* public holiday (n)

jour: à jour up to date

jour: par jour per day *or* daily (adv)

jour: tous les jours every day *or* daily (adv)

journal (m) newspaper (n)

journal (m) *[comptabilité]* journal (n)

journal (m) de l'entreprise house journal *or* house magazine (n)

journal des ventes sales book (n)

journal professionnel *[revue]* trade journal

journalier (-ière) *[quotidien]* daily (adj)

journaliste (mf) journalist (n) *or* correspondent (n)

journée (f) *[de travail]* day (n) *or* working day (n)

juge (m) *[arbitre]* adjudicator (n)

juge (m) *[magistrat]* judge (n)

jugement (m) *[de la cour]* judg(e)ment (n) *or* ruling (n)

jugement déclaratif de faillite adjudication (n) of bankruptcy

juger judge (v)

juridiction (f) jurisdiction (n)

juridique legal (adj) *or* referring to law

jusqu'à *ou* **jusqu'à concurrence de** up to

juste *[correct, exact]* right (adj); accurate (adj)

justificatif (m) *[preuve écrite]* documentary proof (n)

justificatif (m) comptable voucher (n) *[document from an auditor]*

justifier warrant (v) *or* justify (v); account for (v)

Kk

kg (= kilogramme)

km (= kilomètre)

kilogramme (m) *ou* **kilo (m)** kilo (n) *or* kilogram (n)

kilomètre (m) kilometre (n)

Ll

label (m) *[étiquette]* label (n)

label de qualité quality label

laisser entrer (quelqu'un) *[admettre]* admit (v) *or* let in (v)

laisser flotter une devise float (v) a currency

laisser-passer *ou* **laissez-passer (m)** pass (n)

lancement (m) *[sur le marché]* launch (n) *or* launching (n)

lancement d'une société en Bourse floating (n) *or* flotation (n) of a company

lancer *[produit]* bring out (v) *or* launch (v)

lancer à grand renfort de publicité hype (v) *[product]*

lancer une société (en Bourse) float (v) a company

lancer: se lancer dans les affaires go (v) into business

langage (m) (de programmation) programming language (n)

leasing (m) *[crédit-bail]* lease (n) *[with option to purchase]*

lecteur (m) de disques *ou* **de disquettes** disk drive (n)

légal(e) *[juridique]* legal (adj) *or* referring to law

légal(e) *[légitime]* rightful (adj)

légal(e) *[licite]* legal *or* lawful (adj) *or* according to law

législation (f) legislation (n)

légitime rightful (adj)

lettre (f) letter (n)

lettre commerciale business letter

lettre d'accompagnement covering note *or* covering letter

lettre d'affaires business letter

lettre d'embauche letter of appointment

lettre d'intention letter of intent

lettre de candidature (à un poste) letter of application

lettre de change *[money]* bill (n) of exchange (n) *or* draft (n)

lettre de crédit letter of credit

lettre de rappel reminder (n)

lettre de réclamation letter of complaint

lettre de recommendation letter of reference

lettre de relance follow-up letter

lettre de voiture waybill (n)

lettre personnelle private letter

lettre recommandée registered letter

lettre standard *ou* **lettre type** standard letter

levée (f) *[du courrier]* collection (n)

levée (f) d'une option exercise (n) of an option

lever *[supprimer]* lift (v) *or* remove (v)

lever *[percevoir]* levy (v)

lever la séance wind up (v) *or* close (v) a meeting

lever une option exercise (v) *or* take up (v) an option

liasse (f) pile (n) *or* batch (n) *[of orders, notes]*

libeller un chèque *[faire un chèque]* write out (v) a cheque

libérer free (v)

libérer decontrol (v)

libre free (adj) *[no restrictions]*

libre *[personne]* free (adj) *or* not busy

libre *[siège, table, etc.)* vacant (adj) *or* inoccupied (adj)

libre-échange (m) free trade (n)

libre-service (m) self-service (n) (store)

libre-service (m) de demi-gros cash and carry (n)

licence (f) licence (n) *or* permit (n); license (n) *[US]*

licence (f) d'exportation export licence *or* export permit

licence (f) d'importation import licence *or* import permit

licencié(e) pour raisons économiques (be) made redundant *or* (be) laid off

licencié(e): être licencié *[mis à la porte]* get (v) the sack

licenciement (m) sacking (n) *or* dismissal (n)

licenciement (m) *[économique]* redundancy (n) *or* lay-off (n)

licenciement abusif *ou* **injuste** unfair dismissal

licencier *[congédier]* sack (v) *or* dismiss (v) *or* fire (v)

licencier *[pour raisons économiques]* make (v) redundant *or* lay off (v)

licite legal (adj) *or* lawful (adj)

lié(e) par contrat bound (adj) by contract

lien (m) *[relation]* connection (n)

lier *[relier]* connect (v)

lieu (m) place (n)

lieu (m) de réunion meeting place *or* venue (n)

lieu (m) de travail place of work *or* workplace (n)

ligne (f) line (n)

ligne de conduite guideline (n)

ligne de produits *[gamme]* product line

ligne téléphonique telephone line

ligne (téléphonique) extérieure outside line

ligne: en ligne *[informatique]* on line *or* online

ligne: en ligne *[au téléphone]* on the phone

ligne: restez en ligne *[téléphone]* hold the line

limitation (f) limitation (n) *or* restriction (n)

limitation à la liberté du commerce restraint (n) of trade

limitation de temps time limitation; time limit (n)

limitations (fpl) des importations import restrictions

limite (f) limit (n)

limite d'âge age limit

limite de crédit *[plafond]* credit limit

limite de découvert overdraft limit

limité(e) limited (adj)

limiter limit (v) *or* restrict (v)

limiter le crédit restrict credit

lingot (m) *[d'or ou d'argent]* ingot (n)

lingot: (or *ou* **argent) en lingots** bullion (n)

liquidateur (m) liquidator (n)

liquidation (f) d'un société *[ordre]* liquidation (n) *or* winding up (n)

liquidation du stock *[avant fermeture]* closing-down sale

liquidation forcée *[d'une société]* compulsory liquidation *or* winding up order

liquidation (f) volontaire voluntary liquidation

liquider *[dette]* settle (v)

liquider *[écouler]* sell off (v)

liquider *[entreprise]* liquidate (v) *or* wind up (v) *[company]*

liquider du stock liquidate (v) *or* sell off (v) stock

liquidité (f) liquidity

liquidités (fpl) *[disponibilités]* liquid assets (n)

lire (f) *[unité monétaire en Italie]* lira (n)

liste (f) list (n)

liste de colisage packing list *or* packing slip (n)

liste de sélection (de candidats) shortlist (n)

liste noire *[mauvais payeurs, etc.]* black list

liste rouge: être sur la liste rouge be ex-directory *[telephone]*

liste: faire une liste list (v)

listing (m) *[sortie d'imprimante]* computer listing (n) *or* printout (n)

litre (m) litre (n)

livraison (f) *[envoi, marchandises]* delivery (n)

livraison contre remboursement cash on delivery (c.o.d.)

livraison de marchandises delivery of goods

livraison exprès express delivery

livraison gratuite free delivery

livre (m) *[de comptabilité]* account book *or* ledger (n)

livre (f) *[poids: 0.45 kg]* pound (n)

livre (m) *[publication]* book (n)

livre (f) *[unité monétaire en Irlande]* (Irish) punt (n)

livre de caisse petty cash book

livre-journal (m) *[comptabilité]* daybook (n)

livre sterling *[unité monétaire au Royaume Uni]* pound (n) (sterling)

livrer deliver (v)

livret (m) *[de banque]* bank book (n)

livret (m) *[manuel]* manual (n); booklet (n)

livreur (m) deliveryman (n)

local (m) à usage de bureau office space (n)

local(e) local (adj)

locataire (mf) (à bail) tenant (n) *or* lessee (n)

locataire occupant les lieux sitting tenant

locataire principal(e) *[sous-location]* sublessor (n)

location (f) *[immobilière]* letting (n)

location (f) *[logement]* rented accommodation (n)

location (f) *[de voiture, machine]* hire (n)

logiciel (m) *[informatique]* (computer) program (n) *or* software (n)

logo (m) logo (n)

loi (f) law (n)

loi de l'offre et de la demande law of supply and demand

loi de prescription statute (n) of limitations

loi des rendements décroissants law of diminishing returns

long (longue) long (adj)

long parcours (m) *[vol]* long-distance (flight)

longue portée long range

long: à long terme long-term (adj)

lot (m) (d'un produit) lot (n) *or* batch (n) (of product)

louer *[donner en location]* lease (v) *or* rent out (v) *or* let (out) (v) *or* hire out (v)

louer *[prendre en location]* lease (v) *or* rent (v) *or* hire (v)

louer du matériel en crédit-bail lease (v) equipment

louer un bureau *[donner à bail]* let an office (to someone)

louer une voiture hire a car

lourd(e) *[important]* heavy (adj) *or* important (adj)

lourd(e) *[poids]* heavy (adj)

loyer (m) rent (n) *or* rental (n)

loyer élevé high rent

loyer non rentable uneconomic rent

loyer symbolique nominal rent

loyer: sans payer de loyer rent-free

lucratif (-ive) *[qui rapporte]* paying (adj) *or* profitable (adj)

lucratif: (organisation) sans but lucratif non profit-making (organization)

luxe: de luxe luxury (adj) (item)

Mm

machine (f) *[appareil]* machine (n)

machine à affranchir franking machine

machines (fpl) plant (n) *or* machinery (n)

macro-économie (f) macro-economics (n)

magasin (m) shop (n) *or* store (n)

magasin (m) *[entrepôt]* store (n); stockroom (n)

magasin à succursales multiples multiple store *or* chain store

magasin d'usine factory outlet (n)

magasin de demi-gros cash and carry (n)

magasin de détail retail shop *or* retail outlet (n)

magasin de discount discount store *or* discounter (n)

magasin du coin corner shop

magasin: grand magasin department store (n)

magasinier (m) *[entrepôt]* warehouseman (n)

magazine (m) *[périodique]* magazine (n)

magistrat (m) judge (n)

mailing (m) (direct) mailing (n)

main-d'oeuvre (f) *[personnel]* workforce (n) *or* labour (force) (n)

main-d'oeuvre (f) *[travail]* labour (n)

main-d'oeuvre bon marché cheap labour

main-d'oeuvre locale local labour

maintenance (f) *[entretien]* maintenance (n)

maintenance (f) *[vérification]* service (n)

maintenir *[garder, entretenir]* keep up (v) *or* maintain (v)

maintenir: se maintenir *[prix, etc.]* be firm *or* hold up (v)

maintien (m) maintenance (n)

maison (f) *[familiale]* house (n); (family) home (n)

maison (f) *[firme, entreprise]* house *or* company (n) *or* firm (n)

maison d'édition publishing house

maison d'exportation export house

maison mère parent company

maîtrise (f) *[contrôle]* control (n)

maîtriser *[contrôler]* control (v)

majeur(e) *[important]* major (adj)

majoration (f) (de prix) mark-up (n)

majorer (le prix d'un article) mark up (v) (an article)

majorité (f) majority (n)

malentendu (m) misunderstanding (n)

malgré in spite of *or* regardless of

management (m) *[gestion]* management (n)

mandat (m) *[argent]* money order (n)

mandat (m) *[pouvoir, autorité]* mandate (n)

mandat de paiement bank mandate

mandat international foreign money order

mandat postal *ou* **mandat-poste (m)** money order *or* postal order

manifeste (m) manifest (n)

mannequin (m) *[personne]* model (n)

manoeuvre (m) *[travailleur manuel]* manual worker (n)

manque (m) *[pénurie]* shortage (n)

manque (m) *[déficit]* shortfall (n)

manque de fonds lack (n) of funds

manquer *[un train ou un avion]* miss (v) (a train, a plane)

manquer de *[être à court de]* lack (v) *or* be short of; run out of (v)

manquer son but miss one's target

manuel (m) *[livret]* manual (n)

manuel d'entretien service manual

manuel d'utilisation operating manual

manuel (-elle) manual (adj)

manufacturer *[fabriquer]* manufacture (v); make (v)

manuscrit(e) *[écrit à la main]* handwritten (adj)

manutention (f) handling (n)

manutention du matériel materials handling

maquette (f) dummy (n) *or* mock-up (n)

maquette (f) *[modèle réduit]* model (n)

marasme (m) *[crise économique]* slump (n) *or* depression (n)

marchand(e) *[négociant]* merchant (n) *or* dealer (n)

marchandage (m) bargaining (n)

marchander haggle (v) *or* bargain (v)

marchandisage (m) merchandizing (n)

marchandise(s) (f) merchandise (n) *or* goods (n)

marchandises à prix sacrifiés cut-price goods

marchandises dédouanées duty-paid goods

marchandises de première qualité high-quality goods

marchandises en transit goods in transit

marchandises exportées exports (n)

marchandises vendues en catastrophe distress merchandise

marchandiseur (m) merchandizer (n)

marche (f) *[fonctionnement]* running (n)

marche: en (bon) état de marche *[machine]* in working order

marche: mettre en marche *[machine]* start (v) *or* put (v) into operation

marché (m) market (n) *or* marketplace (n)

marché (m) *[affaire ou accord]* deal (n) *or* bargain (n)

marché (m) *[Bourse]* stock market

marché (m) *[place]* market (n)

marché à la baisse buyer's market

marché à la baisse *[Bourse]* bear market

marché à la hausse seller's market

marché à la hausse *[Bourse]* bull market

marché à terme forward market; futures market

marché captif captive market

marché ciblé target market

Marché Commun Common Market

marché des changes foreign exchange market

marché des matières premières commodity market

marché d'exclusivité closed market

marché étranger overseas market

marché faible weak market

marché gris grey market

marché hors cote *[Bourse]* over-the-counter market

marché intérieur domestic market *or* home market

marché libre open market

marché mondial world market

marché monétaire money market

marché noir black market

marché potentiel potential market

marché restreint limited market

Marché unique *[UE]* Single European Market

marge (f) margin (n) *or* mark-up (n)

marge bénéficiaire profit margin

marge brute gross margin

marge brute d'auto-financement (MBA) cash flow

marge d'erreur margin of error

marge nette net margin

marginal(e) marginal (adj)

marine (f) marchande merchant navy (n)

maritime maritime (adj) *or* marine (adj)

mark (m) *[unité monétaire en Allemagne]* mark (n) *[Deutschmark]*

marketing (m) marketing (n)

marque (f) brand (n)

marque *ou* nom (m) de marque brand name

marque de fabrique *ou* de commerce trademark (n) *or* trade name

marque déposée registered trademark

marquer mark (v)

marqueur (m) *[surligneur]* marker pen (n)

masse (f) monétaire money supply (n)

matériel (m) *[équipement]* equipment (n)

matériel de bureau office equipment

matériel lourd heavy equipment *or* heavy machinery

matériel publicitaire publicity matter (n) *or* display material

matières (fpl) premières raw materials (n)

maturité (f) économique mature economy (n)

mauvais(e) bad (adj)

mauvais achat bad buy (n)

mauvais payeur slow payer (n)

mauvaise gestion mismanagement (n)

maximal(e) *[maximum]* maximum (adj)

maximalisation (f) maximization (n)

maximaliser *ou* maximiser maximize (v)

maximum (m) maximum (n)

maximum *ou* maximal(e) maximum (adj)

MBA (marge brute d'auto-financement) cash flow (n)

médiane (f) median (n)

médias (mpl) mass media (n)

médiateur (-trice) (n) mediator (n); ombudsman (n)

médiation (f) *[arbitrage]* arbitration (n)

médiation (f) *[intervention]* mediation (n)

médiocre *[de qualité inférieure]* low-quality (adj)

meilleur(e) *[supérieur]* better (adj) *or* superior (adj)

meilleur(e): le meilleur, la meilleure the best

membre (m) member (n)

mémoire (f) *[informatique]* memory (n) *or* storage (n)

mémorandum (m) memorandum (n) *or* memo (n)

mener *[diriger]* direct (v) *or* conduct (v)

mener des négociations conduct negotiations

mensualité (f) *[paiement mensuel]* monthly payment

mensuel (-elle) monthly (adj)

mensuellement *[chaque mois]* monthly (adv)

menues dépenses (fpl) petty expenses

mérite (m) merit (n)

mériter merit (v) *or* earn (v)

message (m) message (n)

mesure (f) *[dimension]* measure (n) *or* measurement (n)

mesure (f) *[disposition]* measure (n)

mesure de rendement measurement of profitability

mesure de sécurité safety measure *or* safety precaution

mesure de surface square measure

mesure de volume cubic measure

mesure fiscale fiscal measure

mesure: fait(e) sur mesure(s) made (adj) to measure

méthode (f) method (n) *or* procedure (n)

méthode comptable accounting procedure

méthode des coûts marginaux marginal pricing (n)

mètre (n) (carré, cube) (square, cubic) metre (n)

mettre put (v)

mettre en caisse(s) crate (v)

mettre en conteneurs containerize (v) *or* put into containers

mettre une annonce advertise (v)

mettre à jour *[réviser]* update (v)

mettre à la banque bank (v)

mettre à la poste post (v) *or* mail (v)

mettre à pied *[licencier]* lay off (v) (workers)

mettre au point finalize (v)

mettre au point *[développer]* develop (v)

mettre en pratique implement (v)

mettre en vente sell (v) *or* offer (v) (for sale)

mettre fin à *[terminer]* end (v)

mettre fin graduellement phase out (v)

mettre les ressources en commun pool (v) resources

mettre par écrit *[rédiger]* put in writing

mettre son veto (à une décision) veto (v) (a decision)

mettre sous séquestre sequester (v) *or* sequestrate (v)

mettre sur fiches card-index (v)

mettre sur la liste noire blacklist (v)

mettre sur palettes palletize (v)

mettre sur pied organize (v) *or* set up (v)

meubles (mpl) de bureaux office furniture (n)

mi-temps: à mi-temps part-time (adj & adv)

micro-économie (f) micro-economics (n)

micro-ordinateur (m) microcomputer (n)

mieux (adv) better (adv)

mieux: le mieux best

milliard (m) billion (bn) (n)

millier (m) thousand (n)

million (m) million (M) (n)

millionnaire (mf) millionaire (n)

minimal(e) *[minimum]* minimum (adj)

minimum (m) minimum (n)

minimum *ou* **minimal(e)** minimum (adj)

ministère (m) *[du gouvernement]* ministry (n) *or* department (n)

Ministère de l'Economie et du Budget Ministry of Finance; the Treasury *[GB]*

Ministère des affaires étrangères Foreign Office *[GB]*

ministre (mf) (government) minister (n)

ministre (mf) *[d'un ministère important]* secretary (n)

minorité (f) minority (n)

minute (f) *[temps]* minute (n)

mise (f) *[offre]* bid (n) *or* offer (n) (to buy)

mise à jour update (n)

mise à prix *[enchères]* opening price (n); upset price

mise de fonds outlay (n)

mise en chantier house start (n); housing start *[US]*

mise en conteneurs containerization (n)

mise en vigueur *[application]* enforcement (n)

mise initiale *[versement]* initial investment (n)

mise sous séquestre sequestration (n)

mise sur fiches card-indexing (n)

mission (f) commerciale trade mission (n)

mixte mixed (adj)

mixte *[conjoint]* joint (adj)

mobilier (-ière) moveable (adj)

mobiliser mobilize (v)

mobiliser des capitaux mobilize capital

mobilité (f) mobility (n)

modalités (fpl) de paiement modes (n) of payment *or* terms (n)

mode (m) mode (n)

mode (m) d'emploi directions (n) for use

modèle (m) model (n); design (n)

modèle de démonstration demonstration model

modèle déposé registered design

modèle économique economic model

modèle réduit *[maquette]* (scale) model (n)

modem (m) modem (n)

modéré(e) moderate (adj)

modérer *[limiter]* moderate (v)

moderne up to date (adj) *or* modern (adj)

modeste *[peu important]* small-scale

modification (f) *[amendement]* amendment (n) *or* alteration (n) *or* change (n)

modifier amend (v) *or* alter (v) *or* change (v)

moindre *[inférieur]* lower (adj)

moins minus *or* less

moins de less than

moins élevé(e) lower than (adj)

moins-value (f) depreciation (n) *or* capital loss (n)

mois (m) month (n)

mois civil *ou* **mois complet** calendar month

mois: le mois dernier last month

mois: par mois per month *or* monthly (adv)

moitié (f) half (n)

monde (m) world (n)

mondial(e) worldwide (adj)

monétaire monetary (adj)

monnaie (f) *[devise]* currency (n)

monnaie (f) *[pièces]* (small) change (n) *or* cash (n)

monnaie convertible convertible currency

monnaie de réserve reserve currency

monnaie faible soft currency

monnaie forte hard currency

monnaie inflationniste inflated currency

monnaie légale *ou* **qui a cours légal** legal tender (n)

monopole (m) monopoly (n)

monopole absolu absolute monopoly

monopolisation (f) monopolization (n)

monopoliser monopolize (v)

montage (m) *[assemblage]* assembly (n)

montant (m) *[somme]* amount (n)

montant total total amount

montant total de la facture total invoice value

montant versé amount paid

monte-charge (m) elevator (n)

monter *[augmenter]* mount up (v)

monter en flèche soar (v) *or* rocket (v) *or* shoot up (v)

monter rapidement escalate (v)

monter une affaire *[s'établir]* set up (v) in business

monter: faire monter les prix force (v) prices up

monter: se monter *[s'élever]* amount to (v) *or* run to (v) *or* total (v)

moratoire (m) moratorium (n)

mort(e) dead (adj)

morte-saison (f) off-season (n)

motivation (f) motivation (n)

motivé(e) motivated (adj)

mouvement (m) movement (n)

mouvement (m) *[changement]* shift (n) *or* change (n)

mouvement (m) *[flux]* flow (n)

mouvements de capitaux movements of capital

mouvements de stocks stock movements

moyen (m) *[façon]* means (n) *or* ways (n)

moyen (légal) d'échapper au fisc tax loophole (n)

moyen de transport transport facility (n)

moyen(s) frauduleux false pretences (n)

moyen (-enne) average (adj) *or* medium (adj)

moyen (-enne) *[taille]* medium-sized (adj)

moyen (-enne): à moyen terme medium-term (adj)

moyenne (f) average (n) *or* mean (n)

moyenne pondérée weighted average

moyenne: en moyenne on an average

moyens (mpl) *[ressources]* means (n)

multilatéral(e) multilateral (adj)

multinationale (f) multinational (n)

multiple multiple (adj)

multiplication (f) multiplication

multiplier multiply

municipalité (f) local government (n)

muter *[transférer]* transfer (v) *or* move to new place

mutuel (-elle) mutual (adj)

mutuelle (f) (d'assurances) mutual (insurance) company

Nn

N° **1 du marché** *[leader]* market leader (n)

nantissement (m) *[garantie]* guarantee (n) *or* collateral (n)

nation (f) nation (n)

nation endettée debtor nation

nation la plus favorisée most-favoured nation

national(e) national (adj); domestic (adj)

national(e) *[à l'échelon national]* nationwide (adj)

nationalisation (f) nationalization (n)

navire (m) ship (n)

navire-citerne *[pétrolier]* tanker (n)

navire marchand *[cargo]* merchant ship

néant (m) *[zéro]* nil

nécessaire necessary (adj)

nécessiter require (v) *or* need (v)

négligeable negligible (adj)

négligence (f) negligence (n)

négligent(e) negligent (adj)

négociable *[chèque]* negotiable (adj)

négociant(e) *[marchand]* dealer (n) *or* merchant (n)

négociateur (-trice) negotiator (n)

négociation (f) negotiation (n)

négociation (f) *[marchandage]* bargaining (n)

négociations salariales wage negotiations

négocier negotiate (v)

net (nette) net (adj)

niveau (m) level (n)

niveau de réapprovisionnement reorder level

niveau des salaires wage level

niveau des stocks stock level

niveau élevé high level

niveau très bas low level *or* low (n)

nocturne (m) late-night opening (n)

nolisage (m) *[affrètement]* charter (n); chartering (n)

noliser *[affréter]* charter (v)

nom (m) name (n)

nom de marque brand name

nom: au nom de on behalf of

nombre (m) number (n)

nombre impair odd number

nombre pair even number

nomination (f) *[à un poste]* appointment (n)

nomination au niveau du personnel staff appointment

nommer *[à un poste]* appoint (v)

non-livraison (f) non-delivery (n)

non-paiement (m) non-payment (n)

non-résident(e) non-resident (n)

non-satisfaction: en cas de non-satisfaction if not satisfied

normal(e) *[habituel]* normal (adj) *or* usual (adj)

normalisation (f) *[standardisation]* standardization (n)

normaliser *[standardiser]* standardize (v)

norme (f) *[standard]* standard (n)

notaire (m) notary public (n); solicitor (n) *[GB]*

notation (f) financière credit rating (n)

note (f) *[d'hôtel, etc.]* bill (n)

note (f) *[message]* note (n) *or* memo (n)

note de crédit credit note

note de débit debit note

note de frais (de représentation) expense account

note financière *[d'une société]* credit rating (n)

noter *[prendre note]* note (v)

noter *[consigner]* record (v) *or* register (v)

notification (f) *[avis]* notification (n)

notifier notify (v)

nouveau (nouvelle) new (adj)

nouveau: de nouveau again

nouveau départ *ou* **nouvelle orientation** new departure (n)

novateur (-trice) pioneer (n)

nuit (f) night (n)

nul (nulle) null (adj); void (adj)

nul et non avenu null and avoid

numérique numeric (adj) *or* numerical (adj)

numéro (m) *[chiffre]* number (n) *or* figure (n)

numéro (m) *[d'une revue]* issue (n)

numéro (m) *[exemplaire d'un journal, etc.]* copy (n)

numéro de boîte postale box number

numéro de chèque cheque number

numéro de commande order number

numéro de compte account number

numéro de facture invoice number

numéro de lot batch number

numéro d'enregistrement registration number

numéro de référence reference number

numéro de série serial number

numéro de stock stock code

numéro de téléphone telephone number *or* phone number

numéro d'immatriculation registration number

numéro vert *ou* **numéro d'appel gratuit** freephone (n); toll free number *[US]*

numéro: faire un numéro (de téléphone) dial (v) (a number)

numéroter *[pages, etc.]* number (v)

Oo

objectif (-ive) objective (adj)

objectif (m) *[but, cible]* objective (n) *or* aim (n) *or* target (n)

objectif de vente sales target

objectifs à long terme long-term objectives

obligataire (mf) debenture holder (n)

obligataire (mf) *[de bons du Trésor]* bondholder (n)

obligation (f) *[bon du Trésor, titre]* bond (n)

obligation (f) *[emprunt d'une société]* debenture (n)

obligation (f) *[engagement]* obligation (n)

obligation au porteur bearer bond

obligation convertible en action(s) convertible bond

obligation d'Etat government bond *or* Treasury bond

obligation non remboursable irredeemable bond

obligation remboursable par anticipation callable bond

obligatoire compulsory (adj)

obsolescence (f) obsolescence (n)

obsolescent(e) obsolescent (adj)

obtenir *[se procurer]* obtain (v) *or* get (v)

occasion (f) *[bonne affaire]* bargain (n)

occasion (f) *[opportunité]* opportunity (n)

occupant (m) occupier (n) *or* occupant (n)

occupation (f) occupancy (n)

occupé(e) *[téléphone]* busy (adj) *or* engaged (adj) *[line]*

occupé(e) *[personne]* busy

occuper occupy (v)

occuper: s'occuper de attend to (v) *or* deal with (v)

octroi (m) grant (n)

octroyer *[accorder]* grant (v)

officiel (-elle) official (adj)

officiel (-elle) *[en bonne et due forme]* formal (adj)

officiellement officially (adv); formally (adv)

officier (m) de l'état civil registrar (n)

officieusement unofficially (adv); off the record

officieux (-euse) unofficial (adj)

offrant: le plus offrant highest bidder (n)

offre (f) offer (n)

offre (f) *[enchères]* bid (n)

offre au comptant cash offer

offre d'ouverture opening bid

offre de lancement *[promotion]* introductory offer

offre exceptionnelle *[promotion]* bargain offer

offre publique d'achat (OPA) takeover bid

offre publique de vente offer for sale

offre spéciale *[promotion]* special offer

offres (fpl) d'emploi appointments vacant *or* vacancies (n)

offrir *[en cadeau]* give (v)

offrir (de) *[proposer]* offer (v) (to)

offshore offshore (adj)

OIT (Organisation internationale du travail) ILO (International Labour Organization)

ombudsman (m) ombudsman (n)

omettre omit (v)

omettre de (faire quelque chose) fail (v) (to do something)

omission (f) omission (n)

onéreux (-euse) costly (adj) *or* expensive (adj) *or* highly-priced (adj)

OPEP (Organisation des pays exportateurs de pétrole) OPEC (Organization of Petroleum Exporting Countries)

opérateur (-trice) (n) *[d'une machine]* operator (n) *or* machinist (n)

opérateur (-trice) de saisie keyboarder (n)

opération (f) *[affaire]* operation (n)

opération *[Bourse]* operation *or* dealing *or* transaction (n)

opération à terme *[Bourse]* forward dealing; futures (n)

opération au comptant cash transaction

opération clés en main turnkey operation

opération (f) de couverture hedging (n)

opération multidevise multicurrency operation

opérationnel (-elle) operational (adj)

opinion (f) publique public opinion (n)

opportunité (f) opportunity (n)

opposer une demande reconventionnelle counter-claim (v)

opposer: s'opposer à (une décision) veto (v) (a decision)

opposition: faire opposition à un chèque stop (v) a cheque

option (f) d'achat option (n) to purchase

option: en option on option *or* optional (adj)

ordinaire *[courant]* ordinary (adj) *or* usual (adj)

ordinaire *[standard]* regular (adj) *or* standard (adj)

ordinateur (m) computer (n)

ordinateur (m) personnel personal computer (PC)

ordonnance (f) order (n)

ordonner *[classer]* order (v) *or* put (v) in order

ordre (m) order (n) *or* instruction (n)

ordre (m) *[classement]* order (n)

ordre alphabétique alphabetical order

ordre chronologique chronological order

ordre d'achat *[commande]* purchase order

ordre de prélèvement automatique standing order (n)

ordre de virement bancaire *[pour un seul paiement]* banker's order (n)

ordre du jour (m) agenda (n)

ordre du jour: à l'ordre du jour on the agenda

ordre: payez à l'ordre de *[sur un chèque]* pay to the order of

order: ou suivant ordre *[sur un chèque]* or order

organigramme (m) organization chart (n)

organisation (f) *[entreprise]* organization (n) *or* setup (n)

organization (f) *[disposition]* organization (n) *or* arrangement (n)

organisation (f) *[institution]* organization (n) *or* institution (n)

organisation hiérarchique *ou* **verticale** line organization

Organisation internationale du travail (OIT) International Labour Organization (ILO)

Organisation des pays exportateurs de pétrole (OPEP) Organization of Petroleum Exporting Countries (OPEC)

organisation et méthodes organization and methods

organiser structure (v)

organiser *[mettre sur pied]* organize (v) *or* arrange (v)

organisme (m) organization (n)

original (m) original (n)

origine (f) origin (n)

osciller *[fluctuer]* fluctuate (v)

outil (m) tool (n) *or* implement (n)

outiller (une usine) *[équiper]* tool up (v)

outre-mer abroad; overseas

ouvert(e) open (adj)

ouvert(e) à toute proposition open to offers

ouverture (f) opening (n)

ouvrier (-ière) worker (n)

ouvrier (-ière) qualifié(e) skilled worker

ouvrier (-ière) spécialisé(e) semi-skilled worker

ouvrier (-ière) payé(e) à l'heure hourly-paid worker

ouvriers (mpl) qualifiés skilled labour

ouvrir open (v)

ouvrir *[fonder, établir]* establish (v) *or* open (v)

ouvrir la séance open a meeting

ouvrir un compte open an account

ouvrir un compte en banque open a bank account

ouvrir une ligne de crédit open a line of credit

Pp

page (f) page (n)

pages jaunes (de l'annuaire des téléphones) yellow pages

paie (f) *[salaire]* pay (n) *or* wage

paiement (m) *[action]* paying (n)

paiement (m) *[règlement]* payment (n) *or* settlement (n)

paiement à la commande cash with order

paiement à la livraison cash on delivery (c.o.d.)

paiement annuel yearly payment

paiement au rendement *[salaire]* payment by results

paiement (au) comptant *ou* **en espèces** cash payment

paiement avec (une) carte de crédit payment by credit card

paiement d'avance payment in advance *or* prepayment (n); money up front (n)

paiement différé deferred payment

paiement en nature payment in kind

paiement intérimaire *[acompte]* interim payment

paiement libératoire final discharge

paiement mensuel monthly payment

paiement par chèque payment by cheque

paiement semestriel half-yearly payment

paiement symbolique token payment

paiements (mpl) échelonnés staged payments

pair: au pair at par

palette (f) pallet

palettiser palettize (v)

panel (m) de consommateurs consumer panel (n)

panne (f) *[défaillance]* failure (n) *or* breakdown (n)

panne: être en panne break down (v)

panneau (m) panel (n)

panneau d'affichage *ou* **panneau publicitaire** advertisement hoarding (n) *or* display board (n)

paperasserie (f) paperwork (n)

paperasserie administrative red tape (n)

papier (m) paper (n)

papier à lettres note paper (n)

papier cadeau (gift) wrapping paper

papier carbone carbon paper

papier d'emballage wrapping paper

papier en continu *ou* **papier listing** continuous stationery (n)

papier kraft brown paper

papier recyclé recycled paper

paquet (m) *[bloc]* block (n) *[of shares]*

paquet (m) *[colis]* parcel (n)

paquet (m) *[emballage commercial]* pack (n) *or* packet (n)

paquet (m) *[liasse]* batch (n)

paquet d'enveloppes pack of envelopes

paquet de cigarettes packet of cigarettes

paradis (m) fiscal tax haven (n)

paraître *[sembler]* appear (v) *or* seem (v)

parapher *[signer de ses initiales]* initial (v)

parcours (m) route (n)

parfait(e) perfect (adj) *or* A1

parité (f) parity (n)

parrainage (m) *[sponsorisation]* sponsorship (n)

parrainer *[sponsoriser]* sponsor (v)

part (f) *[partie]* share (n) *or* part (n)

part (f) *[valeur mobilière]* share (n)

part du marché market share

partage (m) de temps time-sharing (n)

partage (m) d'un poste (de travail) job-sharing (n) *or* work-sharing (n)

partager *[diviser]* share (v) *or* divide (v) among

partager *[en commun]* share (v) *or* use (v) with someone

partager un bureau share an office

partenaire (m) commercial trading partner n

participation (f) *[contribution]* participation (n); charge (n)

participation (f) *[intérêt financier]* (financial) interest (n) *or* shareholding (n)

participation des employés aux résultats profit-sharing (n)

participation (f) symbolique token charge (n)

partie (f) *[part]* part (n)

partie (f) *[juridique]* party (n)

partie contractante contracting party

partie plaignante plaintiff (n); prosecution (n)

partir leave (v) *or* go away (v)

partir à la retraite retire (v) (from one's job)

partout dans le monde everywhere (adv); worldwide (adv)

passavant (m) *[douane]* carnet (n)

passer à switch over to (v)

passer par profits et pertes write off (v)

passer une commande place (v) an order

passer une écriture post (v) an entry

passible de liable to (adj) *or* subject to (adj)

passif (m) *[dettes]* liabilities (n)

passif exigible current liabilities

patron (m) boss (n)

pause-café (f) coffee break (n)

pavé (m) numérique numeric keypad (n)

pavillon (m) d'exposition *[hall]* exhibition hall (n)

payable payable (adj)

payable à l'avance payable in advance

payable à la livraison payable on delivery

payable à soixante jours payable at sixty days

payable à présentation *ou* **à vue** payable on demand

payé(e) *[réglé]* paid (adj)

payé(e) *[travail]* paid *[work]*

payé(e) d'avance paid in advance *or* prepaid (adj)

payer *[une facture, une note]* pay (v) *or* settle (v) (a bill)

payer *[un employé]* pay (v) (a worker)

payer avec une carte de crédit pay by credit card

payer comptant pay cash

payer d'avance prepay (v) *or* pay in advance

payer des dommages-intérêts *[indemniser]* settle (v) a claim

payer les intérêts d'une dette service (v) a debt

payer par chèque pay by cheque

payer par versements échelonnés pay in instalments

payer: à payer *[impayé]* outstanding (adj)

payer: faire payer charge (v)

payer: faire payer trop cher overcharge (v)

payeur (m) payer (n)

payeur: mauvais payeur bad payer

pays (m) country (n)

pays d'origine country of origin

pays en développement (PED) developing country

pays exportateurs de pétrole oil-exporting countries

pays industrialisés industrialized countries

pays producteurs de pétrole oil-producing countries

péage (m) toll (n)

pénaliser penalize (v)

pénalité (f) penalty (n)

pénétration (f) du marché market penetration (n)

pénétrer *[entrer]* enter (v) *or* go in (v) *or* go into (v)

pénétrer un marché *[s'implanter]* penetrate (v) a market

pension (f) de retraite (retirement) pension (n)

pénurie (f) shortage (n)

pénurie (f) de main-d'oeuvre manpower shortage

PEPS (premier entré, premier sorti) FIFO (first in first out)

PER (coefficient de capitalisation des résultats) P/E ratio (price/earnings ratio)

percepteur (m) tax collector (n) *or* collector of tax

perception (f) des impôts tax collection

percevoir collect (v)

perdre lose (v)

perdre de l'argent lose money

perdre des arrhes forfeit (v) a deposit

perdre par confiscation forfeit (v)

perdre une commande lose an order

performance (f) performance (n)

performance (f) *[efficacité]* efficiency (n)

périmé(e) *[passport, etc.]* no longer valid *or* out of date

période (f) *[durée]* period (n)

période d'essai *[employé]* probationary period *or* probation (n)

période d'exercice d'une fonction tenure (n)

période d'expansion boom (n)

périodique (adj) periodic *or* periodical (adj)

périodique (m) *[revue]* periodical (n) *or* review (n) *or* magazine (n)

périphériques (mpl) (d'ordinateur) peripherals (n)

périssable perishable (adj)

permanence (f) téléphonique answering service (n)

permettre allow (v) *or* permit (v)

permis (m) *[autorisation]* permit (n) *or* licence (n); license (n) *[US]*

permis d'exportation export licence *or* export permit

permis de séjour *[carte de séjour]* residence permit

permis de travail work permit

permission (f) *[autorisation]* permission (n) *or* authorization (n)

personnalisé(e) personalized (adj)

personne (f) person (n); individual (n)

personne désignée nominee (n)

personne: par personne per person *or* per capita *or* per head

personnel (m) staff (n) *or* personnel (n)

personnel (m) *[main-d'oeuvre]* workforce (n)

personnel clé key personnel *or* key staff

personnel de base *ou* personnel réduit skeleton staff

personnel de bureau office staff *or* clerical staff

personnel de direction managerial staff; management (n)

personnel d'encadrement managerial staff

personnel de vente *[commerciaux]* sales team *or* sales force *or* sales staff

personnel de vente très motivé highly motivated sales staff

personnel hôtelier hotel staff

personnel régulier regular staff

personnel temporaire temporary staff

personnel (-elle) *[privé]* personal (adj)

perspectives (fpl) prospects (n)

perte (f) loss (n)

perte de valeur *[diminution]* decrease in value

perte d'exploitation trading loss

perte d'une commande loss of an order

perte nette net loss

perte sèche dead loss *or* write-off (n)

perte théorique paper loss

pertes (fpl) *[gaspillage]* wastage (n)

peser weigh (n)

peseta (f) *[unité monétaire en Espagne]* peseta (n)

petit(e) small (adj)

petit actionnaire minor shareholder (n)

petite caisse (f) petty (adj) cash

petite entreprise small-scale enterprise

petite monnaie small change

petites annonces classified ads *or* small ads

petites dépenses petty expenses

petites et moyennes entreprises (PME) small (and medium-sized) businesses

pétrole (m) oil (n)

pétrolier (m) *[navire-citerne]* tanker (n)

peu not (very) much (adv)

peu actif (-ive) *[marché]* slack (adj)

peu à peu little by little

peu important(e) unimportant (adj)

peu important(e) *[de bas niveau]* low-level (adj)

peu important(e) *[de taille modeste]* small-scale (adj)

phase (f) stage (n)

photocopie (f) photocopy (n)

photocopier photocopy (v)

photocopieur (m) *ou* **photocopieuse (f)** photocopier (n) *or* copier (n) *or* copying machine (n)

PIB (produit intérieur brut) GDP (gross domestic product)

pièce (f) *[morceau]* piece (n)

pièce (f) *[salle]* room (n)

pièce de monnaie coin (n)

pièce détachée *ou* **pièce de rechange** spare part (n)

pièces et main d'oeuvre (PMO) labour and spare parts

pièce jointe (p.j.) *[in letter]* enclosure (n) (encl. *or* enc.)

place (f) *[espace]* room (n)

place (f) *[rang]* place (n)

place du marché marketplace (n)

placement (m) (financier) investment (n)

placement de père de famille blue-chip investment

placement sûr safe *or* risk-free investment

placer place (v)

plafond (m) *[limite]* ceiling (n) *or* limit (n)

plafond de crédit credit limit *or* lending limit

plafond des prix price ceiling

plaindre: se plaindre (de) complain (v) (about)

plainte (f) complaint (n)

plan (m) *[dessin]* plan (n) *or* draft (n)

plan (m) *[projet]* plan (n) *or* project (n) *or* scheme (n)

plan d'ensemble *[d'un immeuble]* floor plan

plan d'occupation des sols (POS) zoning regulations (n)

plan d'urgence contingency plan

plan (m) social *ou* **de développement de la société** corporate plan

plancher (m) floor (n)

planificateur (m) planner (n)

planification (f) planning (n)

planification à long terme long-term planning

planification dans l'entreprise corporate planning

planification de la main-d'oeuvre manpower planning

planification économique economic planning

planifier *[projeter]* plan (v)

plateforme (f) de chargement loading ramp (n)

plein(e) full (adj)

pli (m) envelope (n)

pli: sous pli séparé under separate cover

plomb (m) de la douane customs seal (n)

plus more; plus

plus âgé; plus important senior (adj)

plus-value (f) capital gains (n)

plus-value de change exchange premium (n)

PME (petites et moyennes entreprises) small (and medium-sized) businesses

PNB (produit national brut) GNP (gross national product)

poche (f) pocket (n)

pochette (f) (en papier, en plastique) (paper, plastic) bag (n)

poids (m) weight (n)

poids brut gross weight

poids inexact [faux poids] false weight

poids lourd [camion] heavy goods vehicle (HGV)

poids maximum weight limit or maximum weight

poids net net weight

point (m) point (n)

point (m) [question] matter (n) or business (n) [to discuss]

point de départ starting point

point de vente outlet (n); point of sale (POS)

point de vente électronique electronic point of sale (EPOS)

point de référence benchmark (n)

pointe: de pointe up to date (adj); latest (adj)

police (f) d'assurance insurance policy (n)

police d'assurance-vie assurance policy (n)

politique (f) policy (n)

politique (de fixation) des prix pricing policy

politique budgétaire budgetary policy

politique en matière de crédit credit policy

politique générale (de l'entreprise) code of practice (n)

polycopier duplicate (v)

pondération (f) [indemnité de résidence] weighting (n)

pont (m) bridge (n)

pont (m) [de navire] deck (n)

pontée (f) deck cargo

populaire popular (adj)

port (m) [de mer] port (n) or harbour (n)

port (m) [d'ordinateur] port (n)

port (m) [transport] carriage (n)

port d'attache (d'un navire) port of registry

port d'embarquement port of embarkation

port d'escale port of call

port dû ou en port dû carriage forward or freight forward

port en lourd [charge d'un navire] deadweight cargo

port franc free port

port payé [poste] postage paid or postpaid (adj)

port payé ou en port payé [transport] carriage paid

port pour porte-conteneurs container terminal (n)

portable ou portatif (-ive) portable (adj)

porte (f) door (n)

porte-à-porte (m) [démarchage] canvassing (n) or door-to-door selling

porte-à-porte: faire du porte-à-porte canvass (v)

porte-conteneurs (m) container ship (n)

porte-documents (m) briefcase (n)

porte-documents personnalisé personalized briefcase

portefeuille (f) (d'actions) portfolio (n) (of shares)

porter intérêt bear (v) interest

porter plainte complain (v)

porter une signature bear (v) a signature

porteur (m) bearer (n)

poser sa candidature à un poste apply (v) for a job

poser sa candidature une deuxième fois reapply (v)

positif (-ive) positive (adj)

position (f) position (n) or state of affairs (n)

position (f) [rang] rank (n)

position de force [négociations] bargaining power (n)

position d'un compte (bancaire) bank balance (n)

position financière financial position

posséder possess (v) or own (v) or hold (v)

possibilité (f) possibility (n)

possible possible (adj)

possible *[potentiel]* potential (adj)

possible: aussitôt que *ou* **dès que possible** as soon as possible (asap)

postal(e) postal (adj)

postdater postdate (v)

poste (f) *[service postal]* post (n) *or* postal system (n)

poste (f) *ou* **bureau (m) de poste** post office (n)

poste aérienne airmail (n)

poste centrale general post office

poste restante poste restante

poste: mettre à la poste post (v) *or* put (v) in the post *or* mail (v)

poste (m) *[comptabilité]* item (n) *or* entry (n)

poste (m) *[emploi]* position (n) *or* job (n)

poste (m) *[téléphonique]* extension (n)

poste clé key post

poste d'amarrage *[d'un navire]* berth (n)

poste de travail *[ordinateur]* workstation (n)

poste exceptionnel *[comptabilité]* extraordinary *or* non-recurring item

poste frontière customs entry point (n)

poste vacant *ou* **poste à pourvoir** vacancy (n)

poster post (v) *or* put (v) in the post *or* mail (v)

pot-de-vin (m) backhander (n) *or* bribe (n)

potentiel (m) potential (n)

potentiel (-elle) (adj) potential (adj)

pourboire (m) tip (n) *[money]*

pour cent (%) per cent (%)

pourcentage (m) percentage (n)

pourcentage de remise percentage discount

poursuite (f) *[continuation]* continuation (n)

poursuite(s) (judiciaire(s)) prosecution (n) *or* action (n)

poursuite en dommages-intérêts action for damages

poursuivre *[continuer]* proceed (v) (with)

poursuivre en justice take (v) to court *or* prosecute (v) *or* sue (v)

poursuivre: se poursuivre *[continuer]* continue (v) *or* go on (v) *or* proceed (v)

poussée (f) boost (n)

pousser *[relancer]* boost (v)

pouvoir (m) d'achat purchasing power (n); spending power

pratique *[utile]* handy (adj) *or* convenient (adj)

pratique (f) *[activité]* practice (n)

pratique malhonnête sharp practice

pratiques restrictives restrictive practices

préalable prior (adj) *or* previous (adj)

préavis (m) notice (n) *or* advance notice

préavis (m) *[avertissement]* notice (n) *or* warning (n)

précédent(e) *[antérieur]* former (adj) *or* previous (adj)

précis(e) accurate (adj)

précision (f) precision (f) *or* accuracy (n)

précision (f) *[detail]* detail (n)

précision: avec précision with accuracy *or* accurately (adv)

préemballer prepack (v) *or* prepackage (v)

préférence (f) *[priorité]* preference (n)

préférer prefer (v)

préfinancement (m) pre-financing (n)

prélèvement (m) *[retenue]* deduction (n)

prélèvement automatique *[banque]* direct debit (n)

prélèvement fiscal tax deductions *[from salary]*

premier (-ière) first (adj)

premier entré, premier sorti (PEPS) first in first out (FIFO)

premier trimestre first quarter (n)

première offre *[enchères]* opening bid

première qualité premium quality *or* first quality

prendre take (v)

prendre des dispositions make (v) provision for

prendre des mesures take action

prendre du retard fall (v) behind *or* be late

prendre fin end (v)

prendre fin *[expirer]* expire (v)

prendre la succession de quelqu'un take over from someone else

prendre livraison d'un envoi accept (v) delivery of a shipment

prendre note take note

prendre sa retraite *ou* **partir à la retraite** retire (v) (from one's job)

prendre un appel *[répondre au téléphone]* take a call

prendre un congé take time off work

prendre un risque take a risk

prendre une décision reach (v) *or* come to (v) a decision

préoccupation (f) concern (n) *or* worry (n)

préposé(e) (n) à la réception reception clerk (n); receptionist (n)

préposé(e) à la vente des billets booking clerk

préposé(e)s au(x) comptoir(s) counter staff

près de close to *or* near

présent(e) present (adj)

présentation (f) presentation (n)

présentation (f) *[exposition]* display (n)

présentation *[d'une personne]* introduction (n)

présenter *[donner]* present (v) *or* give (v)

présenter *[exposer]* display (v)

présenter *[une personne à une autre]* introduce (v)

présenter une traite à l'acceptation present a bill for acceptance

présenter une traite au recouvrement present a bill for payment

présenter: se présenter report (v) *or* go to (v)

présenter: se présenter à l'enregistrement check in (v)

présenter: se présenter à un entretien report (v) for an interview

présentoir (m) display stand (n) *or* display rack (n)

présentoir de produits en vrac dump bin (n)

président(e) *[d'une assemblée]* chairman (n)

président(e) *[d'une société, d'un comité]* chairman (n); president (n)

président-directeur (m) général (PDG) Chairman and Managing Director

presse (f) press (n)

prestation (f) *[Sécurité sociale]* benefit (n)

prestation de service service rendered

prestige (m) prestige (n)

prêt(e) ready (adj)

prêt (m) loan (n)

prêt à court terme short-term loan

prêt à long terme long-term loan

prêt bancaire bank loan

prêt bonifié *ou* **de faveur** soft loan

prêt hypothécaire mortgage (n)

prêt immobilier mortgage (n) *[GB]*

prétendre claim (v) *or* suggest (v)

prêter lend (v) *or* loan (v)

prêter de l'argent advance (v) money *or* lend (v) money

prêteur (m) lender (n) *or* moneylender (n)

prêteur (sur hypothèque) mortgagee (n)

preuve (f) proof (n)

preuve écrite documentary evidence

prévenir *[devancer]* pre-empt (v)

préventif (-ive) preventive (adj)

prévention (f) prevention (n)

prévision (f) *[estimation]* forecasting (n)

prévisions (fpl) forecast (n)

prévisions à long terme long-term forecast

prévisions de trésorerie cash flow forecast

prévisions des besoins en main-d'oeuvre manpower forecasting

prévisions des ventes sales forecast

prévisions du marché market forecast

prévoir forecast (v)

prévoir *[prendre des dispositions]* make provision for *or* provide for

prévu(e) projected (adj) *[sales]*

prime (f) bonus (n)

prime (f) *[cadeau promotionnel]* free gift (n)

prime d'assurance (insurance) premium (n)

prime d'encouragement merit award *or* merit bonus

prime de fin de contrat terminal bonus

prime de rendement productivity bonus

prime de renouvellement *[assurance]* renewal premium

prime de risques risk premium

prime de vie chère cost-of-living bonus

prime d'incitation au travail incentive bonus

principal(e) principal (adj) *or* main (adj) *or* chief (adj)

principe (m) principle (n)

prioritaire *[lettre]* express (letter)

prioritaire *[privilégié]* preferential (adj)

priorité (f) *[préférence]* preference (n)

prise (f) de contrôle takeover (n)

prise de décision decision making (n)

prise de position dans les négociations bargaining position (n)

privatisation (f) privatization (n)

privatiser privatize (v)

privé(e) *ou* **privatif (-ive)** private (adj)

privé(e) *[personnel]* personal (adj)

privé: en privé privately (adv)

privé: en privé *[officieusement]* off the record

privilégié(e) *[prioritaire]* preferential (adj) *or* preferred (adj)

prix (m) *[coût]* price (n) *or* cost (n)

prix (m) *[tarif]* price *or* rate (n)

prix à la portée de tous popular price(s)

prix à quai landed costs *or* price ex quay

prix au comptant cash price

prix avec rabais discount price

prix catalogue list price *or* catalogue price

prix compétitifs keen prices *or* competitive prices

prix convenu agreed price

prix courant *ou* **actuel** current price

prix coûtant cost price

prix de clôture *[Bourse]* closing price

prix de détail retail price

prix de facture invoice value

prix de gros trade price

prix de location rental (n)

prix d'émission (d'une action) offer price

prix départ usine factory price *or* price ex works

prix de revente resale price

prix de revient cost price

prix de revient *[coût de production]* production cost

prix de seuil threshold price

prix de soutien support price

prix de vente selling price

prix de vente conseillé manufacturer's recommended price (MRP)

prix d'intervention intervention price

prix d'origine *ou* **coût (m) historique** historic(al) cost

prix d'ouverture *[Bourse]* opening price

prix du billet fare (n)

prix du marché market price

prix du pétrole oil price

prix du transport freight (n) *or* carriage (n) (cost)

prix entrepôt price ex warehouse

prix exceptionnel bargain price

prix ferme firm price

prix fixe set price *or* fixed price

prix fort full price

prix gonflé(s) inflated price(s)

prix imposé set price

prix imposé: politique des prix imposés resale price maintenance

prix le plus bas lowest price; rock-bottom price

prix livré supply price

prix maximum maximum price

prix minimum fixé *[aux enchères]* reserve price *or* upset price

prix moyen average price

prix net net price; all-in price

prix plafond ceiling price

prix raisonnable fair price

prix réduit cut price

prix sacrifié knockdown price *or* bargain price

prix spot *[Bourse]* spot price

prix stables stable prices

prix tout compris delivered price

prix unitaire *ou* **prix de l'unité** unit price

prix: à prix réduit cut-price (adj)

problème (m) *[difficulté]* problem (n) *or* trouble (n)

problème (m) *[sujet]* matter (n) *or* problem (n)

problème (m) de trésorerie liquidity crisis *or* cash flow problem

procédé (m) process (n)

procédé industriel industrial process

procédure (f) procedure (n)

procédure de sélection selection procedure

procédures juridiques judicial processes

procès (m) court case (n) *or* lawsuit (n) *or* trial (n)

procès-verbal (m) minutes (n) (of meeting)

processus (m) process (n)

procuration (f) *[à la place d'un autre]* proxy (n)

procuration (f) *[mandat]* power of attorney (n)

procuration: par procuration by proxy; per procurationem (per pro *or* pp)

procurer procure (v)

procurer: se procurer obtain (v)

procurer: se procurer des fonds raise (v) money *or* secure (v) funds

procurer: qu'on peut se procurer obtainable (adj) *or* available (adj)

producteur (-trice) producer (n)

productif (-ive) productive (adj)

production (f) production (n) *or* output (n)

production intérieure domestic production

production record peak output

production totale total output

productivité (f) productivity (n)

produire *[fabriquer]* produce (v) *or* make (v)

produire *[présenter ou montrer]* produce (v) (documents)

produire *[rapporter un intérêt, etc.]* carry (v) *or* produce (v) (an interest)

produire en excédent *[surproduire]* overproduce (v)

produire un bénéfice show (v) a profit

produit (m) product (n)

produit (m) *[revenu]* revenue (n)

produit d'appel *[article-réclame]* loss-leader (n)

produit dérivé *[sous-produit]* by-product (n) *or* spinoff (n)

produit des ventes sales revenue

produit fini end product *or* finished product *or* final product

produit grand public mass market product

produit intérieur brut (PIB) gross domestic product (GDP)

produit national brut (PNB) gross national product (GNP)

produit semi-fini semi-finished product

produits (mpl) products (n) *or* goods (n)

produits à marque du distributeur own brand goods *or* own label goods

produits concurrentiels competing *or* competitive products

produits de consommation consumable goods *or* consumables (n)

produits dérivés *[Bourse]* derivatives (n)

produits manufacturés manufactured goods

produits maraîchers produce (n)

professionnel (-elle) professional (n & adj)

professionnel (-elle) *[maladie]* occupational (adj) (disease)

professionnel (-elle) *[revue]* trade magazine (n) *or* trade journal (n)

profil (m) profile (n)

profil de poste job description (n)

profit (m) profit (n) *or* earnings (n)

profit: à profit at a profit

profit: faire un profit make (v) a profit

profit: faire un profit brut gross (v)

profit: faire un profit net net (v)

profiter *[se développer]* thrive (v)

profiter de quelque chose *[tirer avantage de]* take (v) advantage of something

programmation (f) (computer) programming (n)

programme (m) programme (n) *or* scheme (n)

programme (m) *[logiciel]* programme (n) *or* program *or* software (n)

programme de recherche research programme

programme pilote pilot scheme

programmer (un ordinateur) program (v) (a computer)

programmeur (-euse) (computer) programmer (n)

progrès (m) progress (n)

progresser progress (v)

progressif (-ive) *[échelonné]* graduated (adj)

progressif (-ive) *[graduel]* gradual (adj)

projet (m) plan (n) *or* project (n)

projet de loi bill (n) *[in Parliament]*

projet pilote pilot project

prolongation (f) extension (n)

prolonger extend (v)

prolonger une traite renew (v) a bill of exchange

promesse (f) promise (n)

promettre promise (v)

promotion (f) *[avancement]* promotion (n) (to a better job)

promotion (f) *[publicité]* promotion *or* publicity (n)

promotion (f) *[offre spéciale]* special offer (n)

promotion des ventes sales promotion

promotion: en promotion on special offer

promotionnel (-elle) promotional (adj)

promouvoir *[donner de l'avancement]* promote (v)

prompt(e) *[rapide]* prompt (adj)

pronostic (m) forecast (n)

pronostiquer forecast (v)

proportionnel (-elle) proportional (adj)

proportionnel (-elle) (à la valeur) ad valorem

proportionnellement in proportion to

proposer (quelque chose, quelqu'un) propose (v) *or* suggest (v)

proposer *[motion]* move (v) (that)

proposer *[offrir]* offer (v)

proposer de (faire quelque chose) propose to (do something)

proposition (f) proposal (n) *or* suggestion (n)

proposition (f) *[offre]* offer (n)

propriétaire (mf) proprietor (m), proprietress (f); owner (n)

propriétaire (mf) *[d'un logement locatif]* landlord (m), landlady (f)

propriétaire légitime rightful owner (n)

propriété (f) *[droit]* ownership (n)

propriété (f) *[maison, terrain]* property (n); house (n); estate (n)

propriété collective collective ownership

propriété en commun *[copropriété]* joint ownership

propriété privée *[droit]* private ownership

propriété privée *[maison, terrain]* private property

prorata: au prorata pro rata

prospect (m) *[acheteur, client potentiel]* prospective client *or* buyer (n)

prospecter *[faire du démarchage]* canvass (v)

prospection (f) *[démarchage]* canvassing (n)

prospectus (m) prospectus (n) *or* leaflet (n)

prospère flourishing (adj) *or* booming (adj)

prospérer flourish (v)

protection (f) du consommateur consumer protection (n)

protectionniste *[tarif]* protective (adj) *[tariff]*

protéger protect (v); safeguard (v)

protestation (f) protest (n)

protestation: en signe de protestation in protest

protester contre quelque chose protest (v) (against something)

protêt (m) protest (n)

protocole (m) d'accord heads of agreement (n)

protocole financier financial agreement

provenance (f) *[origine]* origin (n)

province (f) *[campagne]* country (n) *[not town]*

province (f) *[division de certains pays]* province (n)

provision (f) *[avance, acompte]* advance (n) *or* deposit (n)

provision (f) *[comptabilité]* reserve (n)

provision (f) *[stock]* supply (n) *or* reserve (n)

provision pour dépréciation allowance (n) for depreciation

provisions (fpl): faire des provisions
stock up (v)

provisoire provisional (adj)

pub (f) *[publicité]* publicity (n); (TV)
commercial (n)

pub: faire de la pub (pour un produit)
promote (v) or advertise (v) or plug (v)

public (publique) public (adj)

**publication (f) assistée par ordinateur
(PAO)** desk-top publishing (DTP)

publicitaire advertising (adj)

publicitaire: les publicitaires (mfpl)
publicity people or advertising staff

publicité (f) publicity (n) or advertising
(n)

publicité (f) *[annonce]* advertisement
(n) or ad (n)

publicité à l'échelon national national
advertising

publicité avec coupon-réponse
coupon ad

publicité de produit product
advertising

publicité directe direct-mail
advertising

publicité excessive *ou* **grosse publicité**
hype (n)

publicité: faire de la publicité
advertise (v)

publier publish (v)

publipostage (m) direct mail or
direct-mail advertising (n)

Qq

quai (m) *[gare]* platform (n)

quai (m) *[port]* quay (n) or wharf (n)

qualifications (fpl) professionnelles
professional qualifications (n)

qualifié(e) qualified (adj) or skilled (adj)

qualifié: non qualifié(e) *[ouvrier]*
unskilled (adj)

qualité (f) quality (n)

qualité courrier *[imprimante]*
near-letter-quality (NLQ)

qualité inférieure poor quality

qualité marchande saleability (n)

qualité supérieure top quality or
premium quality

quantité (f) quantity (n)

quart (m) quarter (n) *[25%]*

quartier (m) (d'une ville) district (n) or
area (n) (of town)

quartier commerçant commercial
district

quartier des affaires business centre

quatrième trimestre fourth quarter (n)

question (f) question (n)

question (f) *[point]* matter (n) or
business *[to be discussed]*

question (f) à l'ordre du jour item (n)
on the agenda

quittance (f) *[reçu]* receipt (n)

quitter *[partir]* leave (v)

quitter *[les lieux]* vacate (v) (the
premises)

quitter l'hôtel *[régler la note au
départ]* check out (v) (of hotel)

quitter: ne quittez pas *[téléphone]*
hold the line, please!

quorum (m) quorum (n)

quorum: atteindre le quorum have
(v) a quorum

quota (m) quota (n)

quota (m) d'importation import quota

quotidien (-ienne) daily (adj)

Rr

rabais (m) *[réduction de prix]* price reduction *or* mark-down

rabais: au rabais at a discount *or* at cut price; reduced (adj)

rabais: faire un rabais reduce (v) *or* knock off (v) (price)

rachat (m) *[prise de contrôle]* takeover (n)

rachat contesté contested takeover

rachat de l'entreprise par ses salariés management buyout (MBO)

rachat avec capitaux garantis par l'actif de la société leveraged buyout (LBO)

racheter buy back (v)

racheter une police d'assurance *[résilier]* surrender (v) a policy

racket (m) racketeering (n)

racketteur (m) racketeer (n)

radier quelque chose d'une liste cross off (v)

raison (f) *[explication]* explanation (n)

raison sociale corporate name

raison: en raison de owing to

rajustement (m) *ou* **réajustement (m)** readjustment (n)

rajuster *ou* **réajuster** readjust (v)

ralentir slow down (v)

ralentissement (m) slowdown (n)

ralentissement (m) *[baisse]* decline (n)

rang (m) place (n) *[in a competition]*

rapide fast (adj) *or* quick (adj)

rapide *[express]* express (adj)

rapide *[prompt]* prompt (adj)

rapidement fast (adv) *or* quickly (adv)

rappel (m) *[avertissement]* reminder (n) *or* chaser (n)

rappel (m) de salaire back pay (n) *or* retroactive pay rise (n)

rappeler *[au telephone]* phone back (v)

rappeler (quelque chose à quelqu'un) remind (v) (someone of something)

rappeler une référence quote (v) a reference number

rapport (m) *[compte-rendu]* report (n)

rapport (m) *[taux ou ratio]* ratio (n)

rapport annuel annual report

rapport confidentiel confidential report

rapport d'avancement du travail progress report

rapport de faisabilité feasibility report

rapport intérimaire interim report

rapport qualité/prix excellent good value (for money)

rapporter *[intérêt ou dividende]* yield (v) *or* earn (v) *or* produce (v) (interest)

rapporter *[produire un bénéfice]* bring in (v) *or* produce (v)

rapporter: qui rapporte money-making (adj)

rapporter brut *[faire un profit brut]* gross (v)

rapprochement (m) *[réconciliation]* reconciliation (n)

rapprochement de comptes reconciliation of accounts

ratage (m) *[échec]* failure (n) *or* flop (n)

rater *[échouer]* fail (v) *or* flop (v)

rater *[but, train]* miss (v) (target, train)

ratification (f) ratification (n)

ratifier ratify (v)

ratio (m) *[rapport, taux]* ratio (n)

ratio d'endettement *[effet de levier]* leverage (n) *or* gearing (n)

rationalisation (f) rationalization (n)

rationaliser rationalize (n)

rayer *[supprimer]* delete (v)

rayon (m) department(n) *[in shop]*

rayon (m) *[comptoir]* counter (n)

rayon (m) *[étagère]* shelf (n)

rayonnage (m) shelving (n) *or* shelves (n)

réaction (f) response (n) *or* reaction (n)

réaction (f) *[information en retour]* feedback (n)

réajustement (m) *ou* **rajustement (m)** readjustment (n)

réajuster *ou* **rajuster** readjust (v)

réalisation (f) d'actif realization (n) of assets

réalisation (f) d'un projet realization of a plan

réaliser un projet ou **un plan** realize (v) a project or a plan

réaliser une propriété ou **des biens** [vendre] realize a property or realize assets

réaménagement (m) (d'un magasin, etc.) refitting (n) (of a shop, etc.)

réaménagement (m) (d'une zone) redevelopment (n)

réaménager (un magasin, etc.) refit (v) (a shop, etc.)

réaménager (une zone) redevelop (v)

réapprovisionnement (m) restocking (n)

réapprovisionner: se réapprovisionner restock (v); reorder (v)

réassurance (f) reinsurance (n)

réassurer reinsure (v)

récépissé (m) de douanes customs receipt (n)

réception (f) reception (n)

réceptionner [prendre livraison] accept (v) delivery (of a shipment)

réceptionniste (mf) receptionist (n) or reception clerk (n)

récession (f) recession (n)

recettes (fpl) receipts (n) or revenue (n)

recettes (fpl) [rentrées] takings (n)

recettes nettes net receipts

recettes publicitaires revenue from advertising

receveur (m) [percepteur] collector (n)

receveur des contributions indirectes Excise officer (n)

recevoir receive (v)

recherche (f) [étude] research (n)

recherche des besoins des consommateurs consumer research

recherche documentaire ou **d'information** data retrieval (n)

Recherche et développement (R et D) Research and Development (R & D)

recherche: faire des recherches research (v) or do some research (on)

récipient (m) [contenant] container (n)

réciprocité (f) reciprocity (n)

réciproque reciprocal (adj)

réclamation (f) [plainte] complaint (n)

réclamation (f) [demande ou revendication] claim (n); demand (n)

réclame (f) [publicité] advertising (n)

réclamer [demander] ask for (something)

réclamer [exiger] demand (v)

réclamer (des dommages-intérêts) claim (v) (for damages)

réclamer un droit claim a right

recommandation (f) [conseil] recommendation (n)

recommandation (f) [référence] reference (n) [report on person]

recommander [conseiller] recommend (v) or suggest (v)

recommander (une lettre) register (v) (a letter)

recommander (un produit, etc.) recommend (v) (a product, etc.)

recommencer [reprendre] resume (v)

réconciliation (f) [rapprochement] reconciliation (n)

reconduire un crédit ou **une dette** roll over (v) credit or a debt

reconfiguration (f) (d'un emprunt) restructuring (n) (of a loan)

reconnaissance (f) recognition (n)

reconnaissance (f) de dette IOU (I owe you)

reconnaître [avouer] admit (v) or confess (v)

reconnaître officiellement un syndicat recognize (v) a union

record (m) [meilleur] record (n)

record (m) [maximum] peak (n)

record : qui bat tous les records record-breaking (adj)

recouvrable [récupérable] recoverable (adj)

recouvrement (m) recovery (n) [getting something back]

recouvrement de créances debt collection

recouvrer recover (v) [get something back]

recouvrer une créance collect (v) a debt

rectification (f) rectification (n)

rectifier [modifier ou corriger] rectify (v) or amend (v)

reçu (m) [quittance] receipt (n)

recul (m) [revers] setback (n)

récupérable *[recouvrable]* recoverable (adj)

récupération (f) recovery (n) *[getting something back]*

récupéré(e) *[sauvé]* salvaged (adj)

récupérer *[recouvrer]* recover (v); get back (v)

récupérer son argent recoup (v) one's losses

recyclage (m) *[d'une personne]* retraining (n)

recyclage (m) *[d'un produit]* recycling (n)

recycler *[un produit]* recycle (v)

recycler: se recycler retrain (v)

R et D **(Recherche et developpement)** R & D (Research and Development)

rédaction (f) d'un acte de cession conveyancing (n)

redevances (fpl) *[d'auteur, etc.]* royalties (n)

rédiger *[chèque, facture, etc.]* write out (v) *or* draw up (v) *or* make out (v)

rédiger *[mettre par écrit]* put in writing

rédiger un contrat draw up (v) a contract

rédiger une facture make out (v) *or* raise (v) an invoice

redistribuer redistribute (v)

redressement (m) *[amélioration]* turnround (n) *[making profitable]*

redressement (m) d'impôt tax adjustments

redresser: se redresser stage (v) a recovery *or* rally (v)

réduction (f) reduction (n) *or* cut (n)

réduction (f) *[action]* reducing (n) *or* cutting (n); lowering (n)

réduction (f) *[remise ou escompte]* discount (n)

réduction de prix *[rabais]* price reduction *or* price cut; mark-down (n)

réduction de salaire salary cut *or* cut in salary

réduction des frais cost-cutting (exercise)

réduction d'impôt tax abatement (n) *or* tax reduction (n)

réduire *[diminuer]* reduce (v) *or* cut (v)

réduire *[éroder]* erode (v)

réduire la valeur *[amortir]* write down (v)

réduire le prix d'un article mark down (v) an article

réduire les dépenses cut down (v) on expenses

réduire suivant un barème scale down (v)

réélection (f) re-election (n)

réélire re-elect (v)

réembaucher *ou* **réemployer** *ou* **réengager** re-employ (v)

réemploi (m) re-employment (n)

réévaluation (f) *[augmentation de la valeur]* revaluation (n)

réévaluation (f) *[nouvelle évaluation]* reassessment (n)

réévaluer *[augmenter la valeur]* revalue (v)

réévaluer *[évaluer de nouveau]* reassess (v)

réexportation (f) re-export (n)

réexporter re-export (v)

référence (f) *[recommandation]* reference (n)

référer: se référer à refer (v) to

refinancement (m) d'un prêt refinancing of a loan

refus (m) refusal (n); rejection (n)

refus de faire des heures supplémentaires overtime ban (n)

refuser refuse (v) *or* turn down (v) *or* reject (v)

refuser d'honorer un accord repudiate (v) an agreement

refuser tout paiement waive (v) a payment

régime (m) plan (n) *or* scheme (n)

régime de retraite pension scheme

régime fiscal tax system

région (f) *[zone]* area (n) *or* region (n)

régional(e) regional (adj)

registre (m) register (n)

registre (m) *[grand livre comptable]* ledger (n)

registre des actionnaires register of shareholders

registre des administrateurs d'une société register of directors

registre du commerce et des sociétés **(RCS)** companies' register

règle (f) rule (n)

réglé(e) *[payé]* paid (adj)

règlement (m) *[d'un compte]* payment (n) *or* settlement (n)

règlement (m) *[montant]* payment (n) *or* remittance (n)

règlement avec (une) carte de crédit payment by credit card

règlement d'une dette discharge (n) *[of debt]*

règlement par chèque payment by cheque

réglementaire *[statutaire]* statutory (adj)

réglementation (f) regulation (n)

réglementé(e) par l'Etat government-regulated (adj)

réglementer regulate (v) *[by law]*

règlements (mpl) rules (n) *or* regulations (n)

régler *[un appareil]* tune (v)

régler *[un débit]* regulate (v)

régler *[payer]* pay (v) *or* settle (v) *or* remit (v)

régler avec (une) carte de crédit pay by credit card

régler la note *ou* **l'addition** pay the bill

régler par chèque pay by cheque *or* remit by cheque

régler un compte settle an account

régler une dette pay up (v) *or* discharge (v) a debt

régler une facture pay *or* settle (v) an invoice

régulier (-ière) *[habituel]* regular (adj)

réimportation (f) reimportation (n)

réimportation (f) *[marchandise]* reimport (n)

réimporter reimport (v)

réinvestir reinvest (v)

réinvestissement (m) reinvestment (n)

rejeter *[refuser]* reject (v)

relance (f) *[de l'économie]* recovery (n)

relancer *[activer une commande]* chase (v) (an order)

relancer l'économie boost (v) the economy

relatif à relating to

relatif à l'organisation *ou* **à la structure** organizational (adj)

relation (f) *[lien]* connection (n)

relation (f) *[personne]* contact (n) *[person]*

relations (fpl) *[rapports]* relations (n)

relations entre employeurs et employés industrial relations

relations publiques public relations (PR)

relevé (m) de compte statement (n) of account

relevé de compte bancaire bank statement

relevé mensuel monthly statement

relevé semestriel half-yearly statement

relever (directement) de quelqu'un report to (v) *or* be responsible to someone

relier join (v) *or* connect (v)

reliquat (m) *[reste]* remainder (n)

remboursable *[avance]* refundable (adj)

remboursable *[obligations]* redeemable (adj)

remboursable *[prêt]* repayable (adj)

remboursement (m) *[d'emprunt, de dette]* repayment (n); redemption (n); payback (n)

remboursement de frais reimbursement *or* refund (n) of expenses

remboursements d'un prêt hypothécaire *[versements]* mortgage (re)payments

rembourser pay back (v) *or* repay (v); refund (v)

rembourser une dette pay off (v) *or* clear (v) *or* redeem (v) a debt

remerciements (mpl) thanks (n)

remettre *[à plus tard]* postpone (v) *or* put back (v) *or* defer (v)

remettre *[donner]* hand in (v); hand over (v)

remettre un chèque à l'encaissement cash (v) a cheque

remettre en état *[réparer]* repair (v)

remise (f) *[escompte]* discount (n) *or* rebate (n) *or* reduction (n)

remise à plus tard postponement (n) *or* deferment (n)

remise commerciale *ou* **professionnelle** trade discount; trade terms

remise de base *ou* **remise habituelle** basic discount

remise de gros wholesale discount

remise sur quantité quantity discount *or* volume discount

remonter *[se redresser]* rally (v)

remplaçant(e) replacement (n) *[person]*

remplacement (m) replacement *[item]*

remplacer replace (v)

remporter un contrat win (v) a contract

rémunérateur(-trice) paid (adj) (work); well paid (adj)

rémunération (f) remuneration (n) *or* pay (n)

rémunération (f) *[honoraires]* fee (n) *[for services]*

rémunéré(e) *[compte, etc.]* interest-bearing (adj) (account, etc.)

rémunéré(e) *[travail]* paid (adj) (work)

rémunérer (un compte) pay (v) interest (on account)

rémunérer (quelqu'un) remunerate (v) *or* pay (v) (someone)

rémunérer (un travail) remunerate *or* pay for (v) (work)

rencontrer *ou* **se rencontrer** meet (v)

rendement (m) *[capacité]* capacity (n) *[production]*

rendement (m) *[intérêt]* yield (n) *or* return (n) *[on investment]*

rendement (m) *[production]* output (n); throughput (n)

rendement (m) *[productivité]* productivity (n)

rendement brut gross yield

rendement effectif effective yield

rendement net net yield

rendez-vous (m) appointment (n); meeting (n)

rendre compte de *[faire rapport]* report on (v)

rendre compte de *[justifier]* account for (v)

rendre compte: se rendre compte de realize (v) *or* understand (v)

renoncement (m) waiver (n) *[of right]*

renoncer à *[abandonner]* abandon (v)

renoncer à *[refuser]* waive (v)

renoncer aux poursuites *ou* **à un procès** abandon (v) an action

renouvelable *[crédit]* revolving credit

renouveler renew (v)

renouveler un abonnement renew a subscription

renouveler un bail renew a lease

renouveler une commande reorder (v) *or* repeat (v) an order

renouvellement (m) renewal (n)

renouvellement d'un bail *ou* **d'un abonnement** renewal of a lease *or* of a subscription

renouvellement de mandat reappointment (n)

rénovation (f) *[magasin, etc.]* refitting (n) *or* renovation (n)

rénover *[magasin, etc.]* refit (v) *or* renovate (v)

renseignement (m) (piece of) information (n)

renseigner *[informer]* inform (v)

renseigner: se renseigner enquire (v) *or* inquire (v)

rentabilité (f) *[profitabilité]* cost-effectiveness (n) *or* profitability (n)

rentabilité (f) *[aspect économique]* economics (n)

rentabilité d'un investissement return on investment (ROI)

rentable cost-effective (adj) *or* economic (adj)

rentable *[productif]* profit-making (adj) *or* productive (adj)

rentrée (f) *[recette]* take (n)

rentrée (f) *[revenu]* revenue (n)

rentrer dans ses frais break even (v)

renvoi (m) *[à plus tard]* postponement (n) *or* deferment (n)

renvoi (m) *[d'un employé]* dismissal (n) *or* sacking (n)

renvoi injustifié wrongful dismissal

renvoyer *[licencier]* dismiss (v) *or* sack (v) (someone)

renvoyer *[retourner]* return (v) *[send back]*

renvoyer une lettre à l'expéditeur return a letter to sender

réorganisation (f) reorganization (n)

réorganiser reorganize (v)

réparation (f) repair (n)

réparer fix (v) *or* repair (v) *or* mend (v)

répartir un risque spread (v) a risk

répercussion (f) repercussion (n) *or* knock-on effect

repère (m) benchmark (n)

répertoire (m) d'adresses directory (n) *or* address list (n)

répertoire d'adresses par professions classified directory

répertoire d'entreprises commercial directory *or* trade directory

répertoire des noms de rues *[sur un plan]* street directory

répéter repeat (v)

repli (m) *[baisse ou recul]* downturn (n)

répondant (m) reference (n) *[person]*

répondeur (m) téléphonique answerphone (n) *or* answering machine

répondre (à une lettre, une question) reply (v) to *or* answer (v) (a letter *or* a question)

répondre à la demande *[satisfaire]* meet (v) *or* satisfy (v) a demand

répondre au téléphone answer (v) the phone *or* take (v) a call

réponse (f) answer (n) *or* reply (n)

réponse: en réponse à votre lettre in answer *or* in reply to your letter

reporté(e) *[différé]* deferred (adj) *or* postponed (adj)

reporté(e) *[montant]* carried (adj) forward

reporter *[montant]* carry (v) forward

reporter *[remettre à plus tard]* defer (v) *or* postpone (v) *or* put back (v)

reporter: se reporter à refer (v) to

reprendre *[recommencer]* resume (v)

reprendre les négociations resume negotiations

représentant(e) (sales) representative (n) *or* rep (n)

représentant(e) à la commission commission rep

représentatif (-ive) representative (adj)

représenter *[faire de la représentation]* represent (v)

reprise (f) *[contre un achat]* part exchange (n) *or* trade-in (n)

reprise (f) *[économique]* upturn (n) *or* revival (n) *or* recovery (n)

reprise (f) *[à l'achat d'une maison]* fixtures and fittings *[amount]*

reprocher blame (v)

reproduction (f) copy (n) *or* duplicate (n)

reproduire *[faire une copie]* copy (v) *or* duplicate (v)

réputation (f) *[image de marque]* reputation (n) *or* brand image (n)

requérant(e) claimant (n)

requête (f) *[demande]* request (n)

réseau (m) network (n)

réseau (m) de distribution distribution network

réservation (f) reservation (n) *or* booking (n)

réservation (f) à l'avance advance booking

réservation (f) en bloc block booking

réserve (f) *[argent]* reserve (n) *or* provision (n)

réserve (f) *[entrepôt]* stockroom (n) *or* store (n)

réserve (f) *[marchandises]* store (n) *or* stock (n)

réserve de matières premières stock of raw materials

réserve: faire des réserves stock up (v) *or* stockpile (v)

réserve: sans réserve unconditional (adj)

réserve: sous réserve conditional (adj) *or* qualified (adj)

réserve: sous réserve de subject to

réserves (fpl) *[fonds de secours]* emergency reserves

réserves (fpl) *[provisions]* reserves (n) *or* supplies (n); stockpile (n)

réserves bancaires (bank) reserves

réserves de devises currency reserves

réserves de trésorerie cash reserves

réserves occultes *[caisse noire]* hidden reserves

réserver *[retenir]* reserve (v) *or* book (v)

réserver une table *ou* **une place** book (v) a table *or* a seat

résidence (f) *[séjour]* residence (n)

résident(e) (n) resident (n)

résident(e) (adj) resident (adj)

résiliation (f) cancellation (n) *or* annulling (n)

résiliation (f) *[police d'assurance]* surrender (n)

résilier *[annuler]* annul (v) *or* cancel (v) *or* rescind (v)

résilier un contrat terminate an contract

résilier une police d'assurance surrender (v) a policy

résolution (f) resolution

résoudre un problème solve (v) a problem

respect: non respect breach (n) (of contract, of warranty)

respecter respect (v)

respecter un délai meet (v) a deadline

responsabilité (f) *[charge]* responsibility (n)

responsabilité (f) *[légale]* liability (n) *or* responsibility (n)

responsabilité contractuelle contractual liability

responsabilité limitée limited liability

responsable (adj) *[légalement]* liable (adj) *or* responsible (adj) (for)

responsable (mf) *[chef]* manager (n) *or* head (n) *or* director (n)

responsable de clientèle account executive (n)

responsable de la comptabilité analytique cost accountant (n)

responsable de la distribution distribution manager

responsable de la formation training officer (n)

responsable de la publicité advertising manager

responsable de l'information information officer (n)

responsable de relations publiques public relations man

responsable de suivi progress chaser (n)

responsable du contrôle de qualité quality controller (n)

responsable d'un entrepôt *[magasinier]* warehouseman (n)

responsable d'une équipe de représentants field sales manager

resquiller dans une queue jump (v) the queue

resserrer (le contrôle) tighten up (v) (on)

ressources (fpl) resources (n)

ressources financières financial resources

ressources humaines human resources

ressources naturelles natural resources

reste (m) remainder (n)

rester remain (v)

restrictif (-ive) restrictive (adj)

restriction (f) *[contrôle ou limitation]* restriction (n)

restructuration (f) restructuring (n)

restructuration d'une société restructuring of the company

restructurer restructure (v)

résultat (m) result (n)

résultat (m) *[effet]* effect (n)

résultat net *[bénéfice net]* final result *or* bottom line

retard (m) delay (n) *or* hold-up (n)

retard: être en retard be late; be overdue

retarder hold up (v) *or* delay (v)

retenir keep back (v)

retenir *[de l'argent]* deduct (v) (money)

retenir *[réserver]* reserve (v) *or* book (v)

retenir une chambre reserve *or* book a room

retenue (f) à la source *[impôt]* withholding tax (n)

retenues fiscales tax deductions (n) *[from salary]*

retirer withdraw (v) *[an offer]*

retirer de l'argent de la banque withdraw (v) money from the bank

retirer un gage redeem (v) a pledge

retirer une OPA withdraw (v) a takeover bid

retour (m) *[d'un lieu]* return (n) *[going back]*

retour (m) *[renvoi]* return (n) *[sending back]*

retour à l'envoyeur return to sender

retourner *[renvoyer]* return (v) *[send back]*

retourner *[revenir]* return (v) *[go back]*

retrait (m) withdrawal *[of money]*

retraite (f) retirement (n)

retrancher *[déduire]* deduct (v)

rétribuer *[rémunérer]* remunerate (v)

rétroactif (-ive) retroactive (adj)

réunion (f) *[assemblée]* meeting (n)

réunion (f) *[congrès]* conference (n)

réunion du conseil d'administration board meeting

réunion du personnel staff meeting

réunion du service commercial sales conference

réunir gather (v) together

réunir *[les éléments d'une liste]* bracket (v) together

réunir: se réunir meet (v)

réussir succeed (v) *or* be successful *or* do well

réussir à manage to (do) *or* succeed in (doing)

révéler *[divulguer]* disclose (v)

révéler *[faire apparaître]* show (v)

revendeur (m) *[détaillant]* retail dealer (n) *or* retailer (n)

revendication (f) claim (n)

revendication (f) salariale wage claim

revente (f) resale (n)

revenu (m) *[intérêt, etc.]* income (n) *or* earnings (n) *or* revenue (n)

revenu du travail income (n)

revenu brut *[du travail]* gross income

revenu fixe fixed income

revenu imposable taxable income

revenu locatif rental income

revenu net *[salaire net]* net income *or* net salary; real income

revenu non imposable non-taxable income

revenu personnel personal income

revenus (mpl) *[d'un pays]* earnings (n) *or* revenue (n)

revenus invisibles invisible earnings

revers (m) setback (n)

réviser *[mettre à jour]* update (v)

réviser *[revoir]* reassess (v) *or* review (v)

réviser *[vérifier les comptes, etc.]* audit (v)

réviser une machine service (v) (a machine)

révision (f) comptable auditing (n)

révision de salaire salary review (n)

révision d'une machine service (n) (of a machine)

révoquer revoke (v)

revue (f) *[périodique]* magazine (n) *or* periodical (n)

revue commerciale trade magazine

revue professionnelle journal (n)

risque (m) risk (n)

risque d'incendie fire risk

risque financier financial risk

risquer risk (v) *or* venture (v)

ristourne (f) *[remise]* rebate (n) *or* discount (n)

rompre les négociations break off (v) negotiations

rompre un accord *ou* **un contrat** break (v) an agreement

rotation (f) des stocks stock turnround (n) *or* stock turn (n)

rotation du personnel turnover (n) of staff *or* staff turnover

royalties (fpl) royalties (n)

ruée (f) rush (n)

rupture (f) breakdown (n) *[talks]*

rupture de contrat breach (n) of contract

rupture: être en rupture de stock be out of stock

Ss

SA (société anonyme) *[cotée en Bourse]* Plc *or* plc (Public limited company)

S.A.R.L. (société à responsabilité limitée) Ltd (limited liability company)

sac (m) *[pochette]* bag (n)

sac (m) en papier paper bag

saisie (f) *[confiscation]* seizure (n)

saisie de données au clavier keyboarding (n)

saisir (v) *[un article non payé]* repossess (v) *or* seize (v)

saisir *[des données]* input (v) information (into a computer)

saisir *[des données au clavier]* keyboard (v)

saison (f) season (n) *[time of year]*

saisonnier (-ière) seasonal (adj)

salaire (m) salary (n) *or* pay (n); wage (n)

salaire au rendement payment by results

salaire brut gross salary

salaire de départ *ou* **de débutant** starting salary

salaire horaire hourly wage

salaire minimum (SMIC) minimum wage

salaire net net salary *or* net income

salaire attrayant *ou* **intéressant** attractive salary

salaire payé pendant les vacances holiday pay

salaire régulier regular income

salarié(e) (adj) salaried (adj)

salarié(e) (n) *[employé]* employee (n) (receiving a salary)

salle (f) *[pièce]* room (n)

salle d'embarquement *[aéroport]* departure lounge (n)

salle d'exposition showroom (n)

salle de conférences *ou* **de réunion** conference room

salle de réunion (du conseil d'administration) boardroom

salle de transit *[aéroport]* transit lounge (n)

salle des ventes *[enchères]* auction room

salon (m) *[exposition]* show (n) *or* fair (n) *or* exhibition (n)

salon réservé aux personnages de marque VIP lounge (n)

sanctionner *[pénaliser]* penalize (n)

sans without

sans *[moins]* minus *or* less

sans cesse *[continuellement]* continually

sans emploi *[au chômage]* unemployed (adj)

sans-emploi: les sans-emploi the unemployed (n)

sans-travail: les sans-travail the unemployed (n)

santé (f) health (n)

satisfaction (f) satisfaction (n)

satisfaction dans le travail *ou* **au travail** job satisfaction

satisfaction du client customer satisfaction

satisfaire *[un client]* satisfy (v)

satisfaire *[la demande]* meet (v) *or* satisfy (v) *or* keep up with (v)

saturation (f) saturation (n)

saturer saturate (v)

saturer le marché saturate the market

sauf *[excepté]* except; excepted

sauf erreur ou omission errors and omissions excepted (e. & o.e.)

sauvegarder *[données]* back up (v); save (v) *[computer file]*

sauvegarder *[protéger]* safeguard (v)

sauver (une société) salvage (v)

sauvetage (m) salvage (n)

sceau (m) seal (n)

sceller *[fermer]* seal (v)

sceller *[mettre un sceau]* put (v) a seal

schéma (m) *[diagramme]* diagram (n)

second(e) *[deuxième]* second (adj)

secondaire secondary (adj); subsidiary (adj)

secret (m) secret (n)

secret (-ète) secret (adj)

secrétaire (mf) secretary (n)

secrétaire de direction personal assistant (PA)

secrétaire général(e) *[d'une compagnie]* company secretary

secrétaire intérimaire temp (n)

secrétaire particulière private secretary

secteur (m) sector (n); division (n)

secteur (m) *[domaine]* area (n)

secteur (m) *[d'une ville]* area (n) (of a town)

secteur (m) *[d'un représentant]* territory (n)

secteur difficile problem area

secteur primaire *[industrie de base]* primary industry

secteur privé private sector

secteur public public sector

secteur secondaire *[industrie de transformation]* secondary industry *or* manufacturing industry

secteur tertiaire *[industrie de services]* tertiary industry *or* service industry

sécurité (f) safety (n) *or* security (n)

sécurité de l'emploi security of employment *or* job security

sécurité sociale social security

séduire *[attirer]* appeal to (v) *or* attract (v)

séjour (m) stay (n)

séjour (m) *[résidence]* residence (n)

séjour: carte (f) de séjour residence permit (n)

séjourner stay (v)

sélection (f) *[choix]* selection (n)

sélectionné(e) *[candidat]* shortlisted (adj)

sélectionner (des candidats) shortlist (v) (candidates)

selon *[suivant]* according to

selon échantillon as per sample

semaine (f) week (n)

sembler *[paraître]* appear (v)

semestre (m) (comptable) half-year (n)

semi-remorque (mf) articulated lorry (n)

séparé(e) (adj) separate (adj)

séquestration (f) sequestration (n)

séquestre (m) sequestrator (n)

séquestre: administrateur séquestre (m) sequestrator (n)

séquestre: mettre sous séquestre sequester (v) *or* sequestrate (v)

séquestre: mise (f) sous séquestre sequestration (n)

séquestrer sequester (v) *or* sequestrate (v)

série (f) series (n)

service (m) *[bureau]* department (n) *or* division (n)

service (m) *[pourboire]* service (n) (charge)

service (m) *[travail]* service (n)

service après-vente (SAV) after-sales service

service clients customer service department (n)

service colis (postaux) parcel post (n)

service commercial sales department

service d'entretien service department

service de la comptabilité accounts department

service de la production *ou* **de la fabrication** production department

service de la publicité publicity department

service de reproduction photocopying bureau

service des achats purchasing *or* buying department

service des expéditions dispatch department

service des exportations *ou* **service export** export department

service des réclamations *[assurances]* claims department

service des réclamations *[plaintes]* complaints department

service des relations publiques public relations department

service du contentieux legal department

service (du) marketing marketing department

service du personnel personnel department

service informatique computer department

service postal *[la Poste]* Post (n) *or* postal system

service: être de service be on duty

service: être en service *[train, bus]* run (v)

serviette (f) *[porte-documents]* briefcase (n)

servir serve (v)

servir de *[agir en tant que]* act as (v)

servir les intérêts d'une dette service (v) a debt

servir d'interprète interpret (v) *or* act as interpreter

servir un client serve a customer

servir: se servir de *[utiliser]* use (v)

servitude (f) *[on land]* right (n) of way

seuil (m) threshold (n)

seuil (m) de rentabilité breakeven point

seul(e) only (adj)

seul(e) *[exclusif]* sole (adj)

seul propriétaire (m) sole owner *or* sole trader

siège (m) social *[d'une société]* registered office *or* head office

signaler *[faire rapport]* report (v)

signataire (mf) signatory (n)

signature (f) signature (n)

signature (f) d'un contrat signing (n) of a contract; completion (n) of a contract

signer *[un chèque, un contrat, etc.]* sign (v)

signer de ses initiales *[parapher]* initial (v)

signer en qualité de témoin witness (v) an agreement

simple *[unique]* single (adj)

simple associé junior partner (n)

sistership (m) sister ship (n)

site (m) *[emplacement]* site (n) *or* situation (n)

situation (f) *[état]* situation (n)

situation (f) *[site]* situation (n) *or* site (n)

situation critique *[urgence]* emergency (n)

situation de monopole monopoly (n)

situation financière financial position

situation légale *[statut légal]* legal status

situé(e) situated (adj)

SME (système monétaire européen) EMS (European Monetary System)

social(e) (adj) social (adj)

société (f) *[association ou club]* society *or* club (n) *or* association (n)

société (f) *[immatriculée]* company (n); corporation (n) *[US]*

société (f) *[non immatriculée]* partnership (n)

société à but lucratif profit-oriented company

société affiliée associate company

société anonyme (S.A.) *[cotée en Bourse]* Public Limited Company (Plc)

société à responsabilité limitée (S.A.R.L.) limited liability company (Ltd)

société commerciale trading company

société coopérative cooperative society

société cotée en Bourse listed company

société d'affacturage *ou* **de factoring** factor (n)

société de Bourse firm of stockbrokers

société de crédit finance company

société de crédit immobilier building society

société de location de matériel plant-hire firm

société de services service company *or* service bureau

société de services et d'ingénierie informatique (SSII) computer bureau ; software company

société d'investissement à capital variable (SICAV) unit trust (n)

société en commandite simple (SCS) limited partnership

société exportatrice *ou* **d'exportation** export house *or* export company

société familiale family company

société fiduciaire trust company

société indépendante independent company

société mère *[maison mère]* parent company

société prête-nom shell company

société qui a un fort coefficient d'endettement highly-geared company

sol (m) floor *[surface]*

solde (m) *[d'un compte]* balance (n)

solde (m) *[vente au rabais]* sale (n) *or* clearance sale

solde (m) **à ce jour; solde à reporter** balance carried down *or* carrried forward

solde à moitié prix half-price sale

solde à nouveau; ancien solde; solde reporté balance brought down *or* brought forward

solde à recevoir balance due to us

solde créditeur credit balance

solde débiteur debit balance

solde de dividende final dividend

solde de trésorerie cash balance

solde en banque *[position d'un compte bancaire]* bank balance

solde: en solde on sale; reduced to clear

soldes (mpl & fpl) sales (n)

solder un compte *[arrêter]* balance (v)

solder un compte *[régler]* settle (the balance of) an account

solliciter *[demander]* request (v) *or* ask (v) (for)

solliciter des commandes solicit (v) orders

solliciter un emploi apply (v) for a job

solution (f) *[réponse]* solution (n)

solution de problèmes *[action]* problem solving (n)

solvabilité (f) solvency (n)

solvable solvent (adj) *or* credit-worthy (adj)

sommaire *[approximatif]* rough (adj)

somme (f) *[addition]* addition (n); calculation (n)

somme (f) (d'argent) *[montant]* sum (n) *or* amount (n) (of money)

somme due amount owing

somme totale (grand) total (n)

sondage (m) d'opinion opinion poll (n)

sondage: faire un sondage d'opinion poll (v) a sample of the population

sortant(e) outgoing (adj)

sortie (f) d'imprimante (computer) printout (n) *or* listing (n)

sorties (fpl) *[dépenses]* outgoings (n)

souche (f) *[d'un chéquier, etc.]* counterfoil (n) *or* stub (n)

soulever (une question) raise (v) (a question)

soumission (f) *[pour un contrat, un travail]* tender (n)

soumission cachetée sealed tender

soumissionnaire (mf) tenderer (n)

soumissionner un travail tender (v) for a contract

souple (adj) *[horaire]* flexible (adj) *[hours]*

source (f) source (n)

source de revenu(s) source of income

souscrire subscribe (v)

souscrire une assurance take out (v) a policy *or* an insurance policy

sous-équipé(e) underequipped (adj)

sous-locataire (mf) sublessee (n)

sous-location (f) sublease (n)

sous-louer sublet (v) *or* sublease (v)

sous-payé(e) underpaid (adj)

sous-produit (m) by-product (n)

soussigné(e) (n *ou* adj) undersigned

sous-total (m) subtotal (n)

sous-traitance (f) subcontracting (n)

sous-traitance : donner en sous-traitance subcontract (v) *or* farm out (v) (work)

sous-traitant (m) subcontractor (n)

sous-traiter (v) *[donner en sous-traitance]* subcontract (v) *or* farm out (v) (work)

spécial(e) special (adj)

spécialisation (f) specialization (n)

spécialiser: se spécialiser specialize (v) (in)

spécialiste (mf) *[expert]* specialist (n) *or* expert (n)

spécialiste des techniques marchandes merchandizer (n)

specifications (fpl) specifications (n)

spécifier specify (v)

spéculateur (-trice) speculator (n)

spéculateur à la baisse *[baissier]* bear (n) *[Stock Exchange]*

spéculateur à la hausse *[haussier]* bull (n) *[Stock Exchange]*

sponsor (m) *[commanditaire]* sponsor (n) *or* backer (n)

sponsorisation (f) *[parrainage]* sponsorship (n)

sponsoriser *[parrainer]* sponsor (v)

stabilisation (f) stabilization (n)

stabiliser stabilize (v)

stabiliser: se stabiliser stabilize; level off (v) *or* level out (v)

stabilité (f) stability (n)

stabilité d'emploi security (n) of tenure

stabilité des prix price stability

stable stable (adj)

stage (m) *[étape]* stage (n)

stage de formation course (n) *or* training (n); traineeship (n)

stage (m) de recyclage refresher course (n)

stagiaire (mf) trainee (n)

stagiaire diplômé(e) graduate trainee

stagnant(e) stagnant (adj)

stagnation (f) stagnation (n)

stand (m) *[d'exposition]* stand (n)

standard (m) *[norme]* standard (n)

standard (adj) *[ordinaire]* standard (adj)

standard (m) téléphonique (telephone) switchboard (n)

standardisation (f) *[normalisation]* standardization (n)

standardiser *[normaliser]* standardize (v)

standardiste (mf) (switchboard *or* telephone) operator (n)

standing (m) *[réputation]* standing (n)

statisticien (-ienne) statistician (n)

statistique (adj) statistical (adj)

statistiques (fpl) statistics (n)

statuer *[déclarer]* rule (v)

statut (m) *[position]* status (n)

statut légal legal status

statuts (mpl) d'une société articles (n) of association

statutaire *[réglementaire]* statutory (adj)

stimuler (l'économie) stimulate (v) (the economy)

stipulation (f) stipulation (n) *or* provision (n)

stipuler stipulate (v) *or* state (v)

stock (m) *[marchandises]* stock (n); inventory (n) *[US]*

stock (m) *[provision]* supply (n) *or* stock

stock en fin d'exercise closing stock

stock initial *ou* **stock d'ouverture** opening stock

stocker *[avoir en stock]* stock (v)

stocker *[faire des réserves]* stockpile (v)

stockiste (mf) *[dépositaire]* stockist (n)

stop (m) *[arrêt ou fin]* stop (n)

stratégie (f) strategy (n) *or* strategic planning

stratégie commerciale marketing strategy

stratégie des affaires business strategy

stratégique (adj) strategic (adj)

structure (f) structure (n)

structure (f) en grille grid structure

structurel (-elle) structural (adj)

subalterne (adj) junior (adj)

subir des dégâts suffer (v) damage

subvention (f) subvention (n) *or* subsidy (n) *or* grant (n)

subventionné(e) par l'Etat government-sponsored (adj)

subventionner subsidize (v)

succéder à succeed (v) (someone)

succès (m) success (n)

succès: qui a du succès successful (adj)

succursale (f) branch office

suffisant(e) sufficient (adj) *or* adequate (adj)

suite à *[en réponse à]* further to

suivant *[conformément]* according to

suivant *[en fonction de]* depending on

suivant avis as per advice

suivre follow (v)

suivre une formation train (v)

suivre une ligne de produits carry (v) a line of goods

sujet (m) matter (n)

superdividende (m) surplus dividend

supérette (f) minimarket (n)

supérieur(e) (adj) *[meilleur]* superior (adj) *or* of better quality

supérieur(e) (n) *[personne]* superior (n)

supérieur(e) à (adj) *[plus de]* more than

supermarché (m) supermarket (n)

superviser *[surveiller]* supervise (v)

supplément (m) *[frais supplémentaires]* surcharge (n) *or* extra charge (n)

supplémentaire (adj) additional (adj) *or* supplementary (adj) *or* extra (adj)

supporter *[des frais]* bear (v) *or* pay for (v) *[expenses]*

suppression (f) d'emplois job cuts (n)

supprimer cut out (v) *or* remove (v)

supprimer *[rayer]* cross out (v) *or* delete (v)

sûr(e) (adj) safe (adj)

surabondance (f) *[surplus]* glut (n)

surbooking (m) *ou* **surréservation (f)** overbooking (n) *or* double-booking (n)

surbooking: faire du surbooking overbook (v)

surcapacité (f) excess capacity *or* overcapacity (n)

surcharger *[encombrer le marché]* glut (v) *[the market]*

surcoût (m) surcharge (n)

surenchère (f) counterbid (n)

surenchérir outbid (v)

surestarie (f) demurrage (n)

surestimer overestimate (v)

surévalué(e) overvalued (adj) *or* overrated (adj)

surévalué(e) *[marché]* overbought (adj)

surévaluer overvalue (v) *or* overrate (v)

surface (f) area (n)

surface (f) au sol floor space

surligneur (m) marker pen (n)

surpayer overpay (v)

surplus (m) *[excédent]* surplus (n) *or* excess (n)

surplus (m) *[surabondance]* glut (n)

surproduction (f) overproduction (n)

surproduire overproduce (v)

surréservation *[surbooking]* overbooking (n) or double-booking (n)

surréserver overbook (v) or double-book (v)

sursis (m) stay of execution (n)

surtaxe (f) à l'importation import surcharge (n)

surveillance (f) supervision (n)

surveillant(e) supervisor (n)

surveiller *[contrôler]* control (v)

surveiller *[superviser]* supervise (v)

survente (f) overcharging (n)

suspendre suspend (v) or stop (v)

suspendre les paiements stop payments

suspension (f) *[arrêt]* suspension (n) or stoppage (n)

suspension (f) des paiements suspension of payments

syndicaliste (mf) *[trade-unioniste]* trade unionist (n)

syndicat (m) *[financier]* syndicate (n)

syndicat (m) *[Trade-union]* trade union (n) or union (n)

syndicat de garantie underwriting syndicate

synergie (f) synergy (n)

système (m) system (n)

système comptable accounting system

système d'exploitation operating system

système en temps réel *[ordinateur]* real-time system

Système monétaire européen (SME) European Monetary System (EMS)

système téléphonique automatique international international direct dialling

Tt

table (f) table (n)

tables de mortalité actuarial tables (n)

tableau (m) *[informatique]* spreadsheet (n)

tableau (m) à feuilles mobiles flip chart (n)

tableur (m) *[programme informatique]* spreadsheet (n) (program)

tabulateur (m) tabulator (n)

tâche (f) assignment (n) or job (n)

tachygraphe (m) tachograph (n)

taille (f) size (n)

taille courante stock size

taille normale regular size

talent (m) *[aptitude]* skill (n)

talon (m) *[d'un chèque, etc.]* counterfoil (n) or stub (n)

tampon (m) stamp (n) *[device]*

tamponner stamp (v) *[mark]*

tangible tangible (adj)

tare (f) tare (n)

tarif (m) tariff (n) or rate (n) or price (n)

tarif (m) *[barème des prix]* scale (n) of charges or schedule (n) of charges

tarif (m) *[liste de prix, catalogue]* price list (n)

tarif (m) *[prix d'un billet de train, etc.]* fare (n)

tarif des heures supplémentaires overtime pay

tarif douanier customs tariff

tarif d'un aller simple *[voyage]* one-way fare

tarif en vigueur going rate

tarif horaire hourly rate

tarif postal postage (n); postal charge or postal rate

tarif privilégié preferential duty or preferential tariff

tarif protectionniste protective tariff

tarif réduit cheap rate or reduced rate

tarif tout compris inclusive charge or all-in price

tarifs d'expédition freight rates or charges

tarifs différentiels differential tariffs

tarifs publicitaires advertising rates

taux (m) rate (n); percentage (n)

taux d'amortissement depreciation rate

taux d'augmentation rate (n) of increase

taux de base bancaire (TBB) bank base rate *or* prime rate

taux de change rate of exchange *or* exchange rate

taux de change à terme forward rate

taux (de change) croisé cross rate

taux de change en vigueur current rate of exchange

taux de conversion conversion price *or* conversion rate

taux de croissance growth rate

taux de production rate of production *or* production rate

taux de rendement rate of return; yield (n)

taux de rendement d'une action earnings per share *or* dividend yield

taux d'erreur error rate

taux d'escompte discount rate

taux d'imposition tax rate

taux d'inflation rate of inflation

taux d'intérêt interest rate *or* rate of interest

taux directeurs leading rates

taux d'occupation occupancy rate

taux effectif global (TEG) annualized percentage rate (APR)

taux fixe *[forfait]* flat rate

taxable *[imposable]* taxable (adj)

taxe (f) *[droit]* tax (n) *or* duty (n)

taxe à l'achat purchase tax

taxe à l'exportation export duty

taxe à l'importation import duty

taxe comprise inclusive of tax *or* tax included

taxe d'aéroport airport tax

taxe d'apprentissage training levy

taxe différentielle sur les véhicules à moteur road tax

taxe proportionnelle *ou* **ad valorem** ad valorem tax

taxe sur la valeur ajoutée (TVA) value added tax (VAT)

taxe sur les ventes sales tax

taxe: hors taxe exclusive of taxe

taxe: toutes taxes comprises (TTC) inclusive of tax *or* tax included

technique (f) technique (n)

techniques de gestion management techniques

techniques de marketing marketing techniques

TEG (taux effectif global) APR (annualized percentage rate)

télécarte (f) phone card

télécommande (f) remote control

télécopie (f) *[fax]* fax (n)

télécopie: envoyer par télécopie fax (v) *or* send by fax

télécopieur (m) fax (machine)

téléphone (m) telephone (n) *or* phone (n)

téléphone à carte card phone

téléphone cellulaire cellular telephone

téléphone de conférence conference phone

téléphone interne internal telephone

téléphone mobile mobile phone

téléphone public pay phone

téléphoner telephone (v) *or* phone (v)

téléphoner à quelqu'un call (v) *or* phone someone

télévision (f) television (n) *or* TV

télévision (f) en circuit fermé closed circuit TV

télex (m) telex (n)

télexer *[envoyer un télex]* telex (v)

témoin (m) witness (n)

témoin: être témoin witness (v)

temps (m) time (n)

temps complet *ou* **plein temps** full-time

temps d'ordinateur computer time

temps libre spare time *or* free time

temps partiel part-time

temps de mise en marche (d'une machine) make-ready time

temps improductif *ou* **temps d'arrêt** *[machine]* down time

temps: à temps on time

temps: en temps voulu in good time

tendance (f) trend (n)

tendance à la hausse upward trend

tendances du marché market trends *or* market forces

tendances économiques *[conjoncture]* economic trends

teneur (f) content

tenir une promesse keep (v) a promise

tenir une réunion *ou* **une discussion** hold (v) a meeting *or* hold a discussion

tenue (f) de livres *[comptabilité]* bookkeeping (n)

terme (m) *[période]* term (n)

terme: à terme *[acheter, vendre]* forward

termes (mpl) *[conditions]* terms (n)

termes (mpl) *[formulation]* wording (n)

terminaison (f) *[expiration]* expiry (n) (date) *or* termination (n)

terminal (m) d'aéroport airport terminal (n)

terminal (m) d'ordinateur computer terminal

terminal (m) maritime (pour porte-conteneurs) container terminal

terminal(e) (adj) terminal (adj) *[at the end]*

terminer *[mettre fin à]* end (v) *or* terminate (v)

terminer *[exécuter]* complete (v)

terne (adj) flat (adj) *or* dull (adj)

terrain (m) *ou* **terre (f)** land (n)

test (m) *[contrôle]* test (n)

test de faisabilité feasibility test

test sur échantillon acceptance sampling (n)

tester *[contrôler]* test (v)

ticket (m) *[billet]* ticket (n)

ticket de caisse sales receipt

ticket de prix *[étiquette de prix]* price ticket

tiers (m) *[tierce personne]* third party (n)

timbre (m) *ou* **timbre-poste (m)** (postage) stamp (n)

timbre (m) *[tampon]* stamp (n) *[device]*

timbre dateur date stamp *[device]*

timbrer *[coller un timbre]* stamp (v)

timbrer *[tamponner]* stamp (v)

tirage (m) *[d'un journal]* circulation (n)

tiré (m) *[banque]* drawee (n)

tirer à découvert overdraw (v)

tirer un chèque draw (v) a cheque

tireur (m) *[banque]* drawer (n)

tiroir-caisse (m) till (n)

titre (m) *[action, obligation]* share (n); bond (n)

titre (m) *[d'un livre]* title (n)

titre (m) *[qualification]* (job) title

titre au porteur *[obligation]* bearer bond

titre de premier ordre *[valeur sûre]* blue chip (n)

titres (mpl) *[valeurs]* securities (n) *or* stock (n)

titres d'Etat gilt-edged securities *or* gilts (n)

titulaire (mf) holder (n)

tomber *[avoir lieu]* fall (v) *[on a date]*

tonalité (f) (du téléphone) dialling tone (n)

tonalité 'occupé' engaged tone

tonnage (m) *[d'un navire]* tonnage (n)

tonne (f) ton (n)

tonne (f) (métrique) tonne (n)

tôt early (adv)

total (m) total (n)

total (m) *[montant total]* total amount

total(e) (adj) total (adj)

total général grand total

total reporté running total

touche (f) *[d'un clavier]* key (n)

touche de contrôle control key

touche de majuscules shift key

toucher un chèque *[encaisser]* cash (v) a cheque

toucher net *[gagner]* net (v)

tous frais payés all expenses paid

tous les trois mois quarterly (adv)

tout compris all-in *or* inclusive (adj)

toutes taxes comprises (TTC) inclusive of tax *or* tax included

Trade-union (f) trade union (n)

trade-unioniste (mf) *[syndicaliste]* trade unionist (n)

trafiquer *[manipuler]* fiddle (v) (the accounts)

train (m) train (n)

train de marchandises freight train *or* goods train

train de marchandises en conteneurs freightliner (n)

traite (f) *[lettre de change]* draft (n) *or* bill (n)

traite à vue sight draft

traite bancaire bank draft *or* banker's draft *or* bank bill

traitement (m) de commandes order processing (n)

traitement de(s) données *[informatique]* data processing

traitement de texte word-processing

traitement par lots batch processing

traiter (une commande) process (v) (an order)

traiter avec quelqu'un *[faire affaire]* deal with (v) someone

traiter une affaire *[effectuer une transaction]* transact (v) business

tranche (f) *[d'impôt]* (tax) bracket (n)

transaction (f) (business) transaction (n)

transaction boursière dealing (n) on the Stock Exchange

transférer transfer (v)

transfert (m) transfer (n)

transfert (m) (d'une traite) delivery (n) of (bill of exchange)

transformation (f) *[fabrication]* manufacturing (n)

transit (m) transit (n)

transitaire (m) forwarding agent (n)

transmissible *[cessible]* transferable (adj)

transport (m) transport (n) *or* carriage (n) *or* shipping (n)

transport par avion air transport

transport par chemin de fer rail transport

transport par conteneurs containerization (n) *or* shipping (n) in containers

transports (mpl) en commun public transport

Transports Internationaux Routiers (TIR) Transports Internationaux Routiers (TIR)

transports (mpl) routiers *[camionnage]* road transport *or* road haulage (n)

transporter transport (v) *or* carry (v) *or* ship (v)

transporteur (m) *[entreprise de transports]* carrier (n) *or* shipper (n)

travail (m) labour (n)

travail (m) *[emploi]* job (n) *or* work (n) *or* employment (n)

travail à la pièce *ou* **aux pièces** piecework (n)

travail à plein temps full-time work *or* full-time employment

travail à temps partiel *ou* **à mi-temps** part-time work *or* part-time employment

travail au noir moonlighting (n)

travail au noir *[économie parallèle]* black economy (n)

travail contractuel contract work

travail de bureau clerical work

travail en retard *ou* **en attente** backlog (n) (of work)

travail manuel manual work

travail posté *[travail par équipe]* shift work

travail temporaire casual work

travail urgent *ou* **travail d'urgence** rush job

travail en cours work in progress

travailler work (v)

travailler au noir moonlight (v)

travailleur (-euse) worker (n)

travailleur (-euse) à domicile homeworker

travailleur (-euse) au noir moonlighter (n)

travailleur (-euse) manuel (-elle) manual worker

travailleur (-euse) temporaire casual worker

treizième mois Christmas bonus (n)

trésorerie (f) cash flow (n)

tribunal (m) *ou* **tribunaux (mpl)** court (n) *or* law courts

trimestre (m) quarter (n)

trimestre (m) (juridique *ou* **universitaire)** term (n)

trimestriel (-elle) quarterly (adj)

trimestriellement *[tous les trois mois]* quarterly (adv)

triple triple (adj)

tripler triple (v) *or* treble (v)

troc (m) barter (n); bartering (n)

troisième âge (m) old age

troisième trimestre (m) third quarter (n)

trop-perçu (m) overpayment (n); overcharge (n)

troquer barter (v)

tuyau (m) tip (n) *or* advice (n)

TVA (taxe sur la valeur ajoutée)
VAT (value added tax)

Uu

UE (Union européenne) EU
(European Union)

**UEM (Union économique et
monétaire)** EUM (Economic and
Monetary Union)

un pour cent (1%) one percentage point

unilatéral(e) unilateral (adj) *or*
one-sided (adj)

union (f) douanière customs union (n)

Union européenne (UE) European
Union (EU)

unique *[isolé]* one-off (adj)

unique *[simple]* single (adj)

unité (f) unit (n)

unité (f) *[centre]* unit

unité de mémoire *[informatique]*
storage unit

unité monétaire monetary unit

urgence (f) emergency (n)

urgent(e) urgent (adj)

usine (f) factory (n) *or* plant (n)

usufruit (m) life interest (n)

usure (f) wear and tear (n)

usure normale fair wear and tear

utile (adj) useful (adj)

utilisateur (-trice) user (n)

utilisateur (m) (final) end user

utilisation (f) utilization (n) *or* use (n)

utiliser *[se servir de]* use (v)

utiliser la capacité disponible use up
(v) spare capacity

Vv

valable valid (adj)

valable: non valable not valid *or*
invalid (adj)

valeur (f) value (n) *or* worth (n)

valeur actualisée discounted value

valeur à la cote *[actions]* market value

valeur au pair par value

valeur comptable book value

valeur de l'actif asset value

valeur de rachat *[assurance]*
surrender value

valeur de rareté scarcity value

valeur de remplacement replacement
value

valeur de reprise trade-in price

valeur déclarée declared value

valeur nette net value; net worth

valeur nominale face value *or* nominal
value

valeur sûre blue chip

valeur: sans valeur worthless (adj)

valeurs (fpl) *[titres]* shares (n) *or* stock
(n) *or* securities (n)

valeurs convertibles convertible loan
stock

valide (adj) *[valable]* valid (adj)

valide: non valide not valid *or* invalid
(adj)

validité (f) validity (n)

valise (f) case (n) *or* suitcase (n)

valoir be worth

valoir *[coûter]* cost (v)

variable *[qui fluctue]* fluctuating (adj)

variation (f) variation (n)

variation (f) *[écart]* variance (n)

variations (fpl) saisonnières seasonal variations

varié(e) *[divers]* miscellaneous (adj)

varier *[diversifier]* diversify (v)

véhicule (m) vehicle (n)

vendable saleable (adj)

vendeur (m) *[dans un magasin]* salesman *[in a shop]*

vendeur (-euse) *[dans un magasin]* shop assistant (n) *or* sales clerk

vendeuse (f) saleslady (n); salesgirl (n)

vendre sell (v)

vendre *[commercialiser]* market (v)

vendre à terme sell forward

vendre aux enchères auction (v)

vendre (des marchandises) au détail retail (v) (goods)

vendre moins cher (que) undersell (v)

vendre moins cher qu'un concurrent undercut (v) a rival

vendre son entreprise sell (v) one's business *or* sell out (v)

vendre: à vendre for sale

vendre: se vendre (v)

vendre: se vendre à sell (v): retail for

vendre: qui se vend le mieux best selling (item) *or* best seller (n)

vendu(e) sold (adj)

vendu(e): non vendu(e) unsold (adj)

venir à échéance mature (v) *or* fall (v) due

vente (f) sale (n)

vente (f) *[action]* selling (n)

vente à domicile house-to-house selling

vente agressive hard selling

vente au comptant cash sale *or* cash deal

vente au détail retail (n); retailing (n)

vente aux enchères auction (n) *or* sale by auction

vente avec possibilité de reprise des invendus sale or return *or* see-safe (n)

vente de fin de saison end of season sale

vente directe direct selling

vente en gros wholesale (selling)

vente forcée *[en catastrophe]* distress sale

vente forcée *[liquidation]* forced sale

vente non agressive soft sell

vente par correspondance (VPC) mail order

vente(s) (f) par téléphone telesales (n) *or* téléphone sale(s)

vente réglée avec (une) carte de crédit credit card sale

vente: en vente on sale

ventes (fpl) sales

ventes à terme forward sales

ventes enregistrées book sales

ventes intérieures domestic sales *or* home sales

ventes nettes net sales

ventes prévues projected sales

ventes record record sales

ventilation (f) breakdown (n)

ventiler les frais break down (v) *or* itemize (v) expenses

vérificateur (m) *[contrôleur]* controller (n)

vérification (f) verification (n) *or* check (n)

vérification *[contrôle]* control (n) *or* monitoring (n)

vérification (f) *[inspection]* inspection (n)

vérification comptable *[audit]* audit (n)

vérification générale des comptes general audit

vérifié(e) *[comptes]* audited (adj)

vérifié(e): non vérifié(e) *[comptes]* unaudited

vérifier (v) *or* check (v)

vérifier *[contrôler]* control (v) *or* monitor (v)

vérifier *[inspecter]* inspect (v)

vérifier les comptes audit the accounts

véritable *[authentique]* genuine (adj) *or* real (adj)

véritable *[vrai]* real (adj)

versement (m) payment (n) or instalment (n)

versement annuel yearly payment

verser de l'argent pay (out)

verser de l'argent (sur un compte) deposit (v) money (in the bank)

verser un acompte ou **une provision** pay (v) money down or on account

verser un dividende pay (v) a dividend

verser un intérêt pay (v) interest

véto (m) veto (n)

via [*par*] via

viable viable (adj)

vice (m) **de fabrication** defect (n)

vide empty (adj)

vieux, vieil (vieille) old (adj)

vigile (m) security guard

vigueur: en vigueur [*prix*] going (adj) (price, rate)

virement (m) **bancaire** bank transfer (n)

virement (m) **de crédit** transfer of funds

virgule (f) **(décimale)** decimal point (n)

visa (m) visa (n)

visa d'entrée entry visa

visa de transit transit visa

visa permanent (bon pour plusieurs entrées) multiple-entry visa

viser (à) [*avoir pour but*] aim (at) (v)

visite (f) call (n)

visite d'affaires business call

visite de routine ou **habituelle** routine call

visite imprompue (d'un représentant) cold call

visiter call on (v) or visit (v)

vitrine (f) [*devanture*] shop window (n)

vitrine (f) [*meuble, armoire vitrée*] display case (n) or showcase (n)

voiture (f) car (n)

voiture de location hire car

voix (f) **prépondérante** casting vote (n)

vol (m) [*de marchandises*] theft (n)

vol (m) [*avion*] flight (n)

vol à l'étalage ou **vol dans les rayons** shoplifting (n)

vol charter charter flight

vol régulier scheduled flight

voleur (-euse) thief (n)

voleur (-euse) à l'étalage shoplifter (n)

volume (m) volume (n)

volume (m) [*capacité*] capacity (n) or space (n)

volume d'affaires volume of trade or volume of business

volume de ventes volume of sales or sales volume

volumineux (-euse) bulky (adj)

vote (m) vote (n)

vote par procuration proxy vote

voter vote (v)

voter [*adopter une motion*] carry (v) [*a motion*]

voyage (m) trip (n); journey (n)

voyage d'affaires business trip

voyage de retour homeward journey

vrai(e) [*véritable*] real (adj); genuine (adj)

vrac: en vrac loose (adj); in bulk

VRP (Voyageur-Représentant-Placier) representative (n) or rep (n)

Ww

wagon (m) **(de marchandises)** [*train*] goods wagon (n) or freight car (n)

warrant (m) warrant (n)

zéro (m) zero

zéro: à taux zéro zero-rated (adj)

zone (f) [*région*] area (n) *or* region (n)

zone de libre-échange free trade area

zone dollar dollar area

zone franc franc area

zone franche free zone

zone industrielle industrial estate (n)

zone piétonnière shopping precinct (n)

BILINGUAL DICTIONARIES

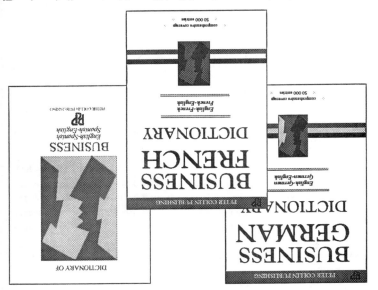

A range of comprehensive, up-to-date fully bilingual business dictionaries. The dictionaries cover all aspects of business usage: buying and selling, office practice, banking, insurance, finance, stock exchange, warehousing and distribution.

Each dictionary includes over 50,000 entries

example sentences   grammar notes

clear and accurate translations   part of speech

Ideal for any business person, teacher, or student

Business French	ISBN 0-948549-64-5	600pp	h/b
Business German	ISBN 0-948549-50-5	650pp	h/b
Business Spanish	ISBN 0-948549-30-0	736pp	h/b
Business Chinese	ISBN 0-948549-63-7	534pp	h/b
Business Swedish	ISBN 0-948549-14-9	420pp	h/b

Available from all good bookshops

or contact: Peter Collin Publishing
1 Cambridge Road, Teddington, Middx. TW11 8DT
tel: 0181 943 3386   fax: 0181 943 1673